Family Wakes Us Up

Family
Wakes
Us Up

Letters Between Expectant Fathers

|||

MICHAEL STONE

MATTHEW REMSKI

ISBN-13: 978-1502474964
ISBN-10: 1502474964

For more information or to order additional copies, please contact
Matthew Remski at threadsofyoga@gmail.com

Cover and book design: Laura Shaw Design, lshawdesign.com
Legal: Julian Porter, Q.C.

for Alix and Carina

September 9th

Matthew,

Last night Carina and I watched a film on Russian water births from the 1970s—wood panels, maroon-fringed things, fur hats. The film begins with a labouring woman and her partner kissing in a glass tub, him rubbing her shoulders with his young hands. Then she reaches down between her legs, the camera filming through the glass, and starts rubbing the baby's head in small circles as it squeezes down and out into the water. Then the arms pop out, seemingly with no elbows. Finally you see the umbilical cord. She rubs the mucus from the baby's eyes, lifts its almost human face out of the water and brings the baby's lips to hers to suck out the fluids. I didn't realize a baby could be underwater for so long.

As we watched the baby suckling at its mother's breast I remembered when my first real yoga teacher, Pattabhi Jois, said that the first inhale is birth and the final exhale is death. I had known that intellectually, but in the moment he said it I felt it in a way that's never left me.

The film, idyllic as I know it was, left me in a mood all night. That beautiful, perfect birth—birth "the way God intended," according to the film's narrator—isn't the way birth goes for so many families.

I slept poorly, realizing that as much as Carina and I have talked about it, I have no idea what to do for the upcoming birth. We are due in seven months. Will I be in the tub with her, rubbing her shoulders and kissing her? Or will I be bringing tea and watching the midwives help her through? Will I be there arguing with doctors about whether we should have a C-section? I was involved in every minute of A's birth. He was born in an iron-frame bed at home. Yet after watching the Russian water births, I now realize how there was an interior life I was navigating during the birth that I've never shared with anyone.

So *yes* to your idea of marking these next months of pregnancy with an exchange of letters. With us both expecting, I'm eager to talk this process through.

In the days immediately following A's birth I was overwhelmed and struggling. I loved him more than anything I'd ever seen, a love broken out of time and space. I still love him that much. At the time though, I felt like my only role was to support his mother. I had no idea what any other role would or could be. I kept telling myself I needed to be a rock. I was 28. I tried to do everything I could to support his mother but I reached a limit. His mother was a decade older. All I wanted was for her to be comfortable. We were surrounded by supportive women and yet there was no talk of how I, the soon-to-be father, could support *and* be supported as we undertook that journey together, and so I turned, as I always have, to my practice: yoga postures, sitting meditation, chanting, studying texts.

I still wake up early in the morning and sit. I light incense, chant, and sway my body side to side until my sitz bones are equally settled in the cushion. I follow the inhale and exhale through the channels of my nostrils and keep my gaze wide and still. I hear Carina stirring in the warm bed in the next room. I'm often distracted by the emails awaiting me in my inbox, but I sit there nevertheless, and sweetly. Thoughts come and go. The release is slow. The mind goes on and on, trying to frame everything that comes through. Grasping, releasing, grasping, releasing—my mind oscillates back and forth between what I want and what I want to avoid. The furnace turns on and off, the birds appear at the window, my son snores lightly in the next room. Every time I lose track of the breath, I start again.

And now this pregnancy marks a whole new beginning.

I've been thinking a lot about fatherhood these days. This new pregnancy excites me, haunts me, thrills me, scares me. I love being a father. It's the best thing that's ever happened to me. A is turning nine, his legs are getting longer and skinnier. He doesn't smell like an infant anymore. Last night when I was helping him fold his clothes into his drawers I felt as if no time had passed since I was guiding his ankles through sleepers. I can't imagine A as an infant anymore, but I also can't envision him as an adult. He studies me sometimes and I'm not sure what he's thinking. He's torn between living in two homes. I'm supposed to give him roots and wings but mostly he wants to be with his mother. It confuses me.

So even though I love being a father, I'm also exhausted by being a father under scrutiny. I know in separation this is common, but the pain of it tugs at me, like skin caught on a thorn. When I pick A up from school I love watching him put on his knapsack, pack his locker, joke with his friends whose mouths are filled with gum, and kiss me when nobody is looking. Sometimes when A is asleep I'll watch him for a few breaths, the muscles around his arm bones, soft and innocent again. I guess we study each other.

This pregnancy is now bringing up old fears, doubts, and pain. My split with A's mother was so painful for all of us. I thought I had healed, but when I see women in the park with strollers and diaper bags, I find myself jaded. I think they look depressed, but I know the sadness is mine.

In the time leading up to A's birth, ten years ago now, I lost my centre of gravity. I was practicing vipassana meditation. My concentration was coming along quite well. In my yoga practice, I was working through the second series (*nadi shodhana*) of the *Ashtanga Vinyasa* yoga system. Meanwhile, I had no idea how to approach the practice of becoming a father. I had no idea what I needed for support. I see now that I was at the frayed end of a long rope. I was using meditation to hone my ability to concentrate, and in that deep concentration I could enter a realm with almost no thought or emotion. It was pleasurable, and mostly a relief. I didn't have to think about my relationships or my doubts.

In my twenties that feeling of groundlessness appealed to me. If I could get into a state of nothingness, I'd be free. This approach definitely reduced stress, but it was itself unstable.My relationships weren't benefiting from this practice, to say the least. And I was scared of dealing with my unhappiness. Doing advanced backbends in yoga wasn't giving me the tools I needed to connect with my partner. I was like two people: the monk and the householder—and they were drifting further apart.

Ten years later, and five years after A's birth, my relationship with A's mother imploded. I was embarrassed that my practice couldn't help me. My heart was shattered. I saw that I was using these practices to avoid the things that weren't working at home.

Now I am living on the same street where A was born, in another house, in a different relationship. I've given up concentration practices in favour of cultivating moment-to-moment mindfulness. I've replaced my youthful longing for transcendence with the practice of being fully present in my life. It's been a long, meandering journey so far, and not, I suspect, so different from your own. We have a mortgage, an old house where every corner is in need of repair, a baby on the way, and I'm determined to do it differently this time around.

I think of practice now in terms of cultivating intimacy. I've come to believe that the whole material world is nothing but relationships, with love as the glue holding everything together. How do I love what's right in front of me, without trying to change it or make it my own? I've come full circle back to the beginning of my practice, but the focus has changed. Now my body, this city, my son, my child-to-be, my life with Carina, the building of community—these are my anchors and my home. In fact, it has never been otherwise. It just took me a while to see it that way.

The Buddha called waking up "going against the stream." Intimacy in family life certainly goes against the stream of our distracted culture. Carina and I are dreaming our home into a monastery. The forms are invisible, but deep down under the old wooden stairs and the trembling furnace, we are building something sacred, and real.

Last night, at the supermarket, an old woman with failing eyes was studying the price tag on a package of eggplant. I walked up to help her and as I approached, her husband stepped in, also frail, and lifted the eggplants up close to one eye and exclaimed: "$2.99! A great deal!" They both laughed. The eggplants went into the cart and they pushed it together toward the next aisle. I followed them for a while.

love,
Michael

|||

September 10th

Michael –

In birth prep class yesterday, our doula asked us to draw a picture of the journey ahead. She asked us to visualize a landscape with a path, to consider what we would need to take with us, and what we knew we had to leave behind. Alix took up red and green and blue pastels and knelt on the floor, unleashing broad strokes on the newsprint. My hand went to a small piece of black charcoal with a sharpened point by use, and started small in the lower left corner.

I began by drawing a window. A writer's window out onto the world. The world shaped by the frame, opening in wider angles according to my closeness, the glass cold to the touch. Every rented room, apartment, house and cabin I've lived in has had a window like this, through which I've poured tens of thousands of hours of my solitude. There is also an inner window, where I've been watching and waiting for a part of my life to begin. For someone to arrive. For a part of myself to open the frame to the larger world of wind and rain. I guess I can call that window my spiritual life.

On the desk beside the window ledge I drew the artifacts of my intelligence: letters, numbers, signs, a ruler. And books. While Alix's arm swept in the long arcs of her coming labour, I was drawing the small tools by which I had measured my ideas about life.

When I told my best friend that Alix was pregnant, he grabbed me by the lapels and said, "Every dryness in your life will finally get some summer rain." The next day, Alix's father said, shaking, through tears, "Now you'll know what all of the words are about, all of this mythology and literature. You'll understand what everybody's feeling and fighting over."

The window will be thrown open as I leave this desk. Rain will splatter in and blur my notes and short out the laptop. I'm leaving so many things behind: my childhood, my extended childhood as an intellectual, my first marriage to a once-dear friend I never see any more. I have a stepdaughter who lives an ocean away.

The love I have is all concentrated right here, but it has frayed edges. What I want most to leave behind is the loneliness I have both cherished and hidden myself in. I've installed a shelf above the changing table and started to freeze containers of bone-marrow for the coming labour.

From the corner of my eye I see that Alix has drawn a strong path down through the woods to the sea.

At seven months, her body is rushing forward into a new state. Her belly is enormous. It takes the lead when she's walking. We go to a restaurant and her belly arrives first and the server asks the belly, "Table for how many?" She's developed a whole new sub-English dialect of grunts and breath-puffs and little moans in the night. She's talking with baby and with the newness of her shape. I've developed a new dialect as well, but it's silent and mainly consists of one repeated question, asked breathlessly, like I'm six years old: *What's happening? What's happening now?*

We were in Mexico on a yoga trip the day we found out Alix was pregnant. She started yelling from the bathroom. *That is definitely a plus sign! Come quick—am I making this up? No I'm not making this up! I've seen a lot of these, and it's never been that totally a plus sign before!* So I had this one awkward instant over wondering exactly how many pee-sticks she'd seen, but then suddenly we were jumping up and down in the nude like two kids on a bouncy bed. We were laugh-crying. I took a picture of the pee-stick sitting on the top of the toilet, flashing its big plus sign. In the picture you can see the yellow water in the bowl. We didn't want to flush it. As if that would hurt the baby! I grabbed her by the arm and said, *Maybe you should stop jumping—the baby!* Then I took a picture of Alix, standing radiant against a window edged with palm fronds. It was the first picture of a new existence.

That night we couldn't sleep. We'd stopped laughing, but the smile and astonishment were cramped into our faces. I felt exhausted. We wrapped up in beach towels and walked down to the roaring sea. We chucked the towels aside and waded in naked. The moon and stars were covered by low clouds. I could hardly see Alix, so I just grabbed on to whatever I could touch. We swam blindly in the warm surf, yelling each other's names, and *I love you.* There was also something dark about it. Like we were baptizing each other into some knowledge of what love does to people.

Then we saw two flashlights bobbing along the shore towards us. It was two cops. They shined their lights on us and we were busted. We ran out to get our towels, laughing. They rolled their eyes and kept walking.

I'll be glad to read your thoughts and let them ground me a bit. This is the first time around for me, at least for this stage of parenting. I can't even think about it without shaking.

love,
Matthew

|||

September 11th

Matthew,

I know something about windows. In fact, this teak desk where I write you from faces a window. To my left is a black meditation cushion; to my right, an altar with a small Buddha statue and an incense bowl. The Buddha sits on an almost-square stone, likely slate, that I found last month on the shore of the Hudson River, just outside Saugerties, New York. In the first hours of the morning the stone is a cold grey but by 7 a.m. the sunlight reveals lines of copper that cut through its edges. When the Buddha is placed on the stone it's off-kilter, and there's no way I can get it to stand straight. In the morning I light incense and bow to the off-kilter Buddha. As with many Chinese versions of the Buddha, the face is female and the body is male. Sometimes I think the off-kilter Buddha is like a marriage: not so holy, but not limited to the mundane either. No matter what I do I just can't get the Buddha straight. Sitting next to the Buddha is our own pee-stick with the positive sign winking through the plastic window.

My office is small and sparse, painted the colour of dry clay, with hundred-year-old chipped baseboards that have probably been painted twenty times. We moved here this year and within four months had conceived. In the corner of this office, under the window, my son's Lego is piled up. He spent all weekend building an F-14 Tomcat—a fighter jet he saw Tom Cruise flying in *Top Gun*. In our rush to get to the first day of school on Monday, he dropped it and I stepped on it. He howled. We argued for ten minutes about how he had to leave it in a pile because we were late for his first day of grade four. He didn't care: he just wanted to rebuild the plane that took him three days to create. So under the window we each have our own altar. His is a blue, red and yellow plastic Lego mess. Mine, I can't get straight.

When Carina was six weeks pregnant she went to the walk-in clinic for an unrelenting bladder infection. She had A with her because I was teaching. It was evening. On the intake form she wrote in blue pen, in large letters:

I AM SIX WEEKS PREGNANT. I AM HERE WITH MY STEPSON.
PLEASE DO NOT SAY ANYTHING. HE DOES NOT KNOW YET.

As soon as the doctor walked in he read the chart and blurted: "So you're six weeks pregnant?" Shocked, A sat up: "You're six weeks pregnant?" He repeated it a few times and then slipped from his chair to the floor.

Carina called me when I was done teaching and a student drove me to meet them at the clinic. A stood there without coming towards me and then let loose every swear word he knew. Then: "You assholes! I don't want another kid! Being an only child is the best part of my life!"

After he calmed down a bit we got in the car and drove west on College Street in total silence. It was June, humid, and I watched as all these young people, likely single and childless, passed by in the bike lanes heading towards Little Italy. Riding one by one, dressed immaculately, upright on their bikes, the evening nothing but possibility. The sky was open and dark. The bright buildings looked like faces. I watched the silver gears, the pedals, the spinning spokes and the hubs at the centre, turning slowly, wondering how to deal with A's upset.

When we stopped at the drugstore, A and I waited on the curb while Carina went to fill her prescription. I told him how I felt when I was his age and learned I was going to have a sister, how I was angry that my parents wanted to do something new, something that wasn't going to benefit me in any way. He started asking me questions about it. Then he said: "I'd rather have a brother, though I know you and Carina are probably going to have a girl. And if you do, I think you should name her Merren."

We played around with ways to spell the name. Merryn. Merrin.

We held hands as we walked to find a snack. Again I noticed the sidewalks filled with young people—getting off their bikes, locking bikes; some with helmets, most without. Jeans tight, skirts short, shirts sweat-stained from the humid air. When A holds my hand I want it to go on forever.

We got back in the car and drove home. Carina was quiet and I could tell she was exhausted. In the back seat, A looked out the open window and watched the city go by. Carina drove the last leg home and I held her hand. Her hands are always warm. In bed that night A came in to kiss me goodnight a second time after I'd already tucked him in. He ignored Carina. It's so complicated.

Your current doula was our doula when A was born. She had us do a similar drawing exercise. I drew a birth scene in which I was standing in the room but there was no ground beneath my feet. There was pencil crayon blood, a relaxed mother post-birth, lots of (paid, professional) women around to support her. But I was alone with no ground. The drawing haunted me enough to prevent me from speaking about it much, if at all. The women were all on one side and I was alone on the other.

When Carina and I learned that we were pregnant, I made plans to go to upstate New York on a silent retreat. I wanted to immerse myself in stillness, ritual, chanting—the monastic life I love. I drove to the retreat centre a day early and spent time in the Hudson River Valley, two hours north of Manhattan, walking, thinking, swimming—alone. I found this square slate rock there, the one the off-kilter Buddha stands on in my office. I knew when I found it that it would make a perfect altar.

It was hot and I dove into Copper Lake, eyes closed, swimming as far as I could without opening my eyes. I'm not a good swimmer, but that whole day all I wanted was to be underwater, where I couldn't see, going forward, trusting that everything would be fine.

When I found that nearly-square stone on the bank, I made a vow to myself that I wouldn't go forward into this next stage of my life without ground to stand on. Not this time. In meditation, I find myself sinking into places that have no solidity, where there is nothing to hold onto, like swimming under water with my eyes closed. But going forward with a family requires a whole different approach. Carina was upset that I left for a long retreat, especially after being away a lot this year, but she also knew I needed to step away.

You think of yourself as a writer. I think of myself as a wayward monk, a priest of a temple with no walls. Not an ascetic yogi in the forest nor a Buddha who left his home. I'm struggling to find ways to bring yogic and Buddhist teachings to life in the city, to make them relevant to child rearing, daily chores, commuting, gardening. This is something I hope we can unpack together, Matthew—how these spiritual teachings, rooted in ancient India and the halls of monasteries in Tibet and Japan, can come alive in our own context. The popularity of mindfulness meditation is complex because we are taking what were essentially monastic meditation techniques and applying them to the mess of everyday life.

No one in my circle of friends believes in reincarnation. I don't believe, like the Buddha did, that the earth floats on water. But I still feel like I'm part of an invisible lineage, a long conversation echoing throughout history on how to live a helpful and meaningful life. Buddhism looks entirely different in Burma than it does in Korea. What's this practice going to look like in this next century? Does the 21st century Buddha live in a home with solar panels? Does the Buddha change diapers? Can a spiritual community hold same-sex marriage as a virtue? What happens to these teachings in Toronto today?

Since I've known you, you've had time to write and think and practice and read. Your stepchild is grown up. Before A's mother and I split I found it difficult to balance practice, research, writing, chores and childcare. It was never well balanced until, funnily enough, his mother and I separated. Then—as difficult as that process was, and is—I found time to be present as a father and also let the inner monk in me come out again. Maybe the most underspoken benefit of separation is that you can finally have more time on your own! Now, Carina and I are talking a lot about how to integrate practice and relationship in such a way that our family can flourish. Carina wants to create a family altar where we light incense together every morning. We say grace before meals. And though Carina keeps suggesting we sit together, it's happening less and less as the demands of cooking, cleaning, and getting A to school, increase.

I think the saying goes something like, "a healthy relationship is two people being alone together." I'd go further than that. A healthy relationship is also not having fixed views about the other. In a certain way I think I can never know Carina fully. How can we ever truly know our partners? I can't even fully know my own self. We are constantly in flux. Maybe it's in that space that love arises?

Matthew, how are you thinking about marrying your craft with your domestic duties? It's easy to say, "the two are one," but I'm not sure it's that easy in practice. Some days I want to drop all these chores, lock the doors, shutter the windows, fill the fridge, and stay in with Carina and talk and rest and make love. Meanwhile the off kilter-Buddha in my office watches over us, turning me around, to face the way our family is growing.

love,
Michael

September 12th

Michael –

In Ayurveda, they say to keep the windows shuttered for the first three weeks of baby's life. Week three is said to introduce the fire element through light and visual form. Week one belongs to sound and space: I bought a small finger-piano to play for baby's first days. It has a gentle and melancholic ring. Week two is touch and the air element and they say this is where baby massage begins, every day. I have all kinds of oil stocked up. Oils I advise for my clients when they are going through their own rebirthing.

Planning ahead with sentimental detail is something I get from the real pro, my mother, who has her own ancient system for arranging things, learned from a working class childhood and surviving so many things. Endlessly industrious, frugal, creatively preparing for every coming storm, good or ill. Sewing, knitting, sanding tiny shingles and railings for the doll's houses she builds meticulously for my niece, keeping the dinner table laid and ready to entertain, scouring garage sales for the next season's necessities. *You won't believe what people just throw away*, she says. It never feels like she's just talking about their things, but about their very labour, or their memories, and that on these Saturday morning suburban lawns, people are losing their dignity by allowing their lives to slip away, one nickel at a time.

Her own memory is a steel trap, holding the entire economy of our relationship and our needs: it will always be her pro bono job to provide and console. Of course I can't always see it like this. She'll call me from fabric stores and antique sales with newsflashes about good deals and to make sure I don't need anything. Sometimes I think I disappoint her by not being able to see as far ahead as she can. But I also know I protect myself from her vigilance when I feel it occlude my future, my fantasy that I can somehow be free of time. It's taken me many years to accept and even enjoy the moments when her love feels like worry to me. It no longer makes me feel like something terrible is immanent. Now it connects me to some wisdom she has about how precious everything is, down to the simple miracle of a wooden toy she'll find on someone's lawn and buy for baby for a dollar, because she knows she'll never see something like that again for such little money.

It's necessary at times to get some breathing room by rejecting the vigilant parent, but in the end it's really good if you can come back to them, because maybe they know more than you do about this fragile web.

Mom sewed some thick curtains to black out the windows in our small apartment. But now she has a broken hip, and I can tell she's worried on the phone at the thought of not being able to climb the stairs to see baby. The head of her femur is totally smashed from a fall a few months back. When she walks with her canes you can hear a sickening grind of gristle and bone fragments. She's waiting for a surgery date, but it won't be for another few months. I see how much pain she is in and realize why such injuries were fatal in earlier times. I imagine my mother seeing our drawn curtains from the car in the street below. Baby comes in October, which is only six weeks away, and we're hoping it will still be warm enough to set up folding chairs on the sidewalk by the car, and maybe a table for tea.

Our neighbour is an old Portuguese lady who is dying of cancer. Everyday her middle-aged children come and sit with her on the front patio in plastic chairs. Before they come she sits alone. Her skin is grey. When they come she gets some colour back. She insists on making them all coffee. It imagine it takes her a long time to scoop the dark coffee into the espresso basket. When they go home in the evening she retreats to the middle room where the TV is always on a 24-hour news channel. When I take our laundry through the lane around the back I can see her through the window, in an easy chair, gazing at the screen, or sleeping. The headlines ticker by.

I'm sure that if my mother comes and we need to set up outside for tea the Portuguese family will lend us their chairs. If it's a Sunday they might offer us some of the barbecue chicken they always make after church. Maybe I'll try to have mom and dad come especially on a Sunday.

Alix always wants to talk with baby inside. She lies on her side on the couch with her eyes closed and her hand cradling the underside of the bump, which week by week is starting to protrude beyond the edge of the couch. Sometimes I'll play the thumb piano beside her, and baby will roll and thump. The best time is at twilight. My teachers used to say that mantras at twilight were most powerful.

My own brother was born when I was A's age. I remember being the diaper-folder. I have a visual memory for most things, but I can't picture exactly how the folds go. I think when they deliver the cloth diapers this week I'll pick one up, close my eyes, and fold it by feel. My hands will remember, and I know I'll be able to change baby in the dark. I've been reaching myself into these semi-conscious tasks, maybe in the same way that baby reaches into a sense of being here, being a thing. Baby doesn't have to fold diapers, or remember to do anything, except learning to be something that moves with and against the world.

There are stacks of unread books on my desk, and a pile of empty Moleskine notebooks as well. But it's the diapers that will be opening now. You're right: I have had time to read and research since you've known me, but there's been something hollow about it, perhaps because books have deferred a deeper need. Even the stuff I'm most entranced by—reading phenomenology and neuroscience through my years of yoga and meditation practice—has left me blank on many days. I open a beautiful book (someone else's life-work and baby) and feel distracted, as though a book asks the body to set aside its own tasks.

This is where I feel conflicted about the yogic ideal of *svādhyāya*. The word is usually translated as "self-study", but it technically means the study of one's one *"ādhyāya"*, meaning "lesson." Back in the day, this referred to that portion of the Veda that a priestly family in ancient India was commissioned to memorize and therefore preserve as a living text. An endless line of boys mimicking their fathers, verbatim.

I imagine we're both questioning the archaic scripts that have been handed down to us. The illusions of romantic fulfillment, and complete emotional transparency. The ideal of the nuclear family bubble. Thinking your partner is there to make you happy, and other forms of co-dependency. Having children because you want to relive your childhood, or have some kind of control over something.

Beyond all that, I have always felt a yawning gap between what is happening in life and every language or model that attempts to describe it. The only scriptures I remember are those that tell me to close the book.

I've been chafing at something else. Self-study puts a strange ceiling on learning. It turns windows into mirrors. In my dreams now I hear a baby cry, and I rush to do something, or I calm myself down, knowing I can't help in the way my instinct tells me. Baby's cry in the night will open something else. It won't come from me, and it will open a part I do not know or did not choose to open. I'm ready to not choose. Funny, now that neuroscience is screwing up whatever we thought we knew of free will: perhaps I am also more ready to sink into every choiceless condition of love, no matter how it feels.

Through the bustle of your own family life you have seen me blessed with a lot of time, and this is true in a stopwatch sense. But it was also time burdened by self-direction, and I'm looking forward to what the tiny new boss will have me doing, and what essential thoughts will squeeze out through the gaps in the storm.

I want to string a laundry line from our second-floor porch to the struggling oak tree in the yard. I remember hanging my brother's washed diapers on the line at my parent's house. In the winter they would freeze stiff and flat as book boards, smelling like powdered milk. My mother told me that when she was a child she'd hang her brother's pants out to dry in the winter and that when she brought them in they'd stand up on their own on the kitchen table. My father, youngest of ten children, remembers his mother feeding the laundry through the rubber rollers that squeezed out the water and how there was a whole basement full of drying racks in their grand old wood-frame house in Detroit, which was burned out and demolished in the 70s.

Tens of thousands of Detroiters today, mostly black folks, grandchildren of sharecroppers who came north to work on factories that globalization has now shuttered, are having their water service turned off. The shock-doctrine technocrats in charge of the bankrupt city have decided to deprive residents of running water if they're a few hundred dollars behind on utilities payments. I'm watching the news and seeing single mothers hauling water from fire hydrants to bathe their children. There's nothing quaint about their laundry lines or the freezing winter. I know none of them have time to write or read letters like this, and I don't know what to do about it, except to remember that resisting oppression is always a call to both the heart and to the pavement.

A few years ago, I started reading everything the radical environmentalist Derrick Jensen has written. I was hooked by the first page I read, in which he says something like: "Every morning I have to ask myself whether it is more important for me to be writing than it is for me to be going out and bombing one of the thousands of river dams in this country that are killing the salmon runs, the lakes, and our forests." So you should know that a part of me is asking a variation of this question every time I sit down to write to you. My attention is riveted to the scale of the very small, but the macrocosm invades without mercy.

When I was a baby, my mother wrote her master's thesis while I napped in the afternoon. I know another woman writer who discovered her daughter would sleep for an extra hour if she kept her awake by running her in the stroller through Trinity Bellwoods park. She finished a book of stories before baby turned two. And my ex-wife, K, who wrote fragments of novels while my stepdaughter, V, slept or made drawings. V, with her tousle of straw-coloured hair and tiny industrious fingers, and K, scratching out a sentence with her right hand and reaching for the teapot with her left, pouring without looking, her heart full of words, her flesh split between the child and the page.

You didn't know me in that other family, which continues in broken form. One of the reasons you've known me as a book-hermit is that I'm a stepfather with an empty nest. V is twenty-three years old now, living in England. K lives there too.

Running with the stroller and writing novels while playing with baby are stories of parents in their twenties, I think. (Privileged stories, as well.) At forty, I wonder if I'll be as driven to multi-task. I may be speaking too soon, but I think I have less to accomplish now. For as long as I can remember, I have had two or three manuscripts in my head, fully formed, creating pressure because writing them out takes an irritatingly long time. My discipline towards writing often reaches a fever-pitch of anxiety.

I often think: "I may die before I finish this book, and then I will be completely invisible."

But the morning after Alix and I discovered she was pregnant, I woke up in the Mexico beach house, mostly relieved of that anxiety. I never was self-made—I understand this now. Studying myself has reached a plateau. I'm never going to know everything I want to know. Perhaps I don't need to finish anything after all.

love,
Matthew

|||

September 13th

Matthew,

It was so encouraging for Carina and I to have you and Alix over for dinner last night. It was our first chance to spend time with another expecting couple since learning we're pregnant. The way you came through the door all excited about the home we've made—investigating the 1950s Westinghouse stove, our new cedar deck, the old lights, the food, the barbeque—I really felt your turn to the domestic, which made me see our home in a new light. I followed you around and as you made an inventory of what we need to finish (drywall, baseboards, windows) I noticed, maybe for the first time, that you are much taller than me, with broader shoulders, and I remembered the time I first saw you, when you lived with K in the east end, when you were thinner, pale, not this vibrant version of Matthew that came through my door excited about everything.

I'm a friend of the mother/writer you referred to in your last letter. She's prolific and inspired. From how I know her, as my neighbour, she seems totally present with her two kids who are both a little older than A. Just yesterday she sent me an email with a list of books she's reading, why I should read them, and details about how they impact the way she thinks about narrative. I mention this because, to me, it seems that the conversation you and I are having is about the way our own narratives are changing. We are both, I think, figuring out how to prepare for the arrival of a child that we want to *change* us. It begins with small domestic chores.

Folding miniature sleeves. Unscented laundry soap. Early morning dishes. Laundering cotton blankets. Walking the frosty grass at the crack of dawn, hoping Alix or Carina can get a few extra hours of sleep.

Remembering taking A in his stroller on this same route, trying to get him to sleep by taking the bumpiest path, which helped him close his eyes, while his mother slept at home. I wasn't practicing yoga in the early mornings anymore so I needed to get out of the house and walk. Daily, my mind spends early mornings in the past.

You said something in your last letter about studying the self. The 13th century Zen thinker and poet Dōgen Zenji speaks clearly about the self:

To study the Way is to study the self.
To study the self is to forget the self.
To forget the self is to be enlightened by all things.

So perhaps there is purpose in contemplating the moods, ideas, feelings, memories, peculiarities and neuroses that we think of as *me* and *mine*. We need to learn how we function—alone and in relationships, in silence and at parties. But, Dōgen says, the purpose is to "forget yourself." Maybe to let go of who you think you are is to be "enlightened by all things." The more we study the self the more we see it's in flux, without, it seems, something solid standing beneath it. The self is a narrative. We are fiction. And here we are writing letters to each other trying to tell the "truth."

If we are made of stories, then old stories can certainly be reworked in the present. When Carina and I give birth to a new baby, I don't want to be thinking about the past as much as I am now. I worry if things with Carina will go the way they did with A's mother, I worry about supporting the family and child-support for A, and I have resentment that A's mother and I never had a chance to talk things through.

When A was born I relished waking up early in the morning to listen to his irregular breathing. I loved the smell of his head resting on my chest. Those moments gave me some kind of relief I can't explain. As his mother slept I'd take him out on long walks in his stroller, on the bike, or when he was tiny, wrapped up inside my down jacket. I walked all the way to Home Depot once at 5 a.m. and bought an extra large thick down jacket just so I could keep A's growing body curled up against mine during winter walks. We walked for hours along railroad tracks, through the west end of the city, in the snow, and often with a hot water bottle tucked between us. Sometimes we were one body, sweating against each other, him humming as I would sing as we walked, or putting my finger in his mouth, before teeth came through, and wondering if he knew they were my fingers or not. When he was nine months I started taking him to St Lawrence Farmers market on Saturdays at five in the morning. I'd balance bags of squash, eggs and greens on the stroller. In the car on the way home he'd sleep as I listened to audio books.

I don't want to idealize laundry and the smell of babies. It's hard work, too, as you know. But I feel more prepared for the hard parts of fatherhood now, much more than I was the first time at least. I was younger, my relationship was rocky and I had lost touch with myself. I was always thinking about how I could make A's mother happy to the point that I lost track of my needs: routines of meditation and yoga, a balanced workload, eating well, time with friends, celebration.

Ten years have passed.

How about you, Matthew? When you became a stepfather, your stepdaughter was four. Certainly you aren't the same self now as when you first met her.

love,
Michael

| | |

September 14th

Michael –

Your question woke me up very early. *Surely I am not the same self.* And yet I am. *But I have lived so many lives.* But there is a through-line, a thread: I think this might be a pre-Buddhist meaning of the term *dharma*. My story has continuity. There's also something continuous about things that are perfectly round. Like the moon, and our partners' bellies.

When we walked into your beautiful old house I started to vibrate with every house I've ever owned and patched up. You're right—I did feel a little like an excited and underemployed contractor. I remembered the horsehair in the plaster-lath of the first old house K and I bought in Montpelier, Vermont. Remembered taking down walls and figuring out how to frame a vaulted ceiling. Or the ruined apple orchard behind the old farmhouse we moved to in the mountains, and how I tried to make money harvesting the field of St. John's Wort that grew yellow in July. I didn't make money of course, but the blood-red oil on my fingers lifted my depression a little bit, and connected me to something that then became my career in Ayurveda. And always the wood: cutting it down, splitting it, laying it up to dry and then smelling the hardened resin under the ice the following year. There is nothing like a wood stove you feed with the work of your hands that gives a clearer sense of how time burns and warms all of these things hurtling into the past.

So I confess I took vicarious ownership of your house for a few hours as well, and worked up a mental tally of the costs you still face before winter. There's a lot of work to do! Trim alone in the kitchen will cost close to a grand if you do it yourself, and it's got to get done or that pretty wood stove will do nothing but suck the cold air in. Anyone who's a writer worth the name can learn to use a mitre box, and enjoy the excruciating pleasure of measuring the eccentric lengths of baseboards along funky old walls. The measurements are like people's stories and the strange angles at which they join.

But I know you don't have the time now, even if you had the skill. In the *Bhagavad Gita*, Krishna says "Yoga is skill in action", and in this case skill would equal time, and time would equal money, and money buys firewood to keep baby warm. Our practice is not just internal now.

It wasn't until the second glass of wine that I let your house be your house again. Funny how adding up flooring costs indicates a kind of responsibility for your life as my friend. But it happens with your family as well. I look at Carina and think about what she'll need in the third trimester and postpartum. I play around for a moment in my mental apothecary, wondering if I'd change the ingredients for her batch of the perineal salve I just made for Alix. Or I feel A's overflowing excitement at being ten, his fascination with his helicopter which is actually a symbol of the complete machine of the world. I want to give him a quiet voice to double your own. I want to tell him the story of how my brother was born thirty years ago, how I saved his life in the lake that day he was three, how we are still connected through all of this change, how he will always be my brother, how even now a part of him clings to my neck with his small arms, wet and shivering and crying his eyes out as I struggle to shore.

Something remains and threads through, even in old Dō-gen's life. When I think of him brushing out that poem you quoted, I can see him in his little post-and-beam study, light slicing down through the rice paper between the slats. I bet he had a favourite lettering brush and a particularly well-worn robe for sitting in in the frosty morning. I imagine these objects might have been even more dear to his sense of continuity, knowing that he never had his own children, as you once told me, knowing that his parents had both died by the time he was ten.

I can't imagine Dōgen or anyone else not hanging onto things. Even this season carries the wisdom of the last time it was this season. This relationship carries a love burnished by the last.

I was twenty-two when I fell in love with K and left my entire life in Toronto to live with her in Europe. I met her in Southampton, England, on my first morning of my first trip abroad on an Arts Council writing grant. It was May. We spent only a few hours together that day. Two weeks later I stood in a phone box in Prague and yelled into the Soviet-era handset that she should come to stay with me where I was writer-in-residence for an art symposium. She came. In July she flew back to the States. After she left I almost died of a fever in the old monastery I was working in. In August I followed her back to Vermont, thinner and burning with change. I met her daughter V and we all stayed together for a week at her family's cottage. In September I sold my books and the few things I had. In October I packed an army surplus duffel bag and flew to Dublin to live with them with a hundred dollars in my pocket and a half finished novel on my dinosaur laptop.

Today it seems I could not be more different from that child on that plane in 1994: alienated from my family, enraged at my uselessness in the world—and what do you know?—unconsciously committed to nothing but remaking family and utility with this strange and beautiful woman and her strange and beautiful child. I plunged into the dream of a wished-for heroism. I loved without knowing who I was. We can do this—we do it all the time—but it's fragile. Knowing more of who I am, which is something I've come to slowly but with groundedness, is the frayed thread that binds frayed edges together. Tonight I find myself in Alix's strong arms. I tell her these stories. *This is what has happened so far. I am a work-in-progress.*

She tells me her stories as well. None of our stories change the temperature of the air on our naked shoulders.

I was such a different person back then, and yet as I write out bits of this story my fingers fly without even thinking, because that different person is still within me. I have told the story many times to myself and to others, with shifts through time, but there's also something stable about it. It's like a raft, anchored in a lake, that I can swim out to, and rest in the sun for a while. So it's not "just a story," as I hear the new-agers say. It seems to wrap around a core of memory that combines with an ever-present intuition—as simple as knowing at a glance that you've only laid up an eighth of the firewood you need for this winter—to form the only self I could ever know.

Last night before sleep I was overcome with a panic and had to hold Alix almost too tightly. She doesn't mind. Alix who now surrounds this sphere of her belly. We call her belly "the moon," "the watermelon," "the world," and I found myself almost clawing at her as though I wanted to get inside with baby and be at source and beginning of things.

She asked me: *Do you feel distant from baby?*

Maybe this is where the invention of the soul comes from: men feeling something raw and essential growing in the women they love, something swelling and invisible, something inaccessible, not inside them, something the woman is holding or withholding.

Not distant. I just can't get close enough.

I soothe myself by singing to Alix's belly. A poem by Blake, a song by Leonard Cohen, an old Catholic plainchant. Alix feels baby wriggle. Baby's head is down, and low, sinking into Alix's pelvis, putting downward pressure on that threshold I've crossed with my upward surge back into love.

Today we're going to the medical supplies store to buy a plastic sheet for our bed to catch the birthwater. We don't have a woodstove in our little apartment, but I have an old oil-circulating spaceheater that I've carried with me since the farmhouse days. I used to sit with my back against it as I wrote or meditated through the Vermont winters. Or I would rest my stockinged feet on it as it tickered away in the garage where I sat and chain-smoked and wrote my novels, trying to suppress the confusion of being a stepfather who was so young, so unprepared. I'm starting to see that I was as unprepared—maybe even more unprepared—for my first experience of family life as you were with A and his mother. I didn't get to bond myself to V's skin and keep her warm in my coat. I just had to present myself to her and hope that she would accept me. But all this was at a time when I was unacceptable to myself. Of course this also means that separating from V did not rip me apart. The stepparent plays such an ambivalent role. So many more people are doing it today than ever before. There's no training for it. Carina is starting to learn these things with A, I imagine.

The midwife said we need a spaceheater for a home birth. It's out in the garage, with all of the other things from my previous life that are with me but have not yet been integrated into this love and family. I'll bring it in later this afternoon and give it a good cleaning.

love,
Matthew

|||

September 15th

Matthew,

It's getting cold here and I too just brought in two space heaters from the garage. One of them I gave to my friend Steve five years ago when my last relationship ended, and I had a few things I didn't think I'd need again. When Carina and I moved into this house Steve gave the heater back to me, saying nothing other than, "Warmth and continuity, Michael. You'll need this."

My father and I once didn't speak for two whole years. I needed to separate from him—physically and psychologically. I wanted my own thoughts. I walked away from a business job that my father approved of and found myself suddenly under pressure to choose something new. I wanted to pause, maybe become a monk. I was starting to visit a meditation centre in Massachusetts to learn how to sit. I had also started psychotherapy. I was reading Joseph Campbell's ideas on the hero's journey and Carl Jung's theories of individuation. After one numb psychotherapy session I said to Anthony, my therapist, "I need a break from my father. He is taking up most of my mind."

Sitting in a wooden chair, the standard five feet away from me, Anthony squinted and said, "I know many men who don't talk to their fathers."

I walked out of that session into the tree-lined streets of the Annex, spontaneously turned south along Huron Street and walked through the University of Toronto campus. It was June, the summer semester was underway, I was working in a bakery full-time, and I imagined myself as a student on campus, en route to class in an old brick building with a smart professor. I watched the students crossing the street and heading into the library. A block later I walked right through the doors of the enormous cement building that is Robarts Library (designed to look like a swan, as my father once told me when we were driving by) and arranged for a library card. Something was carrying me forward. This wasn't pre-planned. I wasn't thinking. With a new blue card in my hand, I took two escalators up to the periodicals room and found two journals—one on Indian philosophy and another on contemporary psychotherapy. I read them cover to cover, devoured them actually. This is what I was hungry for, a life of the mind married to a practice, freedom from my father's ideas of life, success—the expected.

One year later I was back at school.

This theme—that the body knows what to do—returns to me whenever my grand theories of life fail. All it took was Anthony's remark: "I know many men who don't talk to their fathers," and that was that—my body walked straight out of a burning house. I was lucky as well because my uncle Ian, who introduced me to yoga and meditation practice, had just passed away. He lived his life in and out of a mental asylum in downtown Toronto, diagnosed at fifteen with schizophrenia and medicated his entire life until, at fifty, his organs gave up. Soon after his death my grandmother told me that when her husband died (of a heart attack, also in his fifties) money was put away for Ian. Ian never touched it. It was in an account for thirty years, accruing interest. His five siblings received the money and a portion of it came, via my mother, to me. I used the funds to go back to school, but continued working at the bakery.

I woke at 4:30 a.m. in my rough rooming-house apartment on Brunswick Avenue and went to work at the bakery to bake pies, cakes, and bread until noon. I came home, went to school and then practiced yoga and meditation in the evenings. It was the monastic life I craved, right in the heart of the city—few friends, little socializing. When I had school breaks I went on retreats in Massachusetts. I was focused. The places in my heart that were broken and confused now had room to breathe. I detested the bureaucracy of the university but loved my professors, two of whom I spent time with socially, and they became my mentors, showing me their own paths, and this made me trust that whatever I was doing was the right way forward.

One was Ann, an introvert in her late forties from Wisconsin. She loved Keith Jarrett records, Italian food, yoga, meditation, and anything written about psychoanalysis. She taught a course called The Psychology of Religion and when she read William James, sitting on the table at the front of the room, the whole world fit together. I saw in her the richness of melancholy, the way sadness had depth, and she showed me how to live closer to the ground, to listen carefully to what I felt. Eventually we lost touch but just two weeks ago I was on the streetcar in Toronto and I saw her sitting on a bench, legs crossed, watching people walk by. Her body was quiet. I could see her thinking, contemplating street life, body types, and maybe her own visions. I miss her.

When I was stuck or confused, seeking advice from Ann, she'd always direct me back to my body: *Where do you feel that? What would your body do now if you didn't think about it?* Sometimes I thought Ann was more like a choreographer than a psychoanalyst. She didn't always know what to say but she knew that if I moved closer to my body, I'd stumble upon what was truly needed. I am still learning this—we all are.

It took such a long time, maybe four months, for Carina and me to hold hands in public. My arms and fingers, the signal from brain to heart, were thrashed. In the privacy of home, lying on the old wooden floor of my Bellwoods Avenue loft, Carina and I could hold hands, roll around, love each other. When we walked out of the door, I just couldn't do it. I couldn't hold hands with her. The light of day, the faces, the other humans, the sidewalk— the way the world would witness our love was too bright for me. I was still recovering. Carina was patient. Frustrated, but patient. She knew something was growing, that our desire for each other would displace my withdrawn limbs that had crystallized loss. How do we fall down, get back up, and love more deeply? How can we love again after knowing in our bones the unreliability of everything? It took four months to get the trust back, not such a long time in retrospect but still, the body needed time to discover a new language.

Carina knew I was in the Land of Sadness, but she knew time was on our side. She was patient. We went slowly, sheltered by the fact that our bodies knew what was right. She said at that time: "My body was made for loving you." When she said it I started to cry. The mail came through the front door and I went to get it to hide my tears.

love,
Michael

|||

September 18th

Michael –

For me, listening to my body really began one day on a wet rock by a swimming hole. I was naked and shivering. It was probably three or four years into stepfathering. I was at my friend Miles' farm in Vermont. K wasn't there that evening.

Miles was standing on another rock, looking at the water. He's fifteen years older than me. He'd just been through a horrible divorce. We lived in a small town and there were all kinds of vicious lies circulating about him, because people just can't resist taking sides. It's like they're fantasizing about their own divorces, and displacing all their unspoken blame and resentments at their own partners into the court of gossip. Miles was bearing it with uncommon grace. Without thinking, I opened my mouth and asked him "What is fear?" He said "Fear is the absence of love." And he dove into the frigid pond with a warwhoop. I felt a flush of heat to my skin, and dove in as well, drawn by the magnet of water and uncertainty.

Fifteen years later, I stood outside the door of Alix's apartment, feeling like I was crouching on that wet rock again. It was one of our first dates for tea. She opened the door, and held my forearms in her hands. She looked into my eyes, placed her left foot over my right foot, and slowly shifted her weight. Her foot pressed me into the present, and changed my path.

Her apartment is frozen in my memory. A tiny studio, Depression-era, layered with varying conditions of white paint, sparsely furnished, monastic. I looked at her bookshelf and it seemed that it held every important book that I'd either misplaced through multiple moves and life changes, or that I felt slightly guilty for not having made the time to read. The *Collected Wordsworth*, a battered blue copy of Adam Philips' biography of D.W. Winnicott, Alice Miller's *Drama of the Gifted Child*, Sylvia Plath's unabridged notebooks, stories of Mavis Gallant, and everything by D. H. Lawrence and George Eliot. On one of our first dates, we went to the Victoria College used book sale, and brought home bags of classics. We paid for them together and squeezed them onto her little shelf. It was the first part of making a home.

She told me later she loved Eliot's deep generosity as a writer, her meticulous patience in breathing life into every sort of character, high and low. Reading *Middlemarch* had helped her climb out of a depression one spring. One night she read aloud to me the last sentence: "But the effect of her being on those around her was incalculably diffusive: for the growing good of the world is partly dependent on unhistoric acts; and that things are not so ill with you and me as they might have been, is half owing to the number who lived faithfully a hidden life, and rest in unvisited tombs."

She only had two pictures on the wall. One was of that same George Eliot, née Mary Ann Evans. A postage stamp-sized print of a tintype portrait, hanging in the middle of a slightly dirty white wall. I used to stare at it in the early light and wonder what it was like to write under another name. I enjoyed the timeless anonymity of the idea. When Alix moved into the apartment, she didn't change the name card beside her buzzer in the lobby. The card said *B. Moss*. It became Alix's pseudonym to protect "a faithfully hidden life." The other picture was large print of a Matisse nude, a line-drawing that resembles her curviness, but has no face.

How did Alix get to this apartment? How much of of the two of us is still living there? I'm reminded of your fetish for monasteries, or how you spent that winter meditating in a camper van in Algonquin Park. We have rooms and spaces in the past where something unknown grew and changed. And we're all recovering from something.

Yesterday Alix and I detached from our previous families in a way. Last night I had a business dinner, and so she went out to the Beaches to see her parents for a walk and some food. Earlier at lunch I said: *This might be the last time you ever sit with your parents alone, as a child, in your triad.* We both burst into that tearful jag of crying and laughing with realization.

She's an only child. Childhood was dreamy as she tells it, and melancholic, filled with dance and self-consciousness and hiding, and a thousand textures that have dissolved into this presence I love. What a close bond between the three of them! Intense, as it is when there's only one child. They make me think of the Holy Family, how intimate the crèche is. There are no brothers and sisters in that stable. Just the one baby. Only one baby in the world. Her mother, holding Alix and the tiny house and her psychotherapy clients with a precise compassion. Her father, the novelist, watching everything —I mean everything— very quietly, holding people and the world in his eyes and the muscles of his shoulders.

Her dad drove her home and came up to the apartment to see the old rocking chair we'd bought on Craigslist from a woman whose mother had just died. He was able to identify the maker of the chair by looking at it. He wasn't gone a minute before Alix ran downstairs after him, barefoot, eyes moist, to tell him the obvious: *You have been such a good father to me.*

I'd gotten home an hour before Alix, and had started writing a letter to my stepdaughter V. She's an artist.

Dear V—The weather has turned towards fall, but there are still a few hours of summer every afternoon. I've finished a book on yoga that I'm sending to the printer in few weeks, and starting on another book about Ayurveda, although my mind is full of many other things. My mum broke her hip, but she's as industrious as ever. My father's absorbed in her care. My brother is living hand-to-mouth and busking on the streets of Montreal. And we have a baby coming.

I think of you every single day. Sometimes I just close my eyes and envision your flat in the afternoon, and the sound of your scissors making paper cuts, although you might use razors. I even daydream of your cigarette smoke curling in the sunlight. I remember being your age, the pleasure of smoking and art. Of course I only saw your flat when it was empty, and I walked through with your dad and we talked about its strengths and possibilities, like dads should do, although there was really very little to say, for it was in great shape, and you were about to pour yourself into it and make it your own. So when I visualize it now it is still empty and filled with possibility.

This is what being your stepfather has become these days: thinking of you from afar and hoping you are well and trying to feel your life in my heart.

I hope your boyfriend is well and that things between you are good. I miss your dad: please hug him for me. And of course I miss your mother too, not in a way that could change how we have both moved on, but in the way of family grown apart. It's so hard to understand the full story of how this change happened, and why this deep friendship seems so distant now: I hope that something will repair someday. But more than this I hope that she is happy regardless of whether we meet again.

Alix is due on October 9th, which basically means labour can now come at any time. You can imagine how I am preparing soups and potions, and I hope that as you roll your eyes at news of my doctoring you also know I would do anything I could to help you with your own children, if you ever have them, and if I ever have the chance. Life is so short, and I find we have only a small idea of how much we affect each other.

I hope you know you will always be my first child, and that my years with you are a guiding light for better listening as a parent, and that as far apart as we are, I feel your presence.

love, M

The woman who sold us the rocking chair was very concerned about how we were going to get it home. She spent about ten minutes reviewing all possible routes back to our apartment, which was only eight blocks away. As we drove away with the chair tied into the trunk with the length of twine she offered us, Alix said, "That was hard for her, saying goodbye to this chair."

It's a solid chair. Maple, stained blood red.

love,
Matthew

September 19th

Matthew,

Yes we are saying goodbye to many things. The letter to V is beautiful.

Carina wants a rocking chair too. Did you see any others? We've been hunting around on Craigslist, bought a stroller, still searching for a good dresser.

It's 7 a.m., Friday. A is with his mother. Until a few minutes ago I thought I'd have the whole morning free and go for coffee with Natalie, whom I haven't talked to in a few weeks. Washing my face I heard the sound of an incoming message and went straight to the blue screen. It was an email from A's mother:

> I have found live bugs on A's head—I have started treating him. He is not to go to school until he is clear. Could you please get him today by noon at Starbucks as I then have to work after that.

It took a few minutes of pacing my office where my yoga mat is set up to fully accept that my plans today were taking a different course. The switch doesn't happen fast. My synapses are slow today. There are three books on Zen that just arrived in the mail—new translations of old texts—and I want to read them, rest and be alone. The day is clearly heading in another direction. I remember the story of someone asking the monk Basho, "What's your practice?" His response: "Whatever is needed." Or the story of another monk being asking, "What is the teaching of Buddhism?" and his teacher answering, "An appropriate response."

I mentioned Dōgen in my last letter and it's reminding me of so many things. I was in Kyoto in April. It was cold. I was alone. I was happy. I made a pilgrimage to visit the places where he practiced, walked, and on the last days of my trip I hiked up

Mt. Hiei where he was ordained at the age of thirteen. The part of his story I've been thinking about goes like this:

In the 13th century C.E. Dōgen traveled to China to study Zen. His parents had both died, he was struggling with reasons to go forward in his life in the face of loss. Like many other seekers (including the Buddha, whose mother died traumatically seven days after his birth) there are hundreds of stories of young people who were called to the path when they were struck by loss at a young age.

When he arrived in China he met an old man who turned out to be the head cook of a monastery. The old cook had walked twelve miles down to the port to buy fine Japanese mushrooms brought over on Dōgen's ship. Dōgen was puzzled by the distinguished monk and asked him, "Venerable Cook, in your advanced years why don't you wholeheartedly engage practice by doing meditation or studying the sutras instead of troubling yourself by being a cook and just working in a kitchen? What is that position good for?" The elderly cook laughed loudly and said, "Oh good friend from a foreign country, it is clear you have no idea what it means to wholeheartedly engage in practice, to fully engage your life."

Dōgen was bright eyed. He thought monkdom entailed existing in solitude, or being in the company of only kind, quiet people. We all have this fantasy, maybe, that at some point in life the inner monk or nun deep inside all of us is going to enter silence and light candles in the morning. I think you and I have both had periods like this, decades even. The cook is offering Dōgen a teaching here but Dōgen can't see it. What does it mean to wholeheartedly engage the way, even in the practice-position of being the cook? But Dōgen was young, and he had the attitude of a young man, the drive that says, "Get out of my way, no social niceties, I just want to be free."

Now I think differently. As I write these words I imagine Carina nursing. I remember the funny moment after A's birth when his mother's breasts became engorged and then, suddenly, she let down, and out flowed the first delivery of mother's milk. I thought: "Ahh, so this is what breasts are for!" It was as if a woman's body became something entirely new.

Carina is preparing to feed, she's going to be a great mother, and I hope I'm supporting her as best I can. Sometimes I know what to do and sometimes I miss the mark. She wants more massage. She's also upset that I rarely pick up the camera to take photos of her changing belly. It's true, I could be more tuned in. I feel like I'm managing at a macro level, thinking through how to take time off, wondering how A is going to feel, and worried about losing the very rare private hours I have in a day. I'm sure there's more that's stopping me but I see that's a long corridor I don't want to walk down. I do remind myself that the job of the father now is attuning to mother's needs, communicating, remaining present and engaged. I also intuit something stopping me around massaging her more right now. Wait, wait—I can say it more honestly: I'm scared to lose myself to her. To lose track of myself. As I write these words I see an image of A's mother in Mexico and the unreachable look in her eyes the day I saw it was over. The sand slipping away underneath me.

So, practice is whatever is needed. And Carina is articulating her needs. How can I meet them from a place in me that is still shocked by what happened those years ago? The past is always encoded in the present. This is my koan now and mostly I'm keeping up.

It's A's birthday this weekend. He is turning nine, and there's the whole issue of whether we can have his friends over or not, depending on the lice, the nits, the treatment, etc. When my mind starts drifting into frustration that my previous plans are being thrown around, I just tell myself that *this* is practice, that *this* is part of the training—another day in the domestic monastery. Maybe for some people that thought wouldn't help much, but I remember the way the schedule of bells on retreats would remind me that all I had to do was show up, period after period, sitting still or helping in the kitchen, getting out of my warm bed into the cold morning air, hearing the evening bell and knowing there are just two more periods of sitting before sleep. One retreat, in Minnesota, we sat all night to commemorate the Buddha birthday, and I hallucinated colours and triangles within triangles all night without cease. As the sun started coming up I suddenly had a pain in my nose that starting spreading out in all directions, through my teeth and up into my forehead. I opened my eyes and I was on the floor. I must have fallen asleep. I fell forward, right onto my nose. I was covered in blood.

I thought about that fall forward a lot a few years later when A was three months old with a fever and a stuffed nose. He couldn't figure out how to breathe through his mouth so he didn't sleep for more than ten minutes over a forty-eight hour period. Neither did his mother and I. We stayed up, like we were on retreat, and again I was dealing with the same fatigue and frustration, no hallucinations, but I needed to draw on that same shift in story: Michael you are on a retreat, deep in the mountains, and this night up with the baby is your training, the thread from your narrow self to the wider mesh of compassion.

Today is lice practice. It's the nit way. Nit way or gnat way? A nuisance.

(A few hours later . . .)

I was so frustrated combing through A's shoulder length hair that I gave up. With the killer chemical shampoo still in his hair, Carina took over. She has a deeper resource of patience. I'm in the next room typing and Carina is telling A to hold still as she draws the steel comb through his tangled hair. I'm worked up. Here I am writing to you about showing up, about meeting Carina's needs, and I've just totally lost my cool with the nits!

love,
Michael

September 20th

Michael –

I don't remember V getting lice, though I do remember her school being infested, and being on the lookout. I remember just the thought of it made me itchy all over. I remember scratching myself in my sleep.

Like you, I also remember the interruptions into my solitude. In the beginning, at twenty-two, I was just happy to be distracted from my depression, ready to serve this plucky four-year-old with her straw-coloured hair. Ready to be loved and praised by her mother as the helpful and connected young man I wanted to remake myself into.

But within a few years, I wanted my aloneness back. It allowed me, I thought, to get straight with the world. I had trained myself to self-soothe through thinking, brooding, wilting. Writing made me safe. If I could describe life, I could tolerate it in some way. I wrote my second novel in eighteen months, hunched and chain smoking in the garage attached to the tiny house in Vermont we landed in after getting booted out of Ireland for overstaying our visas. I propped my computer on the hood of the car in the dark, isolating myself from dishes and storytime. I remember making and eating dinner, while this impatience surged up: *This is not my family, this not where I am meant to be. And yet I love this woman, this child. Or I should love them. Am I loving them enough? How would I know?*

Often, I wasn't in relationship so much as trying to understand what being in a relationship should look and feel like. I've heard that people on the autism spectrum sometimes have to learn to mimic and then perform social intimacies that they don't quite understand. I think I felt a mild version of that. Fake it till you make it, I guess. The brief moments of making it eventually made the faking part very painful.

As soon as I could, I would excuse myself to go to work late into the night, which meant putting on full arctic winter gear to sit in the mostly unheated garage. I put construction-grade ear-protectors on over my balaclava to block out the excruciatingly tender sounds of mother and daughter getting ready for bed. Part of me hated their bond. It excluded me. But then again, that's what I wanted—to be close, but not too close.

Along with irritation and avoidance came a lot of guilt. I could rid myself of guilt by disappearing into my parka and dark and silence, tapping the keys, restoring order to my internal life by projecting my chaos outward into the world. I could also hide from a commitment, or relieve its pressure at least a little bit. Then I would feel bad about not rising to the occasion, and sink deeper into my garage, and tap harder and faster, and allow the novel to become angrier. It was quite a little feedback loop I had going there.

The absolute law about sitting in my garage was that I needed to have control over when I came out. Cigarettes were also a barrier: if I was smoking, I was untouchable. Being called for help with V's bath or even a goodnight kiss would sometimes provoke a wave of rage that I barely managed to suppress. I remember holding my breath as I kissed her, not only to suppress this emotion that made no sense to me, but in the hope she wouldn't smell my terrible, shameful smoker's breath.

When our relationship was ending, K came back from her therapist one afternoon with a revelation and a sheaf of papers rolled up in her fist. She announced, "You've always had a problem with transitions, going from being alone to being with us. Please read these articles on the links between narcissistic and avoidant personality disorders. I hope you get some help with this if you think you want to go on to have a child with someone else."

I hoped that K's therapist hadn't really pathologized me through her side of the story alone. Still, it was revelatory to step back and remember what I felt in those days and how it related to K's proclamation: *My thoughts are racing about myself and the world . . . this woman does not understand and cannot soothe me... this child does not understand and does not deserve to be exposed to the darkness of my inner world... if I can hide away I'll protect myself from them and them from myself, and I must take charge of when to engage in relationship and when not to... I have no other freedom.*

K was right about me, but many years too late. By the time she found the concepts, I had changed. One of the biggest stresses in relationship might be neglecting to notice that the person you both love and resent in the first few years has become someone different. And there you are, wasting your time complaining about who you think they are, or pining after who they used to be.

I think the fact is that I had few positive self-regulating skills at twenty-two. At twenty-six, I met Buddhism, through K. One rainy night in Dublin she took me to the lecture of some Tibetan guy. He gave some instructions and I started crying uncontrollably. The next day I started meditating. It seemed to be good, but I also used it as a nobler form of self-isolation that I didn't have to feel guilty about. It was *obviously* so virtuous. I know that the sort of Buddhism I met is a big discussion you and I have had through the years. I think you were luckier than I, to run into the mindfulness crowd earlier, while I was zoning out to fantasize about Buddha realms and Tushita heaven so that I didn't really have to face what I felt. But then it did start helping, slowly.

Something tells me that spiritual practice will only soothe a portion of psychic and interpersonal tension, no matter how intelligent and transparent it is. It must contend with the raw fact of being in the right place in the right time, or not. Or, put more softly: being ready or faking it. Faking it can be a powerful teacher, but there are casualties.

I now look at younger men and it seems as if I can smell whether they're ready for fatherhood or not. The ones who are ready have found their breath. They sit at a crossroads where a relatively stable self-identity can meet the uncertainty of the future. The ones who are not are in a tunnel. They need time, a skill, a job, to make money, to be seen. I think the unprepared father feels invisible to his culture. He has not found himself. How can he shine in the eyes of his child? Are we surprised when he hides his darkness in a frigid garage, or at the bar?

It sounds like Dōgen was in the tunnel of the younger man. He was looking forward through the dark, yearning for light, ignoring the mushrooms growing in the damp shit underfoot. Sounds like he needed some time.

love,
Matthew

|||

September 21st

Matthew,

As you know, Alix was here last night with Carina and some of their pregnant friends. It was Tushita heaven! The kitchen was full of women—pregnant women—and A was sneaking around them gathering as many sweets as he could find. Once his pockets were stuffed, he and I went biking to High Park for a few hours, leaving Carina and her friends to cook and talk. "Mostly about clothes not fitting, and sex," Carina would say a few hours later, "things you never talk to *your* friends about." (Wait until she reads this!)

The new playground at the park is majestic, with cedar shakes and a copper roof that's thankfully unclimbable. I pushed A's bum up the hill as he was riding. My father did this with me a lot. He would take me on long rides when I was eight or nine, him on his blue ten-speed with a faded yellow plastic kids' seat on the back, and I with my red Raleigh eight-speed, following along. Sometimes he'd slow down, pull over beside me and reach his long arm behind my bum and give me a push. I'd love the torque, the feeling of suddenly accelerating past him, of being first, the wind, my legs moving faster than I could have pedalled on my own, and the sound of our chains moving us uphill, exhaling, inhaling. Nobody could catch us.

I keep thinking about what you said about "faking it." Carina asks me why I stayed in my last relationship when I was unhappy, not getting what I needed, and unable to express my frustrations. I can't answer. On the outside we looked like a couple in touch with ourselves. I told myself things would get better and I'm sure she did too. I thought that if we split up my life would be worse off. I have enough distance from it now that I can start looking into what happened with more clarity.

I met a Croatian man at the park in his thirties. He was slightly overweight, with an angled pale face, a Metallica t-shirt and sincere green eyes. He was looking after his nephew who was eight years old, two years younger than A. The man told me that when his nephew was being born, the doctor accidently hit his head with the forceps. The baby was in intensive care for four months. He had seizures. When the baby's mother realized how sluggish her child was getting, she took him off medication at one year, started feeding him a diet free of carbohydrates, and he's been fine ever since. He was playing tag with A.

"Now the family is moving back to Croatia," he said, "and since the start of school is this week, they decided to keep him home."

"And you?"

"I'm out of work. I thought I'd get to know my nephew. The time in the hospital was really intense. Now he's eight and he's leaving and I want to get to know him as a regular kid."

We stood in silence for a few minutes, watching A and the other boy swinging on the monkey bars. Then he said: "I wish I could be a father of my own kid. I'd like to know what that's like."

"This is what it's like," I say. I think about his smoking, how he's not taking care of himself, how his family is probably stressed with the move. His nephew is chasing A up the slide. None of the kids are sliding down the twisty orange slide. Either they are climbing up the inside or the outside.

At 7 p.m. it gets cold, we're the last ones in the park, and A and I get on our bikes to leave. The man comes over to me (I still don't know his name) and says, "You're both really lucky." I tell him he's lucky too, but I am just trying to make him feel better.

A and I bike off the hill.

I'm thinking of my father who came to Canada from Poland, after the Holocaust, when he was five. His parents took him to the park behind their home but they couldn't communicate with anyone because they didn't speak English. They were also frightened of people. I'm thinking of our neighbours whose child was born with severe autism, and the woman in the blue house on the corner who died in childbirth. There was the kid in my class in grade two who came to school with a black eye, "from his father," one of the other kids told me, "who hit him." My own father was physical with me but never a black eye or bruises, only yelling, chasing, slamming doors. All week my mind has been straying into these fragmented visions of sick kids and broken ones too.

Later that night I had a dream that the Croatian man was delivering our baby. The doctor said: "She's coming out laughing." The room is full of flowers. There are lots of people around—too many, in fact—and it feels like the lull at a dance when one song has ended and the next has yet to begin. Suddenly everything is quiet and the Croatian man, with an unlit cigarette in his lips, comes over and says: "Everything we think is just words. Words that try to say what it feels like to be here at this time. Now is for dancing . . . "

I'm writing at 6:24 a.m. today, which is rare. This is the time I'm usually trying to fit in yoga or sitting. It's cold out and I thought I'd write you instead, maybe because Alix was here last night, maybe because my letters are taking a while to compose and the house is dead silent and I can't shake this strange dream I had last night.

I understand what you wrote about Alix saying goodbye to her parents. When A was born I felt I was leaving my family and beginning my own. Things with my parents were thorny and I wasn't getting along at all with my brother. But I found that as the years went on, especially when A's mother and I split up, that I became much closer with my family, and with A around they were also getting closer with each other. I think when they saw me broken, I was somehow more available to them, less shielded, and in need of support. They stepped in. Or, maybe I allowed them in.

I used to see my life as a series of separations, or what Jung calls individuation. It's like there are these various births we go through: the first birth of entering the world; our realization that we are not the same as our parents; the sense in our early teens when we start thinking for ourselves, especially about death and wanting to be loved; the process near the end of adolescence of leaving home, and so on. The rituals around those births and deaths help make these transitions meaningful. Having Alix and all the pregnant women in my kitchen last night seemed like one of those rituals.

In a sense we leave home, and in another we never really do. We can't. Our parents are inside of us. We are in them. We may rearrange them in new ways, but their images are built into us. Maybe those images have nothing to do with our parents. Maybe we use our parents as sparks that ignite within us some primordial need to have a father and a mother. And maybe we ignite in *their* souls some deeper pattern of parenting waiting to emerge. I project "father" onto my father the same way he projects "son" onto me.

Our culture has great theories of genetics, the construction of personality and gender, and the influence our family has on us before the age of five. In some private corners of my mind I also entertain the idea that inside Carina a sperm and an egg have found a home to work out a destiny none of us will ever understand. The organism is growing into a world and has already chosen Carina and me as the people he or she needs, as the people who need to meet this lovable stranger. It's like thinking of history backwards.

It's 6:38 a.m. It's September. I am a father. Alix said goodbye to her parents. I looked in the bathroom mirror when I got up and I saw flakes of yellow in my irises. My first thought was "hawk." Then I thought: maybe I am carrying some of this growing organism somewhere in *my* body. Maybe in my eyes. Then

I thought of kids who are born blind, or with only one eye, or yellow eyes—my fantasy life is in the fear loop.

In the Hebrew Calendar it's the New Year. According to A, it feels like winter—he just woke early, came into my office and told me so. These are all so many abstractions to say what it feels like to be here at this time. Now is for dancing. My eyes are going yellow.

love,
Michael

|||

September 22nd

Michael –

Your Croatian friend gets me right in the heart. I'm glad he was able to deliver the baby safely in your dream. I think many men are waiting for the moment when it will be clear that we are no longer endangering what is precious to us, whether it's a partner's love, or a child.

I think of him smoking on the way home from driving his nephew to the airport and wonder if he'll let himself weep, or whether he'll make do with gripping the wheel a little tighter. I hope you run into him again and can tell him your dream.

I appreciate your long view of familial change. My psyche seems to zero in on ruptures and ultimacies, as though I crave bouts of crisis. I associate these with love. It might be a hangover from my Catholic childhood. When crucifixion is your primary iconography for transformation, it's a challenge to develop a subtle view of growth. Religion is a jagged transitional object.

On my mother's side, intimacy is scarred by high stakes. My grandfather was an alcoholic. He came back that way after six years of war in Europe. My mother told me that the British commanders gave their soldiers fresh woolens while digging trenches in Italy, but for the Canadians they just dispersed a ration of rum on the hour. Her story is hers to tell, but I've lived with the echo of that part of her childhood that was punctuated by his chaos.

When I was little I loved my grandfather. A big bear of a man. I loved his cigarettes. I sat in his warm lap and played with the lever on his big old chrome ashtray with the plane on top, making the butts disappear. I loved the smell of his steel butane lighter. We watched the old television for hours: Gilligan's Island, I Love Lucy, Soupy Sales. I could sit with him and just feel time pass safely. Grandparents can be the adults who don't need you to do anything or be anyone but you. I had no idea of all the things that finally got him to AA. It took me a long time to understand where my mother's gallows humour came from. And at a certain point it dawned on me that every bit of creative energy she pours into everything she does carries both the momentum of survival, and an almost giddy joy that life can take a better turn.

But I also remember being the child who wasn't in church and who wasn't part of any family tension—going down to the creek and lying on the clay bank after skipping a thousand stones to get right up close to the scale of the very small. This trickle of water, this dripping blade of grass.

I wonder whether I seek out the rupture for some kind of aesthetic effect. Yes, Alix will be a daughter for as long as her parents are alive, but my heart goes to the flare and irrevocability of the change: she'll never feel *that* triadic energy again, in the same way. It pulls some existential string within me in which death or something close to it makes things both poignant and complete. But it also shows that change for me generally has been an emergency.

I remember seeing King Lear when I was twelve. Lear holds Cordelia and cries *Never. Never. Never. Never. Never.* The iambic foot is reversed into a trochee: the heartbeat is turned inside out with grief. I really am overdramatically thinking of Alix's father here, as I do with my own distance from V. Whatever sorrow we both feel at the passage of time is sweetened by too many things to count. Alix's father seems fine with things changing—a little misty is all. Alix is barefoot on the sidewalk saying hello to a new father as much as goodbye to the old. And V sits by a rainy window in London. I hope she will meet this baby one day, and myself, a new father, an old father, someone who has changed and someone who hasn't.

Trickle of water, blade of grass. How long have you been painting things so softly with your Zen brush, Michael? Its subtle mood gives me space perhaps to use my knives more sparingly.

The split between words and stories and what is happening drove deeper yesterday, a few hours after I pressed send on that email to V. While I was writing it, I had two inner voices: one that spoke from the heart, and one that watched over, wondering and doubting, guessing at her mood, how she would receive this phrase or that, worrying over how her emotions would rise and fall and resolve or not. It's a complex story. She's angry at me for how things ended with her mother. This is the second divorce of parents for her. Her allegiances have been split in many ways, and I'm sure she's just fucking tired of so-called grown-ups. And she spent many months hearing her mother's side of the story alone, forced to play de facto therapist, thrown in at the deep end, unprepared and unboundaried.

So this rich story is turning over and over in my cognitive mind, and I'm searching for the best possible words and lessons and outcomes, but then I look over at Alix as she gasps a little, hand going to her belly, feeling the sharp heat of a pre-labour contraction. And I realize again that underneath the stories of where we've come from and and who loves who and who should have done what and what promises mean and how one wishes things could have gone, the flesh is moving and breathing and growing things.

The garden is on its own time. The womb and placenta and baby are the real calendar here. Our stories can meander and swell and peak and rupture and change and get rewritten over the years, but a gardening season is measured in a set number of days. It takes just about ten weeks to grow a tomato in Toronto.

For babies, forty weeks means forty weeks. Baby's flesh is baby's story. It has rhythm before words.

love,
Matthew

|||

September 22nd

Matthew,

The soft brush of Zen. Carina's kale garden. Alix's swollen belly.

These are the images in my mind as I sit facing the Toronto skyline at the Island Airport. I'm waiting for a flight to Ottawa where I'm teaching for the weekend. I'm also thinking about A's reaction to not being the only child anymore and how best to support him. Maybe I'll pick him up from school some days and spend time alone with him before bringing him home. Maybe we'll need to have some kind of ritual for acknowledging this change in our family structure but I'm not sure what. Across from the ferry is the Island Yacht Club where I took sailing lessons when I was A's age. Maybe I'll take him to the harbour and we can throw stones, heavy ones, flat ones, even shapes that need all our weight to hurl.

On the way to the airport, I stopped at Type Books, my favourite bookstore, to buy a book for the weekend. I couldn't decide between Salman Rushdie's new memoir, written in the third person, or another recently published installment of Susan Sontag's letters (edited by her son). I chose both.

In 1959, Sontag wrote ten guidelines for parenting:

1. Be consistent.

2. Don't speak about him to others (e.g., tell funny things) in his presence. (Don't make him self-conscious.)

3. Don't praise him for something I wouldn't always accept as good.

4. Don't reprimand him harshly for something he's been allowed to do.

5. Daily routine: eating, homework, bath, teeth, room, story, bed.

6. Don't allow him to monopolize me when I am with other people.

7. Always speak well of his pop. (No faces, sighs, impatience, etc.)

8. Do not discourage childish fantasies.

9. Make him aware that there is a grown-up world that's none of his business.

10. Don't assume that what I don't like to do (bath, hair wash) he won't like either.

In my twenties I loved making rules for myself. I imagined them more as necessary constraints, like the ones you need for an art project. In some ways I missed a lot of my twenties because I was so immersed in practice and study. Actually, a few years ago when I was strolling through Williamsburg, Brooklyn, watching the beautiful parade of twenty-somethings on their way past the bookshop I was heading towards, I found myself admiring their pace, the movement of their arms and hands when they spoke to each other, the bustle of the street. I realized how alien social life was to me during my meditative twenties. That night, I felt as if I were finally coming around again to perceiving the world outside myself in a lighter way, one more conducive to socializing. Suddenly small talk seemed as essential as going deep. I fell in love with the architecture of Brooklyn and the busy evening streets. I sat at a restaurant and watched people for an hour.

That night was a turn back towards the extroversion I remembered as a young boy. I don't know too many people who went deep into meditation like I did, or you did, at such a young age. Maybe the world is going too fast now. Who goes on extended retreats anymore? I don't think lowly of that time, not at all, but I'd rather be here at home with my family. Anyways, mindfulness of each moment, which I think of as relational practice, is another kind of devotion. Devotion to Carina and this home, devotion to taking care of my many moods - this is how practice is unfolding now.

Now back to lists. Here's my own, born from my first experience. Nine suggestions for expectant fathers during birth-prep and labour:

1. In the months and weeks leading up to labour, imagine together every possible scenario of how the birth might go, including location, who is in the room, sex of the child, cutting the cord.

2. Let go of all the above.

3. Have lots of food around for everyone who will be there. Liquids especially.

4. Don't be shy about asking others for help.

5. Encourage her to trust her body. The body knows how to breathe and what to do.

6. Take time to step away if the labour goes slowly, and if there is someone else available to the mom. Find your breath, look outside at the sky overhead.

7. Offer to massage her breasts, thighs, legs, shoulders, and feet, but not the nipples so much. Feet are best.

8. Take baths, be close to lakes, rivers or even a pool. Play water sounds on your iPod. Make tea. Talk a lot about water.

9. Have a practice. It's important to connect, everyday, with silence.

What would you add?

love,
Michael

| | |

September 23rd

Michael –

I find Sontag's list a little thin and cold. But I understand it: 1950s feminism was enaged in overthrowing sentimentality. I can hear in her wish for her son her own need: autonomy, a room of one's own.

But when I started parenting I needed mentorship in how to deal with my emotions. Every time V was about to start a new level of school, I would slip into her room late at night and watch her sleep and I would cry quietly. I didn't know how to enter into her world with ease, because I was uneasy in my own. Sontag nails boundaries, but I needed to have every threshold softened.

I haven't helped a partner through labour yet, so all I have to add to your list is my untested Ayurvedic geekery:

— Lots of food? Check. I've made pre- and post-labour bone-marrow broth. Pre-labour broth has warming emmenagogues and downward-moving herbs: cinnamon, saffron, bay leaf, clove, garlic, hawthorne berry. Post-labour broth has vulneraries, antibiotics, and analgesics: white willow, comfrey root, lotus seed, turmeric. We'll simmer sweet potato and carrot into both. I also made lemonade popsicles and stocked candied salmon for labour.

— Food for the soccer team of midwives and doulas coming?
    Check. The freezer is stocked with stewing ingredients,
    the slow-cooker is ready to go, and I've laid up homemade
    chocolates with candied ginger.

— Breasts and nipples? Check. Although it's not very relaxing
    for Alix, I'm happy to say. With olive oil. We've been using
    olive for perineal massage as well. Alix hasn't been able to
    stand the smell of coconut oil from day one. I'm all like,
    "But Ayurveda says . . .", and she pantomimes retching.
    She also can't stand ghee, which I'm taking as a personal
    insult to my Ayur-expertise. Or the spiced chai I make.
    Basically anything she smelled at all during the first
    trimester is now disgusting to her. Except me, evidently. I
    expect we'll have sex during early labour. We can't really
    help ourselves most of the time. Although negotiating the
    enormous belly is getting pretty funny. We're thinking
    of publishing a Kama Sutra for the third trimester.
    "Watermelon Reach-Around"—p. 38.

— Water element? Check. The birthing pool is coming
    soon. Plus warmth. Plus demulcent herbs, especially
    postpartum: licorice, slippery elm. If she gives birth right
    in the pool, I've been wondering about what the water will
    look like as I pump it out into the kitchen sink.

— Practice? Check, I guess. But I don't know what to do
    these days. I sit down to meditate and I'm just making
    lists of what we need, feeling my heart flutter. I roll out
    my yoga mat and can only roll around on the floor. I'm too
    distracted for anything else.

There's some famous midwife who apparently said: *for every
book on birthing you read, you can add two hours on to labour.*
      I used to sculpt my future as well. Also my writing, accord-
ing to artificial constraints. Christian Bök is a friend of mine

—the guy who writes entire book chapters employing a single vowel (*Eunoia* is the name of that book)—and he inspired me along those lines. I think my favourite example is how Milorad Pavic kept The *Dictionary of the Khazars* to exactly 100,000 words, or his *Landscape with Tea,* in which the love story is written in exactly two halves. The man's narrative is written in one direction, and then you flip the book over to read the woman's narrative, written going the other way. The stories meet in the centre of the book.

My first book was an obsessive reverie on pipe organs, in which every page had to be visualized as a pipe. Almost twenty years later, I still work with formal constraints—I'm finishing a book of poems on the Indian rosary that has to have 108 beads. Today, my only formal constraint is: trust Alix. She's feeling hot, and wobbly in the pelvis. I will constrain myself to be open to her sensations. Constraint towards openness is a good model for spiritual practice, I think.

Our cat Krishna knows something's up. We set up a changing table by tacking a beveled changing pad to an old antique dresser. He's been sleeping on it every night, even though he has a half-dozen other places to sleep. Alix frowns at him and says *You know that's for baby, Krishy-roo.* He peers up at her through one eye and doesn't move. *Krishy-roo from Kalamazoo. Do you need a change? Have you got some poopy?* We laugh. He switches eyes and cuddles down closer into the foam.

You'll probably see this letter on your phone during a break between dharma talks. I wonder how well it will harmonize with the formal topic for the weekend.

love,
Matthew

September 23rd

Matthew,

It's cold here in Ottawa and it's taken me two days to realize that this mood I'm dragging around is merely a longing for summer. Actually, for the idea of summer. And in that fantasy I'm carrying a baby. I refused to bring a sweater for the trip, though today I had to put on all the layers I packed.

I travel with a very small black backpack. With my iPad slipped in, it weighs less than eight pounds, I'm sure. I've always felt a quarter domestic, a quarter nomadic, and the rest a mix of breathing and alternating wakefulness and confusion. I'm at home on the road just as I feel at home putting logs in the fireplace. Carina just emailed me a photo of her lying down in front of the wood stove in our kitchen.

Matsuo Basho writes:

The sun and moon are travelers in eternity. Even the years are wanderers. For those whose life is on the waters or leading a horse through the years each day is a journey and the journey itself is home.

Carina and I always joke that when we're at home in routine she's at ease, and when we are in the car trying to find a place to eat in some far away place, I feel at home.

I recall Krishna the cat. One time I was renting your old studio and you had some incense burning outside. When I came in, your door was open and I saw the incense wafting through the patio door and Krishna was lying there in the thick of it, basking in the hazy light. A sandalwood cat.

Today I woke early to meditate. As I was settling in, I realized how practice, like relationship, has so little to do with anything that I consciously think. I sit down and I drop into the way my life moves like water. Timeless—even when I get frozen. This morning I was sleepy, then hungry, then sleepy, then very quiet, then totally in tune with the birds and wind and cars outside, then tired again. Awake, confused, awake, confused—it goes on and on. It doesn't matter how many times a theory rises up and tells me where I am headed or what my life is really like. Theories, too, are just coins rolling away. I think that practice is about staying close to this river of change, coming back to it again and again, and carving a life out of it. Maybe this is all another way of talking about trust. Trust in family again, trust in change, trust in being able to fall down and get back up again. This shifting river is home.

I used to live across the street from the singer Leslie Feist. One day I was walking past her and she waved hello and I noticed she had a tattoo on her wrist. I stopped to see it and it said: HOME. I loved that tattoo and I don't particularly love tattoos. I imagined her touring and looking at that tattoo and remembering that home isn't separate from who we are and what we are doing.

Home is my kitchen, now with no trim and only partial insulation. Home is being 500 miles from Carina and A and the baby, and missing them, and knowing that everyone is okay.

A monk asked Dongshan,
"When the cold visits us, how can we avoid it?"
Dongshan said, "Why not go where there is no cold?"
The monk asked, "Where is the place without cold?"
Dongshan said, "When it is cold, let the cold kill you. When it is hot, let the heat kill you."

"Let the cold or heat kill you"—I love pithy Zen statements like this that I can turn over again and again. Although, I like turning them over in my mind more than I like living them. What gets killed? These stories I have about everything. I remember you once saying that you think Alix is going through a death, a death of who she was before the pregnancy started. It's so true. And, there are so many deaths. The other day I wanted to be alone while A was at school so I could read the new books I'd ordered. The struggle to comb the nits from A's hair was driving me mad. I realized after twenty minutes that there were far too many lice to send him to school. I bought the killer chemical shampoo, washed his hair with far more shampoo than recommended, and then he sat in front of the kitchen window and Carina combed through his hair, picking out hundreds of nits, for the entire school day. Stepmothers should get paid by the hour for this kind of work! He ended up cancelling his birthday party. A day later he was invited to a friend's party and he went, wearing a hat, his hair drenched in olive and tea tree oil. When Carina and I dropped him off at the party, half the other kids were wearing hats too.

I reached a point where I couldn't let the lice kill me. I couldn't slow down enough to comb an inch-wide section of his hair at a time. I wanted it to be over with. Maybe this was all just late-night diaper-changing prep school and I admit to failing miserably.

I've decided to go for a walk now and I'm thinking of you and Alix and your birthing tub arriving, your warmth, your home.

I will step out into the cool fall.

love,
Michael

┃┃┃

September 23rd

Michael –

The weather has turned here as well. We have no woodstove, so I'll have to phone the landlord to have him start up the boiler. I don't want to call him. I guess I resent the fact that I can't turn it on myself.

Before I met K, I'd had a bachelor apartment for just over a year. I moved there after a hard breakup, using plastic shopping bags to move my stuff in. I was very alone. Part of me loved the bitterness. Aside from books, I had paintings and prints from various friends. I didn't have tools, so the pictures never made it onto the walls. They sat at the baseboards, the backings curling with the heat from the smelly electric heaters. I must have looked at them a hundred times, thinking: *I should go to the hardware store and buy a goddamn hammer and some nails.* I never went. Buying tools would have meant investing in a home. I didn't want a home.

There were many times during my marriage with K when I felt I had merged so completely into her life and the life of her child that I thought about those pictures—now scattered and absorbed and almost invisible amongst the many more things that she owned—and whether my path would have felt different had I bought some tools for myself earlier, and hung them. I tried to visualize that apartment as though it had grown beyond the long-term hotel room I made it into.

Years with K gave me some sense of home, but it was never quite mine. I was a guest to her dyad, a guest of her parents, a guest of her ex-husband when we stayed in London. Always a guest of someone older, it seemed, someone with a more well-formed story. I like the idea of Leslie Feist flying around the world with HOME tattooed on her wrist. Yet I wonder if she still feels like someone's guest wherever she goes. She's invited because she sings, after all: *Leslie, you can come to my house because you're a really good singer.* She has to be somebody to earn that invitation. She has to perform something. What if she doesn't feel like it?

I think being a guest means that the table isn't yours to set, the beds aren't yours to make. You aren't the host. You can receive kindness, but you can't receive your own guests. I love that the word *receive* applies to things and people in slightly different ways. Home is where you can receive people, and where people can receive the gift of your home.

By the end of the marriage, I had accumulated a whole shed full of tools in the cottage K had bought out on Cortes Island. Sawhorses, axes, a sledgehammer, a maul, a splitter, shovels, power tools, old wooden shelves where I stored tins of screws and nails, and a mason jar with the extra chainsaw blade curled up in oil. A manual mitre box. A grinder that I used every day to sharpen my spade when I was breaking new garden beds. And a collection of old bucksaws and hand scythes, rusting on their hanging nails, dating back to the first owners, who ran a working farm.

You're missing the idea of summer on the streets of Ottawa. As I remember that shed, I miss the idea of that house and how it vibrated for a few years for me with the possibility of a long-term home. K and I had made extensive plans for the plot and gardens. I spent days in the forest chainsawing deadwood from the paths. I broke about a thousand square feet of sod for garden beds: I wanted to try growing corn. I built ten cold frames out of cedar for April planting, and for basil in the late summer: I slanted the tops at fifteen degrees for the rain to roll off. I built them small enough that K would be able to carry them by herself from the shed to the garden in the spring. We knew there would be many times when I wouldn't be there with her.

K bought the house from a woman named Deborah who had raised her children in it until it was time to move off the very isolated island of 900 for school and to find work. She couldn't bear the loneliness of the island anymore. She had separated from her husband years before. He was a master carpenter, and I would sit on a porch he'd built and admire the joints and the texture of the cedar he'd cut on his Alaska sawmill, which is basically a chainsaw bolted to a workbench with a two-by-four as a guide, left running by keeping the gas trigger pressed with a wire tie-off. A very dangerous set-up. But he made the most intricate cuts with it. I sat there at dusk, gazing at his work, feeling how he'd been there, and how he'd had to leave for whatever reason. I could feel his hands on everything. Deborah had to leave as well, and now lives on a boat, sailing up and down the Queen Charlotte Islands, working as a galley cook for people who want to watch whales or visit the ruins of Haida Gwaii villages—other people's homes, from long ago.

When Alix and I talk about owning a home together, I'm the one who gets all specific. I think of construction, renovation, how many rooms we'd need for what, how much it will all cost, how often things will need paint. Her needs seem completely ascetic in comparison: good food, good windows, relative quiet from the neighbours. It really doesn't matter to her whether we can buy something or not. She'd been renting for the whole eight years since graduating university, most of those years with her ex, a musician who lugs a five thousand dollar instrument to gigs that pay fifty bucks, but loves it. Alix never assumed she would own something, or thought much about needing to own something. Instead what she does is this: every time she wants to tell me something clearly, she puts her left foot on my right foot, just like she did on that first date, as if to say *I don't care where we are. Now we are here.*

So for me now, a home needs a kitchen, and that's about it. If Alix and I travel we rent an apartment where we can cook, and we pack up most of our kitchen to bring with us. The crate of food and spices is much bigger than your 8-pound knapsack. I don't feel I've arrived in a place until I have cooked in it, with my ingredients. I suppose I've learned to take my tools with me— not to hang pictures, but to feed my belly. Actually, now—Alix's belly before mine. Even in some crappy hotel room, I'll bring a hot plate, tea, milk, rice, split yellow mung dal, ghee, salt, garam masala. Two pots: one for chai and the other for kitchari. One wooden spoon, and a sieve for rinsing the rice and mung, and straining the tea. You have to be careful in hotel rooms with hot-plates and fire alarms.

Driving around in a new place looking for a restaurant is actually something I can't stand. I get hungry and untrusting. Somehow it's easy for me to forget that I've never starved. The world has always received and supported me, no matter how homeless, confused, or nervous I am. I know I am lucky in this.

One of my favourite scenes from the movies comes at the end of Bertolucci's *Sheltering Sky*. The heroine, having lost her husband, her friends, her society, and recently escaped from love-slave captivity in the desert, wanders into the Cairo café where she'd begun her journey a year before, and finds Paul

Bowles, the author of the novel and narrator of the film, sitting with a cup of mint tea. He's a very old man in a white linen suit. She floats towards him as the music rises. He looks at her as he would at a daughter and says: *Are you lost?* She breaks into this tearful smile and says: *Yes.*

Some other guy may work the gardens I dug on Cortes, or mend the gate I put up that leads to the forest. I'm sure it's leaning by now. That's his problem. But I should have left him some notes on how I secured it. No matter what we feel about each other, we should always leave each other notes on how to secure things, or loosen them.

Alix sets the changing table. She puts tinfoil in the cradle to train Krishna out of jumping into it. He's an incorrigible cuddler, and we'll be shooing him away from baby nooks for months, I think. The cradle is mine, from when I was a baby. My mother polished it before bringing it over.

love,
Matthew

‖‖

September 23rd

Re: Vacation Reply
Thank you for your email. I am travelling and teaching and not checking my email until October 2nd. If this is urgent please contact my assistant, Bronwyn:
brownwyn@centreofgravity.org
Michael Stone

‖‖

October 2nd

Dear Michael,

It's been a week since we've written—we've both been busy. But I have an hour this afternoon between clients and time is rolling so fast: I'd like to pin a few moments of this dream down.

Alix is due in a week! She's feeling a thousand new sensations: heat moving downwards, baby swiveling knees to the right, a wobble in the pubic symphysis while we walk so slowly on Sunday morning through the crowds at the street fair in Kensington Market. People whirl around us, around her roundness, and she pauses with her hand under her bump, looking down with a furrowed brow.

It's a prickly sensation.

Where?

I think in my cervix.

I shiver up the spine.

My own flesh has become more muscular on her pregnancy diet. I sleep more, like she does, but still steal away to write. I feel most of my changes happening psychically. My flesh will know what to do, I know, but the demands upon it seem too few and too simple. Consider all of the things men feel they have to do because they cannot give birth. We can only stand at the doorways of life for so long.

It's true what they say about last-minute nesting. Alix has been cleaning everything. A dirty cup in the sink is now officially an anxious object. Not irritated-anxious, but excited-anxious. It might never get put away if baby comes in the next ten minutes. I really want to know the brain chemistry responsible for nesting—it's completely automatic. I understand cortisol racing through the bloodstream as the sympathetic nerves engage fear. But nesting is like an autonomic empathy: you know someone is coming for whom the table should be very clean, as if they should be given their start with openness, empty space, and warmth. What could be more gracious in us than mindlessly responding to the needs of someone who isn't even quite present? I think of the chair left open at the seder dinner, for Isaiah to come and sit. Were you traditional enough growing up to have observed this in your family? Or have I made this up?

Alix and I are still floating down the centre of a very strong current, and seeing past lives swirling by the riverbank. Last weekend we went out for lunch with the parents of her ex, with whom she'd lived from the age of nineteen through twenty-nine. They loved Alix like a daughter, and would have loved a grandchild, but her ex didn't want to go there.

Like Alix, he's an only child. I've seen him in pictures with her. He's so good-looking. He's still ready to travel, to be alone and make his singular mark in experimental music. In the pictures they look like easy siblings, molded to each other's late-childhood safeties. Neither of them had driver's licenses: they sat in the back seats of other people's cars for a decade. Alix nuzzles into him and pours her eyes into the camera. He glances at the lens in profile, leaning towards the edge.

He's with an older woman now: a dancer. She's as old to him as K is to me. It's like he took an opposite arc from my own, moving from the woman who was ready to have a family with him to the woman who was self-sufficient. They're not likely to have children. *I think it's what he wants*, Alix says.

Now I'm looking into her ex's mother's eyes over lunch and thinking *I'm standing where he stood*. I feel a bond with her, as though I owe her something. I should keep in touch, and think of a nice gift to send her. I wonder what.

Weird to say: I love her son. I've never met him, but he feels like that part of me who might have continued to choose the outsider's life, devoted to my art, late nights, and working service jobs to pay for it, because my anger is a certain kind of fuel. There is a part of me that wants to stand beyond the culture forever, because it just can't tolerate being told what to do.

Alix and I were talking about thresholds. She could enter labour any hour now, and the waves of trepidation she feels remind her of standing in the wings as a dancer years ago, waiting for an entrance cue, and not quite believing the moment was coming, unable to fathom the possibility of how anyone or anything might move from shadow to light, and increasingly anxious to charge out, breaking the rhythm of the appointed entrance. I remember the same feeling from my years in acting. Chekhov tells you when to enter. The playwright is god. The baby is god.

We can see the threshold, we know we have to cross it, and we can't choose the time or place, and we know we will be ourselves on the other side, changed but continuous, like the baby itself, parting from momma's flesh, but the same. Alix will straddle the threshold and push. I'll be watching, and speaking low, and massaging. I will be necessary to something, perhaps more fully than ever. Except that day I saved my brother from drowning.

My necessity also rises on surges of rage and protectiveness. When we were walking through Trinity Bellwoods Park a few days ago, a homeless guy, clearly psychotic, saw Alix's belly and started to twitch and spit. He growled, *Just cut it out of her* and then turned on his heel and stomped away in his shredded shoes. Alix emerged from her pre-labour dream enough to say, *What was that?*, which relieved me because it meant she hadn't heard. I lied to her—*I didn't catch it.* Then my heart rate shot up even further as I visualized fending the man off and beating him to the ground, seizing his knife.

I've had fear of the labour come and go and come again. Fear that I will be ineffectual, peripheral to the circle of women who are coming. Fear that I will be too emotional to act. Fear that she will turn on me in a rage of separateness, seeing all in a moment what I can't understand, or that she must feel the crisis of our intimacy alone. I'm afraid that baby won't be well in some way.

I'm waiting behind a curtain, listening for the play to give me my cue. She's beside me in the dark, wordlessly running through the dance before it begins. We don't know the steps yet. There's a madman with a knife and I have to talk him down.

love,
Matthew

| | |

October 4th

Dear Matthew,

Being approached by that man in the park must have been terrifying. I have a friend of a friend, a musician, who was walking through that same park a few years ago and was beaten up by a group of young men. I also grew up walking that park with my uncle Ian, who suffered from schizophrenia, but he was calm and didn't have the violent "episodes" that people (wrongly) associate with schizophrenia. Since Trinity Bellwoods Park is only a block from the largest mental asylum in Canada, the park is filled with people wandering around over-medicated or out of their minds.

You know when your Mac computer is falling asleep and that small light glows brighter then dimmer and then bright again? That's how I think of relating to people when they are mad. I always speak to some glow inside them, some sane island, and I have the sense that if I keep talking to that faint island of sanity, it will grow. I learned that from my uncle. If we were ever approached by someone threatening, in the park or the hospital, my uncle would keep his voice calm and talk to the sane part of the one who is threatening. It happened every now and then. But there are times when you need to go for the knife and tackle the person to the ground. When Carina and I met, her backyard opened up onto that same park and I worried about her safety.

You must have wondered: *What's the distance between me and this man? Can I regulate my intense emotions?* All the intense emotions of the everyday are enough to make us insane. It's the everyday stuff that is intolerable to insanity, just like it was for the Buddha who had to walk away from everything.

I am writing to you from seat 34C, the middle seat on a plane at 30,000 feet heading to Copenhagen via Frankfurt. Every year since A was born I've been teaching a week-long workshop in Copenhagen. I've always come alone. Tonight, Carina is with me, five months pregnant now, legs stretched into the aisle, homemade macaroons, crackers, and some goat cheese spilling between us. She keeps reaching over to my left hand and pulling it onto her belly when she feels the baby kicking, though I only manage to feel the odd kick or tumble. She feels constellations in her belly that I can't from the outside. Of course I can't feel her nausea either.

The woman next to us has bad knees and must be wearing several litres of perfume. She exhales with her whole body, like someone walking away from a fight. Nothing seems to be working out for her, the magazines are in French and she is irritated enough that I feel as if I've been put in this middle seat just to help her get through this long flight. There's a teaching in the Lotus Sutra where it's said that the fastest way to Enlightenment is simply seeing each person as a Buddha. Of course it's also the toughest method. How is this woman, whose irritation is as irritating to me as it may be to her, a Buddha? How is that man who approached you and Alix in the park a Buddha? Carina and I make up these intentions sometimes, where we agree that for one week, as a couple, we will practice kindness to every single person we encounter. I can tell Carina's attention is turning inwards more and more. The woman next to me isn't bothering her at all.

You told me when I saw you last that Alix has been organizing house and even folding your sweaters. Carina's starting to do the same. Her socks and shirts are well folded for the first time since I've known her. There are lists everywhere. We can't afford to insulate the third floor so I'm wondering how our bedroom can accommodate the baby in February with its unfinished walls and cold linoleum. My friend Steve, a carpenter, is finishing the trim in the kitchen while we are in Europe. I finally finished cutting all the firewood. But I'll never be able to stock my fridge and freezer with the amount of potions or meals that it sounds like you've already concocted and jarred.

I worry, too, about how to be involved in the birth, mostly because I don't have too many images to draw from. When A was born I was right there with his mother throughout, almost nine hours in active labour. I'd leave every once in a while to get food at the restaurant next door for the doula and midwives. When my mother didn't hear from me earlier in the day she knew instinctively that labour had started and showed up unexpectedly at our house to help. She had the best intentions. But we didn't want her there for the labour and I had to run downstairs to tell her so, which threw me sideways for the last couple of hours of the labour.

My strongest memory of the days following the birth is of isolation and exhaustion. A's mother wanted nobody around the first week, except for a few visits. She wanted me up in the night with her while she was breast feeding and so I was up with her, putting on Chet Baker records and making motherwort tea. I was making all the meals and within two days I was sick with the flu and my mind was in poor shape. Eventually I just collapsed from exhaustion and went on my own to the upper floor and fell asleep until the next day. I called a mentor of mine and he suggested I take a night on my own and get rest so I could support the family again. I felt terrible stepping away so early on, and I heard no end of it from A's mother. It still lingers for me, actually, the way our relationship couldn't tolerate each of us having different experiences. I had the same guilt about bringing that up as I'd had about asking my mother to leave at the birth. My mother was the only person who could have actually supported me, and in retrospect I was angry that I had to turn her away. But instead of getting angry, I felt guilty. I felt I had to be having the same experience as A's mother somehow, and that if I wasn't feeling what she was feeling, she'd feel abandoned.

With the preparation for this birth, I know better what to expect. I just ordered a book on the birth partner's role. It's funny because it arrived in a day and when I opened the package I had an aversion to opening the book. Carina is making plans for a well-stocked fridge, and for her mother to come from the west coast and visit for a month. She's also making a list of friends we can call to help us immediately after the birth. We are going to take a hypnobirthing class together. Carina wants to talk about who will be at the birth, what we need for the home so she feels safe and calm, and who can bring us meals when the baby arrives. She even asked me what I think I'll need for myself. On the one hand I feel relief in helping her plan for a birth that's also being supported by our vast network of friends and, on the other, I'm privately remembering how isolated I felt the last time. She can see in my eyes that I'm haunted. I'm not sure exactly how it impacts her but she must worry about how engaged I'll be when the baby is born.

My sleep is being interrupted regularly at about 3 a.m., and then again an hour later, when Carina wakes up and eats gluten-free crackers in bed. Some nights it's grapes and last night it was yogurt, I think. I'm deep in sleep and then I start hearing crunching within my dreams and the strange smell of goat's milk or sweet fruit. I think I'm dreaming but my nose is twitching and I can smell barns and fields and goats out under the sky. Crackers have a strong effect on me at 3 a.m. Those crackers might be the loudest on the market! Last night I suggested she stop eating in bed. She suggested I roll over and go back to sleep.

Carina is sitting next to me on the plane, wearing an oversized grey wool sweater that has a zipper down the front and falls across her belly in waves. Every week friends come by with new clothes for her to fit her tall frame and swollen belly into. Each day is like an experiment to see what will fit and what won't. We've created some great moments in women's fashion. Of course Alix was the same, I am sure. We're taking photos of our bellies next to each other, and just this week her belly popped forward and she can't see her toes. A is starting to ask her how she feels. He comes home from school and asks about how she is doing and stops to feel her belly before he plays video games. This makes Carina so happy.

Last night, before I was awakened by the smell of goat yogurt, I had a dream where I was in black monk's robes walking down a wooden hallway toward the main hall of a temple. On the way down the hall I passed an open door and could make out a large cafeteria where utensils were being arranged for a large public meal. When I leaned into the doorway to see the utensils (hoping to guess what would be served) I discovered that the utensils were made from the silver and gold of a Buddha statue. The head cook came up to me and said, "We are making Buddha cake to celebrate the birth. *Everyone* is coming."

So for you and me; for our partners, families and this larger community we are part of, something new is coming into being. Fatherhood again. The lives of children we can't possibly imagine yet. More joy, more suffering, more dishes, longer walks, another seat on my bicycle. And of course being stuck indoors sometimes, drop-in play centres, car seats and Lego.

I've always thought it curious that the term the Buddha used to denote meditation is the Sanskrit term *bhavana* or *bhava*: literally, to bring into being. *Bhavana* is a horticultural phrase that refers to cultivation. Making room for life. Cutting away the old ghosts. Matthew, I so want my grief from the end of my last relationship to die and be reborn again in the face of this new kid, in the space of this new family. I want to be surprised and less jaded. I guess I can't feel surprised if I'm jaded.

The flight feels long. Carina has fallen asleep. Now it's my turn. My shoes are untied and the woman next to me is on her third glass of wine. I'm going to close my eyes now and see what comes into being, well aware that Alix is past her due date and at any moment you two will be deep in the energy of something beyond you both.

love,
Michael

October 7th

Michael –

Alix's midnight feedings stopped in the second trimester. She loved juicy pears, so I'd be woken up not only by the smell and the sound but by the occasional splatter of pear juice on my forehead. It was like waking up beside a very large non-grubby raccoon who actually smells good, quietly munching. An animal not only in timing, but also in absolute focus upon the taste and texture of the pear. If I could enjoy a pear as deeply as a raccoon or Alix does, all of my spiritual practices will have been worth it.

By daylight, Alix will talk about her human brain shutting down bit by bit. On that prenatal training weekend, when we were drawing pictures, she drew a picture of herself giving birth: on her knees with her back flexed upward in a bow, and wrapped over and around her was a charging animal in red, its head above hers with its mouth wide with sound. A bear or a wolf.

Learning a little about A's birth makes me wonder how many relationships sustain deep and then hidden trauma from the events surrounding childbirth. It seems like we have so many wounds ripe for exposure during so many moments of crisis. The woman is losing control to an animality she has forgotten or perhaps never known. It is terrifying, and I imagine the psyche dilates even wider than the cervix to receive the broadest impression of her condition: how things are in her world at the level beneath identity. I imagine it registers deep into the tissues: *Did you support me as I lost control? When I became unknown to us both, did you hold the space?*

I wonder if the hair trigger, tactile fear of those days sank in deep for A's mother, and was amplified by each subsequent tension between you, every further consideration of trust or distrust. And now—does that feeling creep into her gut when she so much as sends you an e-mail? Can you feel it? How can she undo it?

But what could you have done differently that week? The only thing I can think of is: be born into a culture in which supporting partners know, perhaps through ritual, the complexity of their role a little better: to merge, to withdraw, to cleave, to observe, to model constancy. Each in its own time. For me, these letters between us are a start.

In a way, Alix and I have developed a kind of conscious distance that might help us remember that even in this most intertwined experience we will be walking different paths. As much as we slammed into one another at the beginning—only a little more than a year ago now—I think we both knew that in some way parallel and even secret lives would continue. For my birthday last November she gave me an antique wooden box, from Japan I think, about two feet wide and eighteen inches high and deep. *This is your private box, for only your secret things, and only you can open it,* she said. When she left for work later that morning I opened the lid on its old brass hinge to look inside, and wept for an hour. Here was someone who was going to let me be whoever I was going to be.

My therapist once said to me, *All of these couples that come to me are so goddam tragic: they want to share everything with each other. But it's a kind of disease. We cannot live without a few hidden things. We have to give ourselves room to live in the fact that we will always in part be unknown to each other.*

I didn't give Alix a box, but I can always smell when she needs her loneliness. Melancholy is a kind of food for her, and I do my best to enjoy it with her, at a distance. It tugs on me, making me want to fix something, but knowing I cannot fix anything makes me love her more it seems.

We've moved into oatmeal season. Put butter and garam masala and sea salt in the saucepan, and then sauté the steel-cut oats until brown and fragrant. Then water. You have to have the lid handy when the water goes in because it will splatter against the hot pan at first. Put in apples at the end. Makes for excellent crapping.

The apples are from our trip yesterday in the car out to the country. Ida Reds are our favourite. We walked through an orchard very slowly, filming a short video for baby about our hopes and fears. How strange that our children will see us from today in HD, 1080 aspect. Their technology won't be so different. They won't know our youth through Polaroid pictures and Super 8 films. It will look to them as though we filmed ourselves yesterday. Long after I'm dead my child will be able to download my books to Kindle or whatever the hell they have then. History is shrinking.

What secrets does Alix think I might have? There is the silent process of digesting the rupture with my first family. I think she knows I must do most of this alone. It happens slowly, beneath language. Like an animal, I can feel the pheromones changing. Krishna is pawing at the rug underneath the waiting cradle.

I don't know how many times I will feel this hole in my chest where these other people once were. How can we misunderstand each other so deeply? I still have my arm around K in a picture on Facebook.

love,
Matthew

|||

October 7th

Re: Vacation Reply
Thank you for your email. Between travelling and time with my family I can't get to all my emails right away. Please be patient.
faraway nearby,
Michael Stone

|||

October 9th

Dear Michael –

Alix can now identify individual threads of labour sensation. She'll have cramping down low, as she does before her period. Shudders through her uterus as we walk slowly. She'll say her pelvis feels like it's moving on about nine hinges. More prickly heat on her cervix, where baby's head presses heavy. She says it's like an orchestra tuning up, and when everything begins to play at the same time, baby will raise the baton and sink into the downbeat.

I've been learning about the chemical dance between mother and baby that initiates labour. They simultaneously release oxytocin to relax and dilate themselves, and prostaglandins to warm and thin the cervix. Some biologists believe that the main process is cued when the baby releases a surfactant protein in the lungs, which completes the preparation for breathing. This protein reduces surface tension in the alveoli, which allows for breath to pass through a porous water barrier into the bloodstream. It also seems to perform an essential immune function against microbes in the lung tissue. In other words, baby begins the mutual release of let-down actions when her lungs are ready to navigate breath, when she is ready for her water to be entered by space, and to have that space fill with air, when she is ready to enter the outside and be entered by the outside. Or he.

Baby has also been hiccupping a lot. Which I couldn't understand at first baby is neither breathing nor digesting through the GI, and I always thought that hiccups were an internal confusion between the pulses of breath and peristalsis. But it turns out that babies hiccup in the womb as a powerful way of developing the diaphragm. And the challenge of yoga or any self-regulatory technique became that much clearer to me: the long, equal, smooth breath of meditation is a long way from the stutter with which our breathing starts. Breath begins in a disorganized fit of learning. Full diaphragmatic breath emerges, I imagine, only when grounded in the perception of safety.

I wanted to pick up a thread from your last note. I love it when you or anybody else quotes Sanskrit, because it shows me how fluid the language is both in our hands and between traditions. I've never heard *bhavana* rendered as "to come into being," but I can see how this would be built from the root *bhu*, earth element. I'm more familiar with the term from late Vedic literature: *bhava* is the word used in astrology to indicate the discrete "field" of sky in which the planets and constellations are seen. These fields are fixed, divided into thirty degrees of arc measuring from the horizon, and are said to contain "moods." A full moon on the eastern horizon is said to resonate much differently from that same moon directly overhead, several hours later. The astrologers translate *bhava* as "house." The houses are types of grounding, portions of earth element that are as different from each other as the earth of different countries. You are sitting, doing *bhavana* on the earth in Denmark—what different roots are beneath us, and what moods do they cast?

The astrologers read the moon as the mood of the emotional-sensory mind. Also as the health of women and children. Tonight, the moon is directly above Toronto, in the tenth house, the house of karma, action, and the father. For you at this moment, that same moon is in a different house, a different country of the sky—the seventh house, on the western horizon, the house of the lover. The astrologer/mythographer in me puts it all together to say: at this moment, your emotional-sensory mind is absorbed and grounded in the otherness of your partner. Maybe you're on a lunch break from teaching. Maybe Carina made lunch, and you're eating together, looking at the western horizon.

Growing up Catholic, I was wired to believe in holy places, which is simply the inverse of considering most of your world to be mundane. The tabernacle, bolted to the cathedral stone, stripped my bedroom and my heart of importance. I was to go there to pray because I myself contained nothing. I carried this attitude into my meditation studies, meticulously creating precious spaces in which I could be okay, trying to rebuild the tabernacle I had blasphemed, and ignoring the basic goodness and support of wherever it was I happened to be standing. *Bhavana* is always available, I suppose, because *bhu* is always underfoot. It's like what you were saying about home.

I'm writing a lot to you because the rest of my schedule is cleared, and I'm just waiting now. Months ago I cleared the week of and after our due date—cancelling my classes and closing my client appointments, thinking this would be the best way to prepare. I just finished writing a book and my mind isn't settled enough to begin another task. The day stretches out before me. I can hear Alix shift in bed. The dawn light is pale, this morning after Thanksgiving.

We have a meeting with the midwife today. We'll go swimming together in the late afternoon. I'm making pennyroyal tea for Alix, with cinnamon. Fairly strong, to warm her uterus. Tonight, as I did last night, I'll give strong thumb-pressure to the Spleen-6 points, midway down her shins, on the inner edges of the tibias. I'll also press down into the tops of her trapezius with my elbows. Those points are said to activate *apana vayu*, the downward moving wind that moves the bowel, and that orgasm and childbirth rides. I remember having an almost-frozen shoulder several years ago, and getting a masseur to dig his elbow into the trapezius with all his weight. My shoulder released, and an hour later I took the biggest shit of my life.

If I visualize moving that sensation forward to a birth canal, perhaps where I feel the front of the perineum connects to the ring of musculature at the base of my penis, I imagine that's a very very small and brief version of what giving birth is like. Jesus wept!

Overhead, the moon is not only in the tenth house, but it's in the constellation of Cancer, representing the mother and the childhood home. Within Cancer it is riding amongst the stars of an asterism called *Pushya*, said to be governed by the deity *Brihaspati*, the lord of children and all things that expand. *Pushya* is also associated with food—specifically banquets of food offered at celebrations. I'm a little manic and seeing magi-

cal connections everywhere. Of course the stars reflect my personal reality! Everything in the world is happening right here!
Here, meaning: in Alix's burning cervix.

The light is coming up. Time to put on the oatmeal.

love,
Matthew

|||

October 11th

Matthew,

We've been obsessed with oatmeal. Carina likes hers with Danish butter and I like mine with cinnamon and lemon peel. At
home I'd add maple syrup but it's a fortune here in Denmark.

It's the final day of teaching and then we're off to Antibes
where I teach at a retreat centre in the hills outside the city.
Carina hasn't been up for walking much—too many sensations
and still some nausea—so we've been cooking in our small,
white apartment, watching the sky from the couch, and enjoying
each other's company as we move around the kitchen. Carina is
from Finland and her family speaks Swedish, as does she, and
listening to Danish all day is giving us ideas about Finnish baby
names. The sky clears occasionally, but mostly it's flat white.
Being away from the household chores in Toronto has me really
focused on both teaching and the pregnancy. I wake early to
practice before the long days of teaching, and when I'm reaching
the closing sequences of backbending and headstands, Carina
rolls in and sets up beside me. The routine is easy. You can hear
the boats in the canal below the windows.

Stone stairs. White petals. Tides. Rolling swells. Five
months pregnant. Domestic pulse. Oatmeal. Spooning in the
morning. Lists of boy names that have to do with bears. Streets
and canals. Wooden boats shaped like kidney beans. Upright
bicycles. No map. Mid-stride. The sky falling into water.

Dreams of my legs ending in streams. Another dream where a man on the canal tells me, *the west always turns east again, so go forward.* His beard was like the one I shaved off this year, but grey.

At home in Toronto my oldest friend Natalie gave a talk at Centre of Gravity in my absence. Tuesday nights we sit for thirty minutes and then a talk. She spoke on projection. She sent me her notes, including this lovely observation:

"We are thrilled by the otherness of our dreams, as if we weren't aware that we are busy creating dreams all the time. We're in the process of projection all the time. Our dreams and fantasies point to a larger life we could experience. They bring us closer to a greater sense of ourselves. Mostly we live in a small version of ourselves. In the Shambhala tradition this small self is called a cocoon. It is a predictable, comfortable, familiar way of being that is also kind of stale. It's like the smell of your armpit: it's comforting and close."

I want realism but I always end up with imagination. There's a Neil Young song I was listening to on the plane where he sings, "I'm a dreamin' man/ guess that's my problem/ I can't tell/ when I'm not being real." I keep having fantasies about having the baby here in Copenhagen, on a houseboat on the canal, with three blonde midwives who speak perfect English and then, right after the birth, Carina's parents come over and surprise her, and then we decide we'll all live together, on houseboats, right next to each other, and when we need food we'll just bike over to the farmers market that sells immaculate vegetables and organic dairy from Finland.

I'm thrilled by my fantasies. What I like about Natalie's quote is it comes back to the idea that fantasy life is not in itself a bad thing. We need a deeper imagination. Imagination allows us to experience ourselves differently. Imagination shows us how we are discontinuous, we are made of stories. That's my situation now. Carina is becoming more and more rooted in the daily schedule of rest, food, and ensuring she doesn't walk too far because the sensations in her pelvis and lower back call her back to earth. Carina's fantasies revolve around Swedish and Finnish baby names. I don't care for any of them yet.

I turn my ideas of the coming baby over and over again until I'm left with the sky, the rain, the boats in the canal—our cocoon of a life on the second floor of this old Copenhagen apartment.

You and Alix are due in a few days. Did I tell you we are expecting a boy?

love,
Michael

|||

October 12th

Michael –

Alix is now three days overdue. I think that as a culture we should really be talking about a "due week" or "fortnight," instead of "date." A distinct date just causes stress, leveraging a whole range of possible future interventions along a mechanistic timeline. At forty-one weeks (counting the literal due date of October 9th), we start twice-weekly ultrasounds to monitor baby. At forty-two weeks, we're supposed to be counseled on the arguments for chemical induction. We're told that the occurrence of stillbirth doubles after forty-two weeks. Which sounds menacing until you hear that this means from one in 1000 to two in 1000 births. What does this mean? What else is going on in that second stillbirth? I don't know much here, but how is that statistic controlled for other variables?

Here's another "doubling": chemical induction raises the likelihood of emergency caesarean delivery by 2.6 times. Interventions lead to interventions. This is as true in birthing as we know it to be in psychotherapy and meditation. And in all of the technical talk it feels like we lose a sense of rhythm, of the woman naturally moving her hips, of the baby feeling its way downwards with little shimmies of the shoulders, pressing the soft fontanelle against the cervix, as if to absorb grounding earth energy into the crown before emerging.

I'm venting because crossing over the date feels like we're entering a zone of communal discourse about this pregnancy that draws power away from the dyad and our intuition, or at least Alix's. But this is one of the prices of social living in general and universal health care in particular: it is for the common good that we begin to heed statistics and probabilities. "There are no statistics for the individual," one of my spiritual teachers once said, foregrounding our capacity for mental and psychic freedom. The problem is that we're not really individuals.

What I do know is that constitutionally, Alix takes her time in everything. Transitions are slow and measured. Where I have torn my way through every change in my life, she seems to have eased her way in. If I were as pregnant as her, the word they use for non-chemical labour onset—spontaneous—would be my style. (Strange that "spontaneous" makes it sound like it's coming out of nowhere. It's a forced word necessary to foil "induction.") But Alix's labour is gathering like a distant storm. And I feel very belligerent towards any talk that suggests she should hurry it along. She is spontaneous, slowly.

No one ever talks about the impact of chemical induction upon baby. Not only for the birthing process, but upon the delicate psychoneurology. What are the results of baby's first interaction with the world being the interruption of the labour dance? How often are we interrupted as children, and then as adults, from processes that are unfolding in their own way? Here are the two longitudinal studies I'd fund if I was rich: the effects of labour induction through the child's 25th year. For boys, the same study, but on circumcision. What does searing pain in the genital region on the fourth day of life teach a boy about the tenderest part of his body?

The wave of worry takes me away from the bright emptiness of this waiting. Isn't it amazing that amidst whatever we think about, the sky still holds us. Alix and I look at each other and one of us will say after a long pause: *Baby is coming.* Neither of us can believe it, so we repeat it, and feel a little goofy.

love,
Matthew

|||

October 13th

Matthew,

Your healthy baby is coming. Of course you're turning over the statistics, you're both excited *and* scared. We should invent an app that rings a gentle bell every time the mind wanders into worry. At the same time I can totally relate to your worry. I could write the Land of Worry Field Guide.

I am no intuitive but I think the birth, however it goes, will produce a stunning kid that will light up your heart. How can we know anything about what's coming? Even the next second is invisible. My only visual sense of our baby is a black and white magnetic image of a pea-sized head and folded limbs, upside down, on a computer screen. Even that image is mixed up with my own baby photos and a few I've seen of a very bald Carina. I guess we are always living this double life of having no idea what's coming next, while at the same time, the brain collages images from the past of what the future could, or should, look like. No matter what our brains worry about, life is this thing that just keeps happening. And do statistics really give us any ground? One of your favorite writers, Jean Baudrillard, writes: "Like dreams, statistics are a form of wish fulfillment."

Carina and I are thinking of you both everyday. I just finished leading a retreat in the twisted wooden hills outside Valbonne in Southern France. There were fifty students and a translator. Carina assisted me though she had to run out every hour to snack in the kitchen. She has celiac disease so she has to prepare her own food because this is a gluten-rich country. Pregnant women can't eat raw cheeses so that narrows her French cuisine down to butter, meat, vegetables and fruit. The mornings were cold so when I woke early to practice I had to turn on the space heater in our bedroom. She stayed in bed and slept and I listened to her sleeping while moving through standing poses, sitting poses, backbends, head stands, savasana. Our travel rhythms are deepening. When I wake up in the morning I consciously think: "Today I'm going to really practice with Carina. We are still building our little domestic monastery." I think it's working.

She doesn't know this yet, but on our last day in Copenhagen when I took the bus to get her some homeopathics in the north of the city, I came across a small jewelry store. I went in. I never enter jewelry stores because neither of us wear jewelry. I looked at rings. In about ten seconds I found a simple ring of white platinum and gold. It's thin and subdued. It was expensive, which made me nervous, but I bought it, tucked it in my pocket, and walked on air to the homeopathy store to get her medicine. The houses had steep clay rooflines and ornate chimneys surrounded by tall gardens and old fences. I held the box in my pocket and decided that I'd give her the ring in France and ask her to marry me, or be engaged, or be my partner for life, or hibernate with me, or maybe I'll just tell her that if she ever gets ill I'll be there loving her, or maybe I'll hand the ring to her and tell her that she is going to be a great mother. I don't know what to propose.

It's beginning to rain here in Antibes now. The seagulls are lined up on the porch railing. We're staying in a flat above the farmers' market and the vendors are packing up. A's mother and I never married. I bought her a ring and when we were up north staying in the small old wooden church we owned, I gave it to her while we were walking in the field with A. She didn't respond with much emotion. She loved the ring. She mostly spoke to me about the ring. She didn't say anything about the relationship.

I felt despair and that night I woke to pee and when I walked out under the stars I cried. I convinced myself it must have been my high expectations and that we had different temperaments, she and I, and I went back inside and lay in bed awake until morning.

It's strange to be pregnant again and to purchase a ring like I just did, and then to have the past return in haunted weighty images that I thought I'd left behind a long while ago. On our first day in Antibes I wanted to give her the ring but I've decided to wait until it's sunny. I have this inkling that I'll see something about our future in my dreams, like I will know for certain that it's time. I can hear my inner romantic looking for signs and I'm laughing as I write this.

Dreams are insolvent. They never finish. The ring this time is not the same as the ring last time. You are four days overdue. Time is passing and, then again, it's not. The yachts in Antibes draw envy. Unmeasured days. Alix folding your sweater.

Carina just came downstairs and sat in front of the tall arched window, watching lightning, leaning back on her hands. The room lights up, then goes dark again, the only light source is the glow of this screen. The box holding the ring is still in my pocket.

Yoga makes new rhythms out of thinking. Did you know the term *vinyasa* comes from the old tantric Hatha practice of "nyasa," where one takes a dream or a mantra and visualizes it as a seed planted in the body, like an internal tattoo. One consciously places one's memories and dreams and credos and mantras inside the cocoon of the body. Then the breath goes down, and when you are ready, it ignites these cherished things and brings them into consciousness in the present. The practice of *vinyasa* is to go in and retrieve these old insights and bring them to life in the embodied present. The breath flows down through limbs and picks up what's needed and brings it up for growth.

Speaking of breathing, I've been walking a lot with Carina. We are talking about the first year of A's life. She keeps telling me that she wants to hear about when A was born and wonders why it's hard for me to retell those stories. My mind goes foggy trying to retrieve them.

I remember when A started teething, accompanied by more and more colds, a few months of occasional fevers, and I thought, "Why on earth am I taking him to these drop-in centres when he only comes home sick?" I'd take him anyway, just to walk along Dundas Street, and then we'd wind our way to Mary McCormick drop-in centre on Brock Street —an enormous sunlit gymnasium full of thousands of kids with runny, bubbly and crusty noses crawling, running, jumping, driving tiny plastic cars, putting their fingers in each others mouths, and riding scooters. There were other parents, slightly older than me (I was twenty-eight), and it was a relief being out of the house.

I didn't talk much with other parents, I mostly just watched people. When A started looking tired I'd give him pumped breastmilk (he nursed until three) and then put him in the stroller with a licorice stick. If you get a stick of licorice, the actual wood, not the manufactured twizzle, you scrape the bark, and you begin rubbing it on your kid's gums, it numbs the gums and it tastes great. A had his own stick and I'd have mine. I'd chew on it and walk him home as he napped in the stroller. I loved walking with him for as far and as long as possible. It gave me time to think. My mouth would go numb and since one of my front teeth is fake, it gave me some relief if that tooth was bothering me, which it does sometimes. But what was I thinking about? Did I avoid thinking about the troubles with A's mother? How I was craving a relationship that was more mutual? I just can't open the door in that memory chamber.

About that tooth. At thirteen, I dyed the front half of my bangs blonde like the skateboarder Tony Hawk, whose urban skateboard videos I studied with the concentration of a Talmudic scholar. I was showing off some skateboard tricks to Barbie Brandis, the blonde older sister of a kid I played hockey with (who chose me as his enemy for some reason I never figured out), and as I lifted the board with my feet, attempting a jump

from the sidewalk to the road, I misjudged the pressure on my
back foot and how much I needed to bend my left knee and so
the board flew right into my mouth. For a minute I felt only
numbness, all through my jaw and nose, then the taste of blood.
I couldn't bear to see Barbie's expression. I turn and ran across
the street into my back door. My mother was in the kitchen. She
looked up and yelled, covered her mouth, put down the knife she
was holding and when I looked down at my skateboard there
was a puddle on the marble floor, dripping from my chin, of
bright red blood, like the kind you squeeze from a makeup tube
on Halloween. My parents rushed me to the hospital where my
front tooth was removed, braces were set temporarily, I received
a root canal (which had to be done a second then a third time
because of an infection), and that was the end of my skateboard
career. My parents took my board away. Thankfully I never dyed
my hair again.

The dentist did such a good job that until I told her, Carina
never noticed that my tooth was false. Tomorrow I'll propose.

love,
Michael

| |

October 14th

Michael –

Alix had steady cramping all through the night. And waves of
emotion. *Will we change to each other?* She feels this more than
I do: it's her body that is splitting apart. All I can think of is how
I can't tell her beauty from her bravery now. Whatever this is,
she's doing it so well.

Baby was always in the room with us. The second time Alix
and I met for tea we talked about having children together. We
were never really only a dyad. Perhaps this is part of why things
moved so quickly. Sometimes I wonder if there will be a price

for that, how much we missed out on getting to know just each other, as each other alone.

But something feels fake about that. We are never each other's alone. That's what romance says, built on the old idea that two essential souls are meeting each other in isolation and will complete each other in some kind of alchemy. But it's never like that. Our selves are social, constructed. We make each other, other people make us. There's no grand design, no perfect outcome. I say this in lectures sometimes and the twenty-some-things look mopey. They should thank me. Understanding this would have disillusioned me years ago, and may have ended my previous marriage far earlier. Funny thing is, it makes me love harder now.

Alix's poop has been slow—just as she remembers it being slow before her period. I stewed one of those Ida Red apples last night with cinnamon and ginger and cider and nutmeg. And snuck in a dollop of that nauseating ghee. She gobbled up the apple mush by candlelight. I smirked that she didn't notice the ghee. She's starting to rock back and forth during every activity.

Carina told Alix by e-mail that you were expecting a boy: I was waiting for you to write it. A boy. We were boys! We had little penises! And look what they've gone and done now.

We didn't ask for our baby's gender from the abrupt Russian ultrasound dominatrix. We wanted a surprise. It probably means that we've had more variance in the fantasies that blossom around who baby will be than you and Carina will. I have gendered the fantasies, for sure: imagining running alongside a little boy on a soccer field, or through the trails of Prince Edward County. Hearing a daughter play piano, or cello. And a fork in the road of possible names. Our list of girl's names has always been longer than our list of boy's names. I wonder if for me at least this is a warning that my expectations for who a son can be are narrower in some way.

I can feel the projection in my gut: my daughter can be anything and I hope she is. But my son already carries the stress of my own childhood. In my semi-conscious projection, he already inhabits a complex world of conflict and vulnerability. I picture him alone, because I had very few friends growing up. I'll have to really work on holding an open psychic slate for him. To see that he is not treading on some thin wire. I wonder if this is the same for you.

Something tells me a brother will be good for A. As I've mentioned, my brother is ten years younger as well. Watching my brother grow up behind me seemed to crystallize certain notions of what a boy needs, and also gave me a longer view of my own life. I could feel his stages in my memory, as though I could work something out through him I hadn't quite finished. I wanted to give him confidence. I wanted him to be able to lose control safely, knowing that an older boy was there to hold him. I saw myself in my brother. And I improvised a very young type of fatherhood to care for him. A practice-run. I wonder if A will feel the same way.

I'm realizing now that you and I were both first-born sons. We had no intermediaries. I think of an older brother as someone tramping down the grasses ahead of you on a long winding hike. Not so that the path becomes easier, but so that we go forward on it knowing someone has been there just before. The younger brother gains the confidence of a broken trail, and the older brother gains the confidence of knowing he can look back and provide care.

The fantasies have fallen off in the last month. Now baby is a wriggling blank, clearly other and unknown. In *The Birth of a Mother*, psychologist Daniel Stern writes that the fantasy baby of the first and second trimesters must defer to the actual baby making itself known in the third. Somewhere inside, we know that the fantasy baby and the actual baby cannot meet, and we have to let the former go.

Spiritual practice for me has given birth to many fantasy babies who have my name. Matthew who has tamed his mind, or sits as an elder in a linen suit in a Cairo café like Paul Bowles, who has developed his intuition through meditation and the Vedic art. Matthew, the good counsellor. Blah, blah, blah. I feel like I'm in a kind of third trimester myself, because my identity has gone quiet and unknown. I've paused all work. The heroes I have wished to be have died to make way for the normal but unknown person I am becoming.

Great story about the ring. My favourite part is how you don't know what you'll say, how you will promise, or what you even have to promise. Even though we don't speak of it out loud, I think we as a culture are finally coming to grips with the fluidity of the promise. People used to talk about the 50% divorce rate as though it were a scandal. But now I hear irony when it's mentioned.

The promise is made by a person who changes, and is as much a commitment to our own sense of continuity as to the ideal of the relationship. *Will you marry me?* seems now to be a way of saying: *I believe these feelings and this attachment are stable within me, it seems as if they are within you as well, and this whole thing is worth nurturing, because we can help each other grow.*

Such a promise is a touchstone for the other things that will change. And when you confess this stability within yourself, this stillness, it is so fragile. It must be met with an equal or at least similar confession from the other, or else you are alone. That's what I feel when I read the hard story of your first proposal. You disclosed something about yourself: *this is where I am stable.* For whatever reason, A's mother couldn't meet you there. Your joy twisted in on itself and soured. It seems like you left the proposal in the sky, and now you're pulling it back down.

My inner romantic had a ring made in May by the German guy on Markham Street beside the Victory Café, where Alix and I spent summer evenings drinking beer in our twenties, ten years apart. I chose a Celtic knot design. It has three strands interwoven. And one of the tiniest diamonds he had. The box rubbed in my pocket throughout our babymoon trip to Europe in June. I too waited for the right time, which happened to be at dawn in a sleeper car on an overnight train rolling into Paris from Venice. I just handed it to her. I didn't ask a question, although we had spoken for months in quieter moments about marriage. When it came to the moment it didn't seem like speaking was the right thing. The ring spoke. *This is who I feel I am to you now.* A circle of three strands.

On Saturday night we went out to the sports bar around the corner to watch the Tigers beat the Yankees in twelve innings. Fuck the Yankees! We met our doula on the sidewalk. The day before she'd met with Alix for tea and suggested that we take some meaningful pilgrimages in these last days. So we told her we were heading to Duff's. She didn't really take it in, until we explained we both loved baseball. Also that we weren't going to eat chicken wings there—we'd had dal and rice at home. Then she got it. I drank beer and Alix crunched on ice. And the twenty-something waitresses hovered around the belly, praying there would be something they could do to help. People were cheering at the screen, our faces were glowing, the waitresses flitted around Alix like those bluebirds flitting around Snow White.

Alix and I both played ball as kids, pretty competitively. I pitched and caught, played first base and right field. My spine is still curved rightwards from pitching and my right shoulder is still clicking with scar tissue. Alix has a great arm. Last year around this time we drove up to Algonquin Park. The farmhouse we stayed in had a shed with dusty croquet and badminton sets, and two gloves, and a ball. We both threw hard and stung each other's glove hands, like we were testing each other. On Christmas day we dug her dad's glove and her old glove out of her parent's front closet and played catch on the boardwalk.

We returned to that boardwalk yesterday, for a quieter pilgrimage. Alix woke up saying: *I want to go to Riverdale Farm to see the animals, and to the beach.* We drove in silence through the light traffic of Sunday. Alix turned to me and asked if there was anywhere I'd like to go in these last days of waiting. My mind was blank. I thought briefly of the churches of my childhood, but felt no real yearning. There are no goats in St. Michael's Cathedral. Our mangers today are our public parks. We gazed at the cows and nuzzled the goats. One momma goat poked her nose through the slats to sniff at the belly.

Before sleeping last night, Alix said, "My body feels fully three-dimensional now. My spine feels as intelligent as my face, my eyes."

love,
Matthew

|||

October 15th

Matthew,

We had a lull in our sex life for over a month and this week it's picked up a little. This means A has been on the iPad after school more often. Today it's come to an end again. Carina's bladder infection is too uncomfortable for her and now a yeast infection is making fermented experiments between her groins. So this email is for you, dedicated to all future fathers who need to walk down to the local herbal dispensary and make the proper concoction to ease the suffering of their lover's vagina. I will let you know how it works . . .

Okay, here is the yeast-busting suppository blend:

YOU'LL NEED:

½ cup coconut oil
½ cup of powdered herbs: mix of goldenseal, slippery elm and echinacea
Thyme and lavender essential oils
Calendula oil (not an essential oil—an infused oil)

THEN:

— Melt coconut oil on low, don't let it boil. remove from heat

— Mix oil with herbs

- Add 7 drops each of thyme and lavender oil

- Add 2 tsp of calendula oil

- Let it cool (even in the fridge) until it forms a thick sticky dough, add additional powder if necessary.

- Smile in the kitchen as you're doing this. Let her know this is fun for you. Don't tell her you're going to publish the recipe one day.

- Roll it out on a cutting board sprinkled with slippery elm powder, roll into an index finger-wide 'snake.'

- Cut into 1-2" pieces, wrap each in foil, and refrigerate until firm.

- Insert one bolus into vagina each night before bed (she can do this herself). Have a towel under her for the night in case it leaks out. Repeat for a week.

There are so many rituals we're moving through right now: pregnancy, my marriage proposal, and vaginal caretaking. Did I ever tell you about the Jukai ritual we do in Zen?

In Zen, there is an old tradition called Jukai. Enkyo Roshi, my teacher in Manhattan, mails me a bag with sewing instructions, black thread, sheets of black cotton and a long line of green thread in a small bag. I was to sew a *rakusu*. The *rakusu* is a traditional Japanese garment worn around the neck of Zen students who have taken the precepts or lay ordination. It's made of sixteen strips of cloth sewn together into the shape of a rice patty and worn around one's neck like a bib. In the old Chinese Chan tradition, Buddhist monks were persecuted and so they sewed their robes into these brick-like patterns and wore them hidden under their jackets. The Buddha is said to have renounced the wearing of fine robes, insisting that his students make their robes from pieces of cast-off white burial cloth found at funeral sites, and then dyed with saffron as a disinfectant. The

Buddha wanted robes to be made from discarded material. The way I interpret it, the Buddha was making a gesture to welcome in and include whatever was being compartmentalized.

So, over four months I had alot of help sewing my *rakusu* into the traditional rectangular shape. On the back collar, there is a final embroidered stitch with green thread in the shape of two pine needles. One pine needle is meant to be straight and the other is meant to be broken. It reminds me of my life. Sometimes straight, sometimes broken. It reminds me of the off-kilter Buddha on my desk at home. After sewing the *rakusu*, Roshi took it and on the back of it, she signed her name and then my new Dharma name: Sho-ken. The name comes from the second paragraph of the Heart Sutra. 'Sho' means bright, 'ken' means seeing.

When I study with Roshi, when I sit by myself, or when I do any other formal practice, I always wear the *rakusu*. The *rakusu* changes my relationship to whatever I'm doing. Wearing the *rakusu* is training. It's a reminder that my commitments are as close to me as my eyelashes. I try to do whatever I'm doing with concentration, and with both hands.

Jukai is a commitment to the Precepts, which actually sound like good guidelines for child-rearing:

1. Recognizing that I am not separate from all that is. This is the precept of **Non-Killing**.

2. Being satisfied with what I have. This is the precept of **Non-Stealing**.

3. Encountering all creations with respect and dignity. This is the precept of **Loving Conduct**.

4. Listening and speaking from the heart. This is the precept of **Non-Lying**.

5. Cultivating a mind that sees clearly. This is the precept of **Not Being Ignorant**.

6. Unconditionally accepting what each moment has to offer. This is the precept of **Not Talking About Others' Errors And Faults**.

7. Speaking what I perceive to be the truth without guilt or blame. This is the precept of **Not Elevating Oneself And Blaming Others**.

8. Using all of the ingredients of my life. This is the precept of **Not Being Stingy**.

9. Transforming suffering into wisdom. This is the precept of **Not Being Angry**.

10. Honoring my life as an instrument of peacemaking. This is the precept of **Not Thinking Ill of Awakening, the Teachings, and Community**.

I've always seen the precepts as not only as prescriptive, but descriptive of the way a Buddha would function in this world. They are also good guidelines for family life. They are my compass. Last night, while Carina was lying down feeling nauseous, I felt stirred up that I was washing dishes again with two loads of laundry on the go to boot. So, I put on my *rakusu*. I've decided that whenever this domestic monastery gets overwhelming, especially the chores, I'm going to wear my *rakusu*.

There is so much to do in the garden. A's clothes are everywhere. The baseboards, which you reminded me need finishing, still haven't even been installed. The compost stinks. Whenever I'm faced with this urgency, I'm going to put on my *rakusu* like I'm wearing new eyes.

When I was thirteen—the loneliness set in, the aloneness you talk about in your letters. Stacking three steel garbage cans upside down one on top of the other, I'd climb up the black iron ladder that led to the school roof three stories up, around 7 p.m. as the sun set. I could smell the new asphalt of the school track, the trees in early May, pollen, the unlit cigarette behind my ear, and the pressure in my chest, the force that always visits when I'm alone, its pressure turning inward, from my ribs to my lungs—underwater, fear, separateness. I'd smoke a cigarette, watch the sunset, study the canopy of trees from above, watch cars pulling into the driveways—nice cars, ones I'd never own, belonging to large families with kids who did all the right things, who found paths through school and social life that I couldn't figure out for myself.

I realize as I write this that it was the first time I realized that my thoughts weren't my own, but were my father's—the inability to fit in, worrying about being poor again, enjoying the design of nice cars but being unable to afford them, stressing about not knowing how to manage feelings of intense isolation. These were his post-Holocaust thoughts. I lay on my back on the flat gravel and tar roof, feeling the tiny pebbles under my shoulder blades, the two flat areas of my back that were getting stronger every month, watching the sky above where a few stars appeared like jewels. The whole scene was beautiful and painful at the same time. I wanted to be alone and I wanted to fit in. I wanted to be part of what everyone else seemed to be part of, but I didn't know what that was, or if I liked it. My uncle Ian, my best friend, who lived in what was then called the mental asylum, taught me to how to sit still. But even in stillness I longed for a connection, to anything, maybe a person, another family, a different school, a girlfriend. Anxiety and I were bound together for life, at least until university. The anxiety never showed up with others, only when I was alone—leaving a party early, walking for hours in the ravine downhill from my home, smoking cigarettes at dusk on the schoolyard roof.

A is approaching the age at which I began this descent into anxiety and loneliness. I don't see it in him though. He can be introverted at times, and he says he feels alone when he takes the streetcar (which he just did by himself for the first time), but I don't see in him the desperation I felt at his age or the melancholy.

I could be wrong. Maybe he's better at hiding his loneliness than I was. Maybe he's sneaking off on his own or worrying about his life in ways I'm not picking up on. I have to be honest that it would serve my own image of being a good parent to believe that everything is fine.

I drive by Forest Hill Junior School maybe once every few years, on my way uptown. As I come up over the Spadina Road hill, heading north, approaching the crosswalk where my friend Hannah told me, in grade four, that she would never be my girlfriend, I look to the right at that old brick building, the flat roof, the track, the hill I slid down every recess in winter—and I'm relieved those years are over. Sometimes instead of continuing straight up Spadina to the house where my mother now lives (she is happily remarried), I turn left onto Elderwood Drive and slow the car down as I pass my old home. The new owners have painted the brown wooden window frames green, the walkways have been re-landscaped, the old Japanese maples are cut back, and the scene just doesn't hold much for me anymore. But I keep going back, to see if anything is there, something like a key, an explanation for my melancholic memories of childhood. Or maybe it's that I need to see myself now in contrast to that old loneliness, as if I'm comparing my life now to those older images of myself, so I can tell that thirteen-year-old boy that it all turned out okay, that my son now is not me then, that I transformed the constant loneliness, that I created a family, that anxiety doesn't haunt me anymore, that it's okay now. Mostly.

All this is flooding my mind as I prepare to ask Carina to marry me.

love,
Michael

October 15th

Michael –

Your letter about the pressure of being thirteen makes me think that everything we do in practice—for me it started with piano and then the pipe organ in darkened churches, and then poetry, all before I'd even heard of meditation—is to internalize social anxiety, oppression even, and make of it a pearl, note by note, line by line, breath by breath.

At thirteen I felt like an open wound walking around, alive to every cruelty and contradiction. I remember the feeling of my body: slender and tremulous. My neck felt very long. It always hurt from all the reading and music. My glasses were always smudged it seemed. It felt like I was always trying to look out and around them, past the blur, but then into the fuller blur of my short-sightedness. My long neck and greasy face would flush with intense heat whenever I was called *faggot*. I remember how that heat could overflow so mindlessly into a flurry of fists. There were about three other boys who I remember wanting to literally kill when rage overtook me.

If we manage such a transition, and every other, we are called healthy, functional. If we can't—if the oppression is too heavy, the emotions too intense, the resources too scarce—we're primed for drudgery, addictions, the endless cycle of outbursts and consolations and a lot of just hanging on. We generally over-value our agency in the matter. We need each other so much. And those we are meant to depend on can be so lost.

You give a good yeast recipe: I've made similar boluses for my clients, although I use licorice powder instead of slippery elm, and I add turmeric to the powders—in equal measure. When I have it, I also add a good anti-yeast herb called *shardunika* in Sanskrit and *gurmar* in Hindi ("killer of sweet"). Alongside the boluses, equal parts of turmeric, licorice, and shardunika are taken orally with warm water.

Yeast during pregnancy is particularly hard because the woman is usually craving building foods, which have the same kind of sweetness that provokes the yeast. The first trimester especially is a tissue-building time: it's hard to use anti-yeast bitters when everything wants to be grounded and growing.

Get a recipe, give a recipe. Yours was for the vagina, mine's for the mouth.

Pre-and-post natal broth:

FOR BOTH, START WITH:
5 lb marrow bones (organic beef)
3–4 gallons spring water
1 C red wine or ½ C of balsamic
3 beets, washed and chopped
3 onions, peeled and chopped
salt to taste

FOR PRE-NATAL (LABOUR INDUCING) BROTH, ADD:
12" cinnamon stick
12 cloves
8 cloves garlic
2 bay leaves
4-6 kefir lime leaves
as much saffron as you can afford

FOR POST-NATAL (VULNERARY) BROTH, ADD:
2 T fennel seeds
¼ C lotus seeds
4" fresh ginger
2 T turmeric
3 T comfrey root, cut and sifted (a traditional addition, but I tell clients to use their own discretion here, as there are studies that worry about the potential toxicity of comfrey)

I'm thinking about that thirteen year-old on the roof. Maybe you've grown this large community around you to take care of him. The most thriving urban Buddhist community in the country, where hundreds of people come and consider their condition, and form deep bonds with each other.

But they can't form deep bonds with you. Not on equal terms, anyway. Not like in these letters. They think you're this way or that way. What does Michael think? Michael this, Michael that. People hang on your words and probably fantasize about the serenity of your mental states. As much as I can see that you don't want to be an authority or object or symbol of something, the fact is that you are, and this means you're always standing apart from people a bit. Feeling your way into their relationships and struggles, but from afar. You're still on that roof in the sunset—perhaps it's the middle of the night now—and I wonder if you would know how to do it any other way.

love,
Matthew

|||

October 17th

Matthew,

Our last day in France, full of quick closed-mouth kisses. Short kisses to say, "it's so good to be here with you, right here, now." Short kisses to say, *thank you.*

In your letter you end by talking about my role as a teacher, its loneliness, and the constant need to step out of the projection the role sets up. I wish I had a step-by-step method for projection-busting, like the one created for yeast infections, but I don't. More and more I try and keep my friendships and the people who study with me separated. I have an ongoing private conversation with myself where I check in and see what projections I've fallen for and what's real. It's exhausting sometimes. I catch myself being five years old and wanting to be liked. At least a performer gets to dress up and create a character through which to sing or act. I have to teach as myself. And though I have deep bonds with my students, especially the ones who consistently come on silent retreats, I wouldn't call them when I'm down, or write them emails about my sex life. So this community grows, it's true, but my more intimate social sphere has not. Sometimes I fantasize about moving somewhere where I don't teach so I can have more anonymous relationships with people. Maybe it's one reason I love travelling.

I miss A. On my iPhone I have a photo of him helping me shave.

Below the window here there's a man smoking beside his son who is sound asleep in a blue pram. If I turn west, away from the street where we are staying, there are about fifty yachts registered to the Cayman Islands. Almost half of them have their own helicopters. I take photos of them for A who is obsessed with helicopters and all machines that fly. Carina calls it the harbor of the one percent.

It's not lost on me that this is the same body of water that hugs Syria, where only a year ago peaceful protest marches broke out across the country. The images of those marches are still burned into my mind. When I was watching those events unfold, expecting to see the protesters face water cannons or batons at most, I remember being horrified to discover that Assad's government was firing lethal rounds. When the protesters were arrested, they were tortured and mutilated and then left in public places as a warning, as a message to a mangled human race. It all turned into a very long and bloody campaign, one that I am losing track of because I just don't understand it any more. The young Syrian protesters are still fighting back but nobody has come to their aid.

Carina and I are swimming in the sea every day. Her swollen belly shares the same waters as the warships not far from here.

My parents met at a pool on Toronto Island run by the

Island Yacht Club. My mother was a member and my father was a lifeguard. They met in an argument: he wouldn't let her swim without a bathing cap. Three years later my parents were taking me to the same pool. When I turned five I managed to get my leg stuck in the tiled ladder and I couldn't get out of the pool. My head was submerged and my father jumped in and somehow squeezed my foot from the small crevice in which it was stuck. All I remember was my father's strength, the chlorine, bubbles, gasping for breath, and looking up at last to see my father's red beard and the sky.

I never took to swimming. This past year I've been thinking about swimming a lot, so every day I am heading out to the sea, sometimes with Carina and sometimes without, and teaching myself front crawl. I'm using all the muscles I love from forearm stand practice in the Ashtanga yoga sequence. Holding my breath underwater is fabulous. I must admit that I also had to spend an hour on the iPad learning that sharks in the Mediterranean have only struck about forty times in the past century. I did the math in my mind for the first few laps, imagining how many millions of people swim here each year. Carina is also worried about the sharks that don't actually exist. How much of falling in love is about sharing these spectacular dark fantasies? I love the feeling of the waves coming up over my shoulders, the saline sting in my eyes, and the exhalations pressing me forward against the current that I imagine draws France towards Syria. Since Carina became pregnant I'm doing a lot of things I've always wanted to do. I even took one ballet lesson, but the music was awful.

I want to try new things, not one thing in particular, but a million things—from going back to school to living rurally; from working with young people to visiting Japan again. Maybe we'll move out west? Secretly I also have this worry that when the baby comes I'll fall back into old relational habits again. I was twenty-six turning twenty-seven when A's mother and I met. She was a decade older. Strangely, I was experiencing that feeling women talk about, where in their thirties the biological clock starts telling them that it's time for a baby, and so they either switch relationships or begin looking at their partners as potential caregivers. That happened for me at twenty-five. I thought I would leave everything behind and become a monk and also, I wanted to have children.

I walked home one night from Natalie's house. She had just broken up with her long-time boyfriend. I thought about the three women I was attracted to, including her, and my mind was going back and forth between seeing myself lying on a couch with each one of them. In one scene there's a baby girl, and I see myself, skinny and sitting in lotus, in a rural temple, maybe in Japan or India, with nobody else around. In the monk fantasy I'm sitting most of the day, and reading old scriptures written on thin linen paper. There are strange insects, long paths through the forest, and food is simple but someone else is cooking. The fantasy would continue for a long time, often, but on this one night, walking from Natalie's house, along Bloor Street back to my loft in Kensington Market, I decided then and there to stop dating, to get focused on choosing someone, finding that someone, searching for that woman I could build a family with. I kissed Natalie in her bathroom. But for sure, I knew we would never have babies together. A gear was shifting into place. For the next two years I saw possible partners only through that lens.

When A's mother and I met, she had just come to the end of a pop music career and hadn't even thought about kids. None of her friends had kids, even though they were all at least a decade older than me. It was the only thing on my mind. The first overnight date we had, camping under an enormous orange moon, I wondered whether we could have kids together. Even the first time we made love I was thinking about kids.

Now I'm in France, and I couldn't feel further from that time. More than a dozen years have passed. Those days seem young and confused. Where did those fantasies come from? Why did family win out? How does one know when to listen to the body and when to follow images, prophetic dreams, or little voices that whisper "go forward," or "stay away," or "she is the one to have the baby with." A Jungian analyst, my university teacher Ann Yeoman, once said to me, "Michael, you are very intuitive. However, intuition is either 100% right or 100% wrong."

This is what intuition has felt like for me: the time I knew it was safe to take LSD from a stranger, which was the same night that Jennifer, at the same party, had her wallet stolen. The night I knew not to go into a convenience store but did anyway, and three older boys started pushing me around, terrifying me, but at the right moment, I saw the door and ran as fast as I could across the road, and found three friends somehow standing there, at one in the morning, and I was safe. Or the night I had a dream of surfing on a river in British Columbia, wearing camouflage, and the tail of the river opened into a vast ocean, and as I surfed into the wide vista I looked back at the rainforest, filled with animals, and when I awoke from the dream, and put my clothes on, I walked down the road past a garage sale, where sitting on someone's porch was a painting of a young man in camouflage standing with a surfboard with the Canadian rainforest in the background, exactly as it was in the dream. I didn't tell anyone. These synchronistic events happen again and again, even now, and I listen as best I can. When Carina and I started dating it scared me that everything I felt when we were together was right.

It's late afternoon, it's raining and I'm going to go swimming again.

Waves on my back. Asking Carina to marry me. You and Alix waiting swollen. No sharks. Underwater where nothing gets recorded. Everything in the sea nameless. Our unborn kids, also nameless. Granite steps down to the water. French cigarette smoke at the laundromat. Finnish baby names.

love,
Michael

October 19th

Matthew,

I haven't heard from you in a few days. If Alix is in labour than maybe this letter should become a new chapter in our collection. I am in Sweden now, teaching at a small yoga centre in Gottenborg. It's wet and cool. When I meet new people at the centre where I'm teaching I silently pronounce their name, secretly trying out each one as a potential baby name. I woke at 4 a.m. and rolled out my mat to practice, only because I knew I wasn't going to fall back asleep. Of course I wondered about you for the first hours of the morning, hoping the birth is going smoothly. Is it?

I only have grey glimpses of A's first week, maybe because I slept so little and had that nasty flu. A was so light, hardly a feather, and I'd hold him with one arm while bringing tea from the kitchen to the upstairs room that we cleared out as a space for resting and breast feeding. We listened to Chet Baker constantly for those first few weeks. I loved the feeling of holding him and moving my arms in slow swells and watching calm come though his tiny body, his eyes either falling asleep or scanning mine. The feeling of breathing and swaying my body and how it transferred rest into his, is the primal memory I have of A and me—half-remembered songs and Chet Baker's soothing trumpet in my ears, coursing through my hands and through A's tiny frame.

Carina and I parted at the Nice airport. She flew back to Toronto and I've come here to Sweden for three days of teaching before following her home. The white sky has fissures of grey in it. The yellow leaves look bright even though they are only half alive. The day is dreamlike. I guess every day is dreamlike, full of expected things that won't happen and unexpected things that will—like a birth, perhaps?

Anything I write today will be small in comparison to what's happening for you. And yet there is a dimension to what's happening in your life that is exquisitely ordinary. Watch the thousands of people in an airport—so many parents, so many births, so much worry and magic.

One of the lessons about spiritual practice that I've learned over the years is to take the most special things that I do and treat them as totally ordinary: lighting incense, chanting, bowing, saying prayers with Carina—totally ordinary. Then, I take what is most ordinary and draw it up into something holy: tying shoes, dishes, laundry, sleeping, banking. What is mundane is given special attention and what on the surface seems religious is treated as mundane. This trick of the imagination changes intentions for the better. It brings my practice into regular routine. I need these reminders because my emotional life seems all over the place. Sitting is the only way I can settle. This morning I listened from my small room to the sound of my hosts in the kitchen down the hall, feeding breakfast to their seven-year-old who has a cold. They speak Swedish so I have no idea what they were saying. I imagine this is what Carina's family sounded like in her early years. In meditation the breath falls and gets quieter and quieter until some point when the filters fall away and my mind feels stable. Funny, on the iPad on which I'm writing, the word *fall* was revised as *fail*, which makes a much better sentence: *the filters fail away.*

A Chinese teacher named Panshan wrote:

In the universe, there is nothing.
Where will we search for the mind?

Sometimes I sit because I want to explore the unfindability of mind. The space of not-knowing. Other times, like today, I sit because my mind is racing and my emotions are bouncing off every thought that comes through me. When Carina and I were skyping last night I was hardly paying attention. I don't sit to get answers. Just to clear a space. Even when I'm still and a thought arises, especially if preceded by some question I have, it's usually clear that a thought is not what I need. It's easy to see in practice. But what about as a parent? When I had a hard time with A this year—to clarify, it was actually a hard time with his mother—I wrote to my teacher Enkyo Roshi and described the situation. She wrote back and said:

You don't need any advice.

I am thinking about you and Alix regularly.

love,
Michael

|||

October 19th

Michael –

5:28. At 1 a.m. this morning, Alix's water broke! It was thrilling to see her looking down at the kitchen floor in amazement. Crystal clear water, silky to the touch, a vague sweet smell. I got down on my hands and knees to look for meconium, the fetal poop they're worried about causing infection when the woman is overdue. There was nothing.

I have a few minutes now while the oatmeal cooks, and Alix moans softly and dozes through early contractions. It rained all day yesterday, into the night: there's downward water everywhere. I have to wake her up soon to page the midwife and report, to see if we should cancel the ultrasound we have booked for two hours from now.

I've been out of touch because we've been in Labour-Induction Boot Camp here, hiking all over the city, hunting down spicy food, dancing in the living room. There's so much in your letters to respond to, and I trust the important threads will come back when these waves subside. You're going to ask Carina to marry you. I press down on Alix's sacrum and she moans with relief and pleasure.

Going to the ultrasound will get us both moving in the light morning rain. And I want to see baby on that grey screen one more time before he or she is in my arms.

One thing about the ultrasound department at the hospital is that you're in line with very sick people on stretchers. Last time, there were two old men on gurneys. One who stared terrified at the ceiling and had the sour smell of cancer. But when the other was wheeled past me, he looked at me and winked. His skin was drooping and grey. Alix was on my arm. It was all I could do to take in their condition—I couldn't even smile at them. So maybe I'll get to see baby on that screen, but also make eye-contact with these men at the end of things, to try to see what we're sharing, if anything.

Thank you for holding us in your heart.

love,
Matthew

|||

October 19th

Matthew,

Indeed you are in my heart and I'm in suspense, of course, though I certainly don't expect you to write now. I'm in the Gottenborg airport leaving Sweden on my way back home to Toronto. I just announced, "Her water broke!!!" to everyone in earshot. Now I have my head buried in the keyboard because I'm being stared at.

Carina just sent me sexy photos of another punk haircut (she keeps shaving the sides of her head) and I'm eating dark rye with two thinly sliced potatoes on the top covered in a slimy piece of herring. The fish goes down smooth and I chase it with an espresso. I woke early, as I've been doing all trip, working on backbends to keep my spine supple while travelling, and then did some pranayama and sat still. After I sat I checked my emails. Everyday since Carina flew home to Toronto she's been sending me hot photos. In the last photo she wrote: "Here is another picture. Say goodbye to my twenty-something legs. And my breasts are never going to look this good again. Enjoy!"

Right now I am sending you continuous love through space and time. Maybe I should send you a sexy photo? I wish I knew what your new apartment looked like so I could visualize you and Alix together there. I hope everything is happening as smoothly and safely as possible. I care for you both. I want to write and write and build a bridge of letters to your new family—an attempt to accompany you in real time. Everything is going to go well. In no time you'll be watching your kid sleeping. Someone told me that until your child turns 14, they always look like an infant when they sleep. It's true with A. When he sleeps he looks like he's a month old even though his feet smell now.

One night, before I left for this trip, after A fell asleep, I opened the door to his room and lay down on the blue carpet next to him (actually, at first I lay down on a sharp corner of Lego). For a while I lay on my side, then my back, then I sat up and watched him sleeping. I hadn't done so in years. The streetlight lit his arm with its blonde hair and three or four freckles near his wrist. He had marker on his fingers, a little on his neck, and he was snoring as usual, maybe from the litres of yogurt he consumes daily.

He is reading Johnny Cash's biography, in the form of a graphic novel—it's in bed with him—and his eyelashes are long and stunning. Outside the cars bump over speed bumps louder than usual, and I can hear Carina shutting the lights off downstairs. A's room smells like the laundry detergent from his mother's house, and this upsets me sometimes, reminding me of a tear in my life, especially in my bond with A. But tonight there's just his breathing, my tired arms, and his beautiful skin. Separation is this exacting line that cuts across everything, making a mark in the timeline, like the transition from B.C.E to C.E.

Next to A's bed is a video his friend Alice gave him. My mind drifts to Sam, my closest friend when I grew up. Her family had a very large house that resembled an oversized English cottage, and sometimes when I told my parents Sam and I were going out, I'd go to her home instead and, in the basement in the dark, we'd lie on her brown corduroy couch holding hands and listening to Neil Young. We'd kiss and talk. She was a lot like a boy, dressing in plaid button down shirts, boys' jeans and suede desert boots. She was a stellar piano player. We were fourteen. She was the first girl who I really experimented with, though she was less ambitious than me. I always thought kissing her was like kissing a boy, that her body was more like mine than it was like other girls' at school or camp. But when we held hands and listened to music, I never felt alone. She wore a tight t-shirt instead of a bra, and grey wool socks—never a dress—and she rode a boy's bike. She taught me how to smoke. She was far cooler than boys.

Her mother was especially kind to me. Upstairs she'd make snacks in the kitchen. I so wanted to live in that kitchen, in that house, with her family, at the top of the hill. They had more money than us, and then there were her relatives, also in large homes, with kids a little older than I, spread out through the neighbourhood. Her father had a very old green Porsche 911. It wasn't even fancy, it was simple and had paint bubbling at the bottom of the doors. I loved parking my bike in their garage, which was always open, and peering at the worn leather seats in that car, imagining myself driving it, with Sam in the passenger seat, out into the forest north of the city, on a long road trip, the boxer engine behind us—free.

A few years ago I learned that Sam was gay, her parents were divorced, and after her father's mining company was shut down in a lawsuit over environmental regulations, he was caught breaking into the condominiums of elderly neighbors and stealing their money and jewelry. I haven't seen Sam since those days. I forget why we lost each other. Sometimes when I drive past that house I still long for the feel of that wooden kitchen, the fireplace, that large sink under a wide window opening to enormous maple trees. And I would still love to have that old green rusty Porsche.

I spent a lot of my life wanting to join other families, live in their homes, do whatever they did. At night I would roam in the dark and see lamps lit in foreign living rooms, people moving about, tall gates in backyards that I couldn't see over. I wanted to see what happened behind those gates.

But where the story doesn't add up is that I also felt alien to those other lives—the privileged cloistered, Jewish families. When I had more than two hours free, I'd make my way down to Kensington Market, alone, and find solace amongst the leather shops and skateboarders.

Now we have two skateboards in the house—one for me and one for A. We skate irregularly. I'm afraid of injury. Anyways Matthew, it's time for sleep. And for you also, if possible, because any day now you two have a child coming into this world.

I asked Carina to come walk with me down to the small beach at the bottom of the the city. I tucked her ring in my pocket. We got two blocks and then she had to pee. She walked back up the two flights of stairs to the apartment and didn't come down. I fingered the ring in my pocket. Finally, I ran up to see what was going on and she was eating as much as she could from the fridge. Again, we left the house, the ring in my right pocket, and walked ten minutes to the sea. She told me she was still hungry. She went to get a drink, and again I stood waiting for her, nervous, excited, unsure how to ask her her to marry me. Finally, with enough food and several trips to pee, we were sitting by the water at the foot of Antibes, I turned to face her and said: "Will you marry me?" I'd never been so nervous. Tears welled up in our eyes. She said "Will *you* marry *me*?" We cried and laughed and I gave her the slim ring from Copenhagen.

love,
Michael

October 21st

Dear Michael.

Jacob Cale Remski.
Born 10/20/2012 at 10:18 a.m.
St. Joseph's Hospital, Toronto.

love,
Matthew

| | |

October 22nd

Dearest Matthew and Alix,

This is wonderful.
Jacob Cale.
Please let me know if you need anything. I know you have
lots of food stored away and plenty of friends to support you
both but if you, Matthew, need a walk or someone to talk with
or even if you want to go for a fast sauna, let me know—I am
around the corner. I know you know your job now is to be close.
That's all. Your heart was just born again, too.

love,
Michael

| | |

October 29th

Dear Michael –

Oh boy a sauna would be really good, especially in this damp
edge of the hurricane that's sweeping across our city. As well
as the hurricane within me—to smell that bright hot cedar and

have it dry this torrent of weeping between Alix and me: of so many layers of recognition, of the labour trauma I won't be able to write about for some time, of the aura around his tender flesh and irregular infant breathing. A sauna, maybe next week, but not before uncle Michael and auntie Carina come around to visit. Maybe you can bring A as well?

It's early morning. I don't even know what time it is. The clock says 4:37, my flesh says *stay awake forever—you can't miss any of this*. My eyes are burning with bright exhaustion. Baby's nursing and sleeping well, but it feels like I'm going through my own birth, and the labour has taken this whole nine days so far. Whenever I think I'm settling in for complete silence, I hear him breathe like another person within me, someone I have forgotten until now, someone coming in a dream, but no dream has ever pulsed so hot.

Jacob and Alix were separated nine days ago, and now they are finding each other again. She curls him into her, he reaches for her with his mouth. He wriggles on her stitched up belly in ways that make her gasp: *he did exactly that inside me.*

I was also separated from Alix during the labour. She disappeared into a trance I will write about one day. Now Jacob pulls us towards each other. But within the triad, the two of them tight together, they ground each other. Watching her as a mother, as new to mothering as he is to breathing, is like watching ocean finding shore. She studies him in minutest detail, but then her flesh goes to him without thought.

He comes from the distant land of inside her. How did he ever seem so remote, so far away? He rests between us, nodding off at Alix's swollen breast. For now, the sexual charge that has zipped between us from the beginning broadens and slows down and now swaddles itself around him.

Everything is satisfied, but I cannot sleep. Jacob, you are sleeping for me. You are the dreaming child without time who soothes this waking man surrounded by clocks that make no sense.

Of course he is not me at all. He is new. He gets to come into this light and shadow and sound and texture for the first time, as if he were inventing perception.

Alix's nipples cracked and bled on the second day in the hospital—we think because he has such a powerful suck and his latch wasn't catching her whole aureole, and the colostrum wasn't enough for him. I found pure lanolin for her to daub on and we joked about barnyard smells. But what really helped was when the midwife came for her first visit and helped Alix correct the latch.

Linda, the midwife, was delighted to come. We'd had most of our prenatal meetings with her, but she wasn't at the birth—a younger substitute was on call. Linda is in her fifties, and was jolly throughout the home visit, chuckling at Jacob's fat-folds, and answering every question with "It's a baby! You'll figure it out! Sometimes things are tough or things go wrong, but it's very rare. This is the best thing in life, and we can miss it if we worry too much!" She kept laughing, shrugging her shoulders, and saying "It's a baby!", as though it was the only thing anyone would ever have to remember.

I boiled fenugreek seeds and fed them to Alix to help her milk along. As soon as she took the first spoonful, the milk began to drip down onto her belly. I found fresh fenugreek leaves at my favourite Indian grocer. I told the Sri Lankan guy I've known for years it was for breast milk and he grinned with betel-juice-stained teeth and gave me a pomegranate as a new fatherhood gift.

I steamed the fenugreek leaves and dressed them in lemon and olive oil and salt and we both chewed it down. I fell asleep trying to figure out how fenugreek works according to Ayurveda (pungent, bitter, downward-moving—but how does it target the breast?) and then I rubbed my face in the armpit of the shirt I've worn for three days and the unmistakable scent of fenugreek smacked me. The herb has permeated my lymphatic system, and is wafting from the nodes under my arms. Bitter caramel.

Fenugreek is pushing our lymph. It must flavor the milk as well, and give baby a little extra sleepy heat.

I put a lot of turmeric in Alix's recovery broth as an anti-inflammatory and antibacterial, and it's turning Jacob's early poo a bright yellow-orange that stains like sunshine. The changing pad is a loaner. I hope Jennifer doesn't mind if we return it as though some Burmese monk with a colour-bleeding robe had borrowed it.

I'll tell you one thing: bonding is a crisis. The biological imperative is for it to happen as soon as possible. Within hours of Jacob's birth the flood of emotion had burned his face into my brain. Sitting here in the next room, I can picture him more clearly than my mother or father, more clearly at moments than Alix. His face is already etched on my bones as if he'd put his entire life-force into communicating just one thing to me: *I'm here because of you. Look closely.*

For a few hours, Alix had waves of tension contract within her cuddling: *is he okay, is he safe?* And to me: *I need you close.* All when I couldn't possibly get closer without crawling into her womb, where this strange new empty space is.

I understand even more now the unbearable physical and emotional attachments our spiritual paths go on to try to correct or soften, but I reject even more now all the bullshit of it being some kind of weakness. Life bangs out promises in every heartbeat. The smallest thing voices an incredible demand: *you are not your own anymore, you will care for me more deeply than you have ever cared for yourself.* This intense attachment—*I would open my veins for you over and over again*—has got to be the root of empathy. Where else would we begin? How do we learn to spread it out? Connect to others who feel it as well?

In the *Mahabharatha*, Kunti makes love with the sunrise and gives birth to Karna, who grows up thinking he's a bastard and so struggles with feelings of abandonment throughout his life. Kunti never reveals her secret to him, but showers him with adoration to compensate. But in her overbearing love she has an insight. She says "Whenever a mother favours her own children over the children of another, war is near." Karna never realizes that when the sun shines upon him, he is feeling his source. Every morning by the river, his father shines upon him, and he does not know it. Later, at battle with Arjuna, his chariot wheel is stopped in the mud. He dismounts and sits in the sun, waiting for the arrows to pierce him. He has so many silent moments with the sun.

Jacob's breath stutters in his sleep as the storm rolls in. The midwives told us this is normal. His breath will shudder, gasp, hiccup, sigh, jitter, skip a beat, then smooth itself out. His diaphragm is learning its many moods and tools. Learning to pivot, to be resilient, to absorb the thrusts and parries of his infant dreams. His diaphragm, which has no insertion or attachment points, a muscle as continuous as the nervous system.

Later in life we sit down to meditate and watch the breath to smooth its arc. But this is meaningless to someone disconnected from the full range of breath-strokes, with all of their giddiness and fear. It makes me think that yoga couldn't make sense without grounding in the eccentric and asymmetrical movements that remember these infant reflexes. And I don't know how rich the mental posture of *metta* could possibly be without the crushing, jealous, hyperpersonal attachment that marks the first relationships of life. We reach for peace through love, but love begins in this ecstatic confusion. I transcend nothing.

Jacob grimaces in his sleep and the bright yellow poo fills his diaper, propelled by a series of loud wet farts. He is unbearably beautiful.

love,
Matthew

November 4th,

Dear Matthew,

The best news! A healthy baby is the best news. Eleven pounds? Is that like eight pounds of baby and a few pounds of ghee? Carina and I would love to come see you two and the ghee-baby.

Maybe you need to be held too? I imagine a hundred versions of the traumatic delivery and when you're ready to talk it through, even small bits, please let me know.

There's been a hurricane of labour in your life, and the winds here in Toronto are intensifying. New York is in darkness in Hurricane Sandy's wake. I am supposed to go there Saturday to study with my teacher for three days. We are going to do koan practice together. She's seventy-one. It's impossible work. I visit her and present the koan I am currently working with. More on that later. But for now she just wrote:

> Still no power at the zendo or at our apartment. The city is a bit of a mess in terms of transportation, etc. We are waiting to hear if there will be power, but we may not be open on Sunday.
>
> When there is no power, there is no water, and being on the eleventh floor, no elevators, safety lights, etc.
>
> love to you,
> Roshi
>
> P.S I am writing from an NYU library—I have no power, phone, nor internet . . . just carrying water up my ten flights is good exercise . . .

Roshi is trapped in Manhattan without power—it's as if she is in a long labour herself. Like all old bald people, Roshi looks like a baby. I imagine her in her eleventh floor walk-up like I picture my son upside-down in Carina's belly. One of her students just sent me a photo of an old gate in front of a Brooklyn brownstone with an extension cord, power bar and note saying: *We have power. Please feel free to charge your cell phone.*

Kim, whom I'm supposed to stay with in the East Village, has been displaced from her building because there's no power there either. And my friends in Brooklyn can't figure how to get me from the airport to the city because everything is shut down—the whole infrastructure. So maybe I'll end up being home with Carina, who all week has needed more massage through her lumbar spine. I'll cook. We haven't been walking together in a week because the winds have been so intense. How are the trees near your place?

Last night we took A out for Halloween, and despite both wind and rain there were so many kids out. I couldn't believe how many branches there were, strewn all over the lawns. I'm going outside now to clean up the debris in our yard.

There is a hurricane inside you. And as you said, you feel like you need to stay awake forever. I remember exactly the same sentence when A was born, but I had nobody to say it to.

I'm working on the famous koan called "*Mu*." It's not the first time I've struggled with this. It's from a story that took place in China more than a thousand years ago:

A student asked Zen Master Zhaozhou, "Does a dog have Buddha nature or not?" Zhaozhou said, "*Mu*."

The word *Mu* means "no."

The method with Roshi is that she wants me to sit down face to face with her and *show* my response. No explanations. "Just *show* me *Mu*," she said, while her face lit up. I presented it to her. She smiled. Then she said, "Let's keep going. Now tell me: How old is *Mu*?"

I stumbled. I paused. I looked to the left then back at her and suddenly I was in my head again, thinking around for a response. She shook her head. "Maybe next time."

Then she told me to go home and when I am with the baby or with Carina, to ask myself: "How old is *Mu*?"

The koan can go in many ways. Does life have an underlying nature? Do all sentient beings have an essence? Do I? If so, what is it and how do I express it? And how old is that nature? Or, perhaps there is no underlying nature, as the literal translation suggests. Then, how old is the nature of something that has no nature, and how old is the nature of that something which is me? How old is Jacob Cale? How old or young is this moment in time?

I don't want to share all the details of my process except that I've been meditating on this koan throughout the day. I say to myself: *Mu* or *No*. Then I say: *how old is this?* The question relays again and again in my mind throughout the day, like one pool ball hitting another. What I've started to believe is that the attention I bring to the question is really a form of love. The koan process, for me, anyways, is bringing love to each moment. Who ever thought that turning over a question again and again could bring love about?

You were so worried about birth stats. That's a koan also. Jacob is a koan. One Zen master wrote:

The only koan
That really matters is
You.

love,
Michael

|||

November 6th

Dear Michael –

Time is micro to the baby, and stretches out, like breath, over time. I've been tugged into baby's biorhythm as he slides slowly from nocturnal to diurnal, and as each nursing governs a whole digestive cycle. He sleeps for three hours at a time at most, which is not enough to feel either the depth or the angst of sleep. How strange that he has his entire lifespan before him, yet every cycle is so accelerated. But he is working hard and without cognition towards survival. Alix was reading an article about how elite athletes crumble under the physical demands and energy outputs that infants make every day: this constant reaching, clutching, lurching backwards, craning, holding and releasing the urethral sphincter, twisting out gas, and bearing down on the bowel.

I'm writing of Jacob, although I've become shyer of using his name. It is so clear that there is no person here yet, but a radiant and writhing tangle, a microsystem of weather, no self at all. People ask me what he's like, as if he has a personality or character, and I am blank. How do you describe the immediate? I'm more than blank, actually. It's slightly irritating how quickly we want to pin our projections onto infants, starting with the thickest projection of all: that we are independent selves.

His name seems too personal to me. But I can use the gendered pronoun: his penis swells and shrinks with waves of aliveness. Baby is a he.

What is remarkable is to feel my own selfhood erode in this wind, broken down by changing plans and pivots in necessity. Change, feed, bounce, change, feed, feed, console. I myself cry, and sleep, shallow sometimes, sometimes deep. How perfect is this: the developmental psychology is shared between parent and baby: baby strips away a father's self so that he can find his own personhood. And what can I even say of Alix's change?

I am absolutely convinced now in the absence of the soul or *atman* or anything eternal and abstract except for the pulse of life that connects the thrust of sex between Alix and I last January to this shuddering breath today. There was a windstorm that night. She said: *Make a baby with me*. She said it as though our lives depended on it, but she didn't need to say it.

We emerge out of movement and stuff. Life doesn't come from somewhere else. It is its own writhing cause. We feel it all the time, if we can get beneath our disguises. We become selves not because we are uniquely destined, but because we come to see and know each other. At only seventeen days old, he's almost focusing his eyes directly into my own eyes. I, in my eroded selfhood, am almost focusing my eyes into his. It doesn't seem right that he should be named before he can name me.

Why the soul? Why the Self? Why the *atman*? What is this story about? I'm starting to understand what Roshi is doing with you in that koan practice. She's getting you to strip away your language and your conceits and your presumptions and all the ways in which you try to console yourself instead of digging deeper into the present moment. And it's all happening in relationship with her. You're sitting with this big old baby in a robe, and she's making you say *Mu*, over and over again. It's so funny!

Life is a koan: enormous and palpable, immediate and inescapable, vast and tiny. Dissociating into a cognitive fantasy of possessing a self or soul or getting the job that our father wanted us to have relieves us of the crush of the present moment, which, if we live it as a baby does, is an endless swirl of pressures, shadows, textures, vibrations—all internal as much as external, with no instructions for telling them apart. The baby is the world. It is incomprehensible, until the organizing fiction of the self seems to create a version of the world that we believe will be navigable.

love,
Matthew

|||

November 10th

Matthew,

Koan practice, like the lived experience of relationship, is teaching me how to stop grasping. Not holding on to "Michael," "father" or anything else I identify with. The key is safety. I feel safe enough with Roshi that I can be vulnerable with her. She always shows me some other angle I wasn't seeing. I'm grateful for this relationship. I'm lucky she can send me emails like, "You don't need any advice," and that she kicks me out of interviews when I'm not seeing the point. She once said, "When you leave an interview with me, don't go to the bathroom or have tea. Just go as fast as you can back to your cushion and sit still because usually the answer to the koan appears in the second after you've presented something to me."

I'm learning how to meet her. I have to learn it again and again.

I found my teacher Enkyo Roshi when I was on a retreat at the Insight Meditation Society and came across a publication called the Insight Journal, in which Enkyo Roshi was interviewed. In the interview the editor begins by posing this question to her: What is your practice?

Her response: *Manhattan*.

Centuries earlier a monk asks Yun Men: What is Buddhism?

Yun Men: An appropriate response.

And one more, Matthew: two monks are in the kitchen of a monastery. They are preparing the ingredients for the meal, measuring water and flax and grains. As one monk lifts the bag of flax onto the scale, the other asks him: What is Buddha?

And the monk, lowering the bag to the scale, looks up and says: Three pounds of flax.

Three pounds of flax. Maybe you might answer Jacob Cale. Or joy. The practice of parenting is immediate. It's not a thing. It's not a state. Every letter you have been writing says the same thing: what happens when we stop trying to find the perfect state? What happens when intimacy is our practice? What is *Mu*?

How much does three pounds of flax really weigh?

There's a whole protocol of walking into the interview room with Roshi that prepares me for this moment of encounter. We bow to each other twice and I sit three inches from her knees. A candle burns to my left. When I joke that Carina and I are creating a domestic monastery, it's not that we have rituals in our day or that we bow twice to one another, it's that we are both interested in this same kind of engagement, this intimacy that is immediate. It's the most important thing. It's the heart of my life. As far as I know, it's the same for Carina. In relationship, aren't we always asking of each other: Show me yourself, show me who you are?

Carina has gone to Vancouver for a week. I'm trying to get some plastering done on the cracked walls and ceilings before the baby comes, so the house is covered in a two-inch layer of dust. It's turned cold outside. My son is sleeping at my mother's house.

When I got home tonight to find the house empty, I thought it was a perfect chance to write and tell you about Carina's swollen belly, her trip to see her parents, the hilarious episode of her arriving in Vancouver and her sisters insisting that they take her straight away to try on wedding dresses. ("When they brought out the veils," she said, "I feigned nausea and we left.")

I re-read your letter. I didn't know this about fenugreek. The only thing I know about fenugreek is that it turns Ethiopian food yellow. And Alix's nipples in the hospital? I wish I could have told you about cabbages. When A's mother was engorged in the first hours after the milk came in, I ran to the store and got three large cabbages. We put the concave leaves on her breasts and her breasts were so hot they steamed the leaves in two minutes. We went through a few cabbages in a day!

Oh. But I just realized that you're talking about cracking, and I'm talking about engorgement. Shows you how much I know. Anyway, I hear you.

What happened at the hospital?

love,
Michael

November 16th

Michael –

I can't tell you what happened at the hospital yet. I need to get clear on it. I need to hold Alix for several months and listen for whenever she's able to speak about it. I have my version, and she'll have hers. A big part of love, I think, is allowing our different versions of our stories and of each other to be separate and braided at the same time. I remember Rilke describing two trees standing separate on a hill, with their roots intertwining in the earth below.

One more thought. With no self in my arms, no self wriggling on the changing table at three in the morning, no self sleeping in the snuggly in my coat as we walk through the November leaves, no self squirming on my naked lap as I slather him with coconut oil and then let him stretch his limbs in the warm bath, no self craning his head up with grunts and groans, no self gazing at me and then beyond me to other patterns in space, no self straining and rooting for my lover's breast: who or what is it that I love with this crushing love? No one is here, but the world pours into this twelves pounds of baby, and I cannot tear myself away. I am jealous, shielding, teeth on edge, my muscles quivering around his as they quiver. Who or what do I love here? There is no self. Nothing mediates this shared and wordless grip. Or maybe I am afraid for this other self to exist.

In other news, I'm coursing with adrenaline. I sneak out to the gym whenever I can and run twice as far and twice as fast and lift twice as much as I ever have before. What's happening to me?

love,
Matthew

|||

November 16th

Matthew,

You always have one more thought. Thoughts always follow one another—one more, just one more! When I first learned chanting, I chanted from the Yoga Taravali which begins: *Vande Gurunam Caranaravinde*. It basically means that I bow to the plurality of teachings that have two lotus feet which are my own.

It's a great chant. Every teacher and teaching in time and space exists within my own two feet. In the commentary I learned that we have two feet called *Krama* and *Vikrama*: step and counter-step. The idea is that for every step, we need another; for every thought we need another. No thought can frame the whole thing. Ever. Every idea has a counter idea and every technique has a counter-technique, and every good idea eventually becomes a bad idea.

I remember that thing about names. When A was born and this baby was in our midst, it was so strange to give him a name. I would practice saying his name over and over to make sure it resonated, connected and had traction. It did. But for the first few days the name seemed like an overlay, a superimposition on this life force that had taken over and rearranged everything. It was far too large to have a name. I had no idea what he was, what my life had become, what he needed.

The Buddha didn't teach *no* self. He taught *not* self. The difference is spectacular. The Buddha taught that everything comes into the world embedded in conditions. Nothing is born alone. The conditions change. There is no essential "thing" beneath those conditions. It's not that there is no self, it's that nothing belongs to "me" and "mine." So when you look at your child's face, and the ten thousand moods that move through it, you can see how none of it belongs to a person that stands behind him. We are just moments in time. Imagine that. Imagine looking at everything, even your hands or your car, and seeing each thing as just a conditioned moment in time. Nothing belongs to me. Nothing is mine. Nothing you can point to is the essence of you, of Jacob Cale, of the wind tonight or the cold branches outside. *No-self* would be too strong a position, a denial, a reverse theology. Instead, *not-self* asks you to look further. This is powerful stuff when it's felt in the bones.

Here is how Nagarjuna says it:

Clinging is to insist
On being someone;

Not to cling
Is to be free to be no one.
To be someone is to be
Self-conscious, impulsive,
Thinking, feeling a body,
Which is born, ages, dies,
Suffers torment, grief, pain,
Depression, anxiety.
Anguish emerges
When someone is born.
Impulsive acts
Are the root of life.
Fools are impulsive
But the wise see things as they aro.
When confusion stops
Through practising insight
Impulsive acts will cease.

—(from *Verses from the Center* by Stephen Batchelor)

What I like about Nagarjuna is that he doesn't really have a position. A self-conscious self is willed into being and yet we can't find the core of a mind inside a body inside a world. No "thing" is given primacy. I could say more but you are feeling it now and that's more important. You are a father because you have a son. But he does not belong to you. You are alive because you breathe. But the breath is not yours, only another wind. Not self, not self.

Soon the white calm of winter will be here. Soon I hope to make tracks in the snow with you and our kids. In the meantime I'm sitting at Pearson airport. Another airport, waiting for an announcement that my flight is ready for boarding, or it's delayed, or it's in limbo, because it's arriving from Montreal or Halifax or Asia. Hours and hours of my life (I'm scared to actually count the total number) have been spent inhaling and exhaling in airports, planes, taxis, hotels where the windows can't open, mostly travelling to teach, almost always alone. There were the frequent trips from Toronto to Ottawa, where I have likely spent a total of thirty days this decade, likely the same number in Montreal and Madison, Green Bay, and half that number in Portland, Paris, Los Angeles and Guelph. For almost ten years in a row I've spent the first week of October in Copenhagen. Then there were the four trips to Greece, and within those trips there was a month on the southern shores of Crete with A, three years old, wandering naked by my side on an empty beach. I woke early in the mornings in Crete and practiced alone on a patio with the moon hanging overhead, the June winds set adrift from Northern Africa and they were so strong that one day I saw a sheep being blown across an unpaved mountain road.

Miami, Asheville, Gottenborg, London, Calgary, Edmonton, and at least three months of my life in Manhattan. I lived in Vancouver for two years and outside Detroit for less than a year. Twice, Carina and I spent several weeks of autumn in Antibes, living in flats as close as possible to the farmers' market. We hope to go there again and again to celebrate our anniversary, if time and money allow. I have travelled to teach mostly, and so it's been a way of being in other cultures, parachuting into communities, in a way I could never afford on my own. Seawalls, birds, trains, taxis, fields, cobblestones, white lines down the freeway, more taxis and waiting, waiting, waiting.

The concourse, the gate, the jetway, the bridge. "A shopping mall," my father says, "with planes in it." My father is an architect and now he consults with airports as they redesign their interiors to maximize shopping. He helps Starbucks figure out how to build their stores on budget. "The lease," he says, "is always five years, so that's how long the construction materials need to last. In other words, we build with the cheapest materials because when the lease is up, everything gets thrown out."

The Denver airport, where I stopped a few weeks ago, is the strangest. It's designed under enormous white tents and strung up with sophisticated cables and steel girders that "replicate the Rocky Mountains," my father says, but it's a stretch to see the 450-acre site that way. A business person can fly in for a meeting and never see Denver, the inner city, or inhale the crisp Colorado air.

There are infinity sinks and endless marble in the Charles de Gaulle airport in Paris, intricate wooden floors in Copenhagen and an organic bakery in Madison. LaGuardia and Washington D.C. are monuments to the crumbling infrastructure of the U.S.

Meditation comes spontaneously walking under the enormous torqued ellipses forged by my favorite artist Richard Serra at the Toronto airport. Carina and I walked through those ellipses, then around them, holding hands, waiting to board our flight to Copenhagen, while pregnant. She was stunning. As usual that year she had her hair shaved on either side, with a short and messy top, and when she wore her fading jeans and Converse I wanted nothing other than to walk beside her, anywhere, in airports or the by the windy canals in Copenhagen. Today I miss her. Another airport, waiting.

Difference in landscape blends into the sameness of global capitalism. There is an oddness to my life. Travel, domestic duty, then disappearance. I don't make my living where I live. Airports are designed to make you feel everywhere and nowhere. My identity is erased in an airport. Is this the same as the not-self of Buddhism? What's the difference between my Buddhism and the Buddhism of Tibet in 1959 where the practice had to integrate watching the destruction of everything while managing some kind of faith? Airports are, in many ways, destroying local life. With a credit card symbolizing something that used to be called money, we can go anywhere at any time. Or, we think we can.

With climate change intensifying, our kids will certainly not travel as much as we do.

love,
Michael

November 18th

Dear Michael –

No, they won't travel as much. If they take any interest in Buddhism, they'll have to nurture it locally. We've been lulled into thinking it's our birthright to observe the world from 30,000 feet, seeing sameness in airports and touristy differences in cobblestones. The groundlessness of late capitalism allows us to explore and perhaps amplify the ephemeral side of meditation. But the catastrophic climate change that is coming will drive this new global Buddhism back into the forest, where the instability of life can still be measured out in cups of rice and water.

We were having a rough night about a week ago. Three weeks of three- to four-hour stretches of sleep had suddenly given way to baby J being up every hour to nurse, although he didn't want to nurse deeply, it seemed, and if he dropped off to sleep it was with a lot of twitching and snorfling. I made gripe water from peppermint and fennel, and Alix and I took turns bouncing him on the Pilates ball while he hollered with endless energy. She started singing "Ninety-nine bottles of beer," and when I took over I would pick up with the right number. At one point we switched the song to "Ninety-nine bottles of milk," but then I said, "He doesn't need any more milk—he's already congested." We barely managed to laugh.

Then I suddenly realized that I was holding this hot little wriggling proto-person and my soothing sounds were building into a story of what was going on inside him. I began to speak to him as though he was thinking thoughts like mine. I was asking him questions about what he was worried about. Mayor Ford? Another depressing start to the Leaf's season? Climate change?

Through it all I started to see how the self is constructed, from the outside in. It's beautiful, but also slightly creepy.

I am making him into a container or channel for my own thoughts. It's not enough to let him be a swirl of sensations that crests and falls. Because his feelings are impinging upon my sleep, I looked for reasons behind and within his behaviour, and, absurdly, I begin to reason with him, as though he understands time or cared about waking up the neighbours. I began to attribute intentions to him, as though there is an adult trapped within this infant flesh who really wants something specific. I begin to imagine that there are words and sentences in him that he cannot speak, or that he is withholding from me. I endowed him with an internal monologue less mature than my own. I am giving him an ego structure—and finding fault with it already— perhaps because I don't know how else I would recognize him to bond with him. But absolutely none of this is true.

What is most eerie about beginning to construct an internal, willful, aloof self for my son is that it is fuelled by frustration. It is so easy to create the other as the thing that is obstructing your needs, and then to attribute willfulness to it. It is so easy when you are tired and underfed to look at this beautiful hollering child and make subtle accusations: *You don't know what you want. You're confused. You're really angry.* It's as though there's a part of us that literally creates otherness through our own stress. The friction of being depended upon is relieved by believing that the other could somehow take care of themselves, if they only got it together.

And yet: does self-regulation begin to occur through these very same cues? Are these smallest movements towards an ego structure that learns to expect relief from gas or hunger, and so can self-soothe for a while, initiated by hearing the parent speak from their own internality? Will Jacob's language-mind evolve to answer my need for him to be a self? Will it evolve to hide from me, and my needs?

It feels like the "I" is a type of bacterial flora, and I am inoculating him with it, so that we can come to some kind of understanding. If we could only remember that we endow each other with personhood, and do not make ourselves.

Baby Jacob's self is shimmering into evidence on his skin. Maybe if I say the word "I" enough, or his name enough, individuation enters his ear, reaching into his deepest brain. I want to be there to see that first moment of self-satisfaction and wonder in which the penny drops for him, and he says *I am Jacob. I am me.* Then we will be equals in the core problem of life.

I remember my father singing to me a Peter, Paul & Mary song. "Day is Done," written by Peter, whose surname is Yarrow, and who actually looks a lot like my father. It was perhaps the sweetest way I could have been made a channel of an older self I would try to model. I became a self more through relationship with my father than with my mother, from whom it was harder to individuate. The first time I clearly remember hearing and understanding the song, I didn't hear the "my son" in it as being addressed to me. I heard it as though *I* were the father, as though I could pretend to care for myself, as though I could sing myself into the kind of person who would be able to comfort others.

> *Tell me why you're crying, my son*
> *I know you're frightened, like everyone*
> *Is it the thunder in the distance you fear?*
> *Will it help if I stay very near? I am here*
>
> *And if you take my hand my son*
> *All will be well when the day is done*
>
> *Do you ask why I'm sighing, my son?*
> *You shall inherit what mankind has done*
> *In a world filled with sorrow and woe*
> *If you ask me why this is so, I really don't know*
>
> *And if you take my hand my son*
> *All will be well when the day is done*
>
> *Tell me why you're smiling my son*
> *Is there a secret you can tell everyone?*
> *Do you know more than men that are wise?*
> *Can you see what we all must disguise through your*
> *   loving eyes?*

And if you take my hand my son
All will be well when the day is done

What if this song is at the heart of my desire to be a therapist and a teacher? It holds the wish to empathize, to witness, to encourage. It is good self to have been conditioned by, or conditioned into, in those endless moments of gentleness and warmth, listening to my father's off-key voice, in the middle of the night, in a rocking chair.

love,
Matthew

|||

November 30th

Dear Matthew,

Just home from walking alone in High Park. We went looking for a stroller at that strange marketplace called a "baby store," which these days feels more like the Genius Bar at the Apple store. After learning about forward-facing/backward-facing options, handlebars that adjust for height, optional coffee mug, running tires or knobby ones, headlight, sunscreens, rain screens, winter booties, fifty kinds of warranties—and all these options in "organic"—I needed to be alone near trees. I wanted to *become* a tree actually. Or a forest of them in this bitter winter wind. It feels like it's been windy since early October. I want to disrobe the entire pregnancy, remove accessories, walk for a hundred days until the baby comes and then go out to get what we need *then*. Oh, and like every November, my wrists and knees are a little sore. I've been meaning to ask you what I can do for sore joints in November (other than good fatty broths).

I think we are going to buy the B.O.B tricycle style stroller which I also got for A. They are cheaper on Craigslist. Carina and I started arguing in the store because she wants the baby to face her and I want him to face the world. I took the position of "I've done this before, so I'll just make the decision." Although, she might be right because the B.O.B. stroller has very little room for groceries. While we were arguing, I realized I hadn't eaten lunch. She looked at me and said: "We aren't making any decisions because your eyes look crazy. You haven't eaten. Let's go eat." I said, "Fine, but I'm right."

I had a blue tricycle stroller with A. When he was about two and Whole Foods opened in Toronto, I took him one cold winter day and we went shopping. He didn't want to be in the stroller so I carried him. Because I couldn't push both the stroller and the shopping cart, I ditched the cart and put our groceries in the stroller. Just before we paid I couldn't recall whether we needed whole or crushed canned tomatoes so I pushed the stroller past the cash registers to the front door to use the pay phone. I dropped in a quarter to call A's mother for a reminder and just as I finished dialing we were surrounded by two men and someone who looked like the store manager. They pulled out cards and announced they were undercover agents and I had just been caught shoplifting. "What are you talking about? My groceries are right here in the stroller, you can see them and I'm just making a phone call, I'm not even done shopping yet."

"Please step over here, sir," and they pulled the cart out into the centre of the doorway, in front of all the cash registers, to make a scene, and starting taking out the items one by one, writing up the whole episode, like I was being given a ticket. I realized I was going to be arrested. So I told them to stop, and I started pushing the cart towards the cash. I pulled out my wallet as a gesture that I was ready to pay and then A started crying. Finally a second store manager, a woman wearing yoga clothing, came to the rescue. She watched the whole episode and explained to the agents that it seemed fine to let us go. We walked out with an empty stroller and never returned.

I love you no matter what, I said to Carina last night. Then I got down at her navel and said the same thing to the baby: *I love you no matter what.*

My mother picked up a new car seat and Carina's sisters sent us a suitcase of tiny booties, overalls, soft-cotton-everything.

After talking with you Sunday night about how nuclear families are impossible, I went to bed trying to visualize the birth of the nuclear family; making a film in my mind to see how we ended up here in this house, in 2012, trying to find a way to include a larger social realm in the upbringing of our new kid. Can a couple and baby be a whole world for each other? Is that enough? I won't let Carina stow her art supplies away in the basement just so she can mother. How will we divide our labour?

Last week when I confided in one of my mentors that I'm nervous about creating "an impossible nuclear model," she said: "That's good to feel. Do what the Buddha did. *Don't* leave home."

love,
Michael

|||

December 4th

Dear Michael –

Your mentor is a card. Funny thing about Gautama—he left his wife and baby and extended family in the middle of the night. That's how Zen language rolls, I suppose. Leaving everything becomes, "Don't leave home."

What is she actually saying? That if you manage your internal reality—your "home", everything will work out? I understand the point, but why do so many so many of the rhetorical gestures of spirituality depoliticize our choices? There are structures and systems at play from which none of us are free. The spiritual aphorism gives a temporary relief from considering the political difficulty at hand. It's a kind of stress-reduction sleight-of-hand. But it's not actual advice. It doesn't provide insight into policy, although we often pretend it does. How many times have we walked away from teachings and retreats wondering *Now what the hell do I do?* The problems of the nuclear family or climate death won't go away through a more positive attitude, any more than consumerism will. At most, a positive attitude buys us some clearer thinking time.

Sore joints. Barring any "nested" inflammation—I think your diet is pretty clean—it's probably not an issue for cleansing. In Ayur-land, we'd say that the earthy-watery-joint-juice has withered with the cold, dry season. Internally: increase ghee, bone marrow broth, and simmered milk tonic with dates and turmeric and cinnamon and slippery elm. You can also sauté okra in ghee with salt, turmeric and garlic. For a real lube job, let it cool and blend with comfrey root tea and bang it down. Externally you can apply castor oil wraps. Rolled gauze bandages work best: one joint at a time because it's messy. The oil should be hot to just below the point of discomfort.

Ayurveda is messy. We've been applying raspberry leaf to Alix's belly to tighten up the spongy after-pregnancy skin. It has a noticeable effect in just a few applications. I think we could make our millions if we can figure out how to make an apron that will hold the poultice intact and not disturb people's Ikea-clean surfaces. There aren't many folks out there who are willing to be smeared with herbs everyday and have them dripping all over the floor. Oiling is another happy mess. For the last ten years, my bathtubs have been covered in a sheen of sesame. And every wooden floor has paths of bright patina snaking from room to room from the padding of oily feet. Then there are the oily enemas.

Increasing oil in your diet will probably settle meditation, but it might also give you some extra weight. Have you gained any weight along with Carina? I must have gained twenty pounds as Jacob built up his eleven. It feels really good. I feel less like a boy. I've had to replace some pants. Many people have told me how much better I look—more settled.

Except for K, who broke her silence with me last week with an email to say that she'd seen two promo videos of mine over the last two months, and she thought I looked ill, and that I should make an appointment for a physical ASAP. I was bewildered: I've never felt more settled or stronger or in-my-body. How am I looking different to her? I'm heavier for sure, bearded, but also stronger and less apologetic about taking up space. I suppose this could look like sickness, in the form of the unexpected, or something that feels intrusive. I'm not the person she knew and loved when he was twenty-two or thirty-two. That guy withered away, and here I am.

Re: the nuclear family problem. I think that privacy is its real allure and capital. It serves men more than women, which is why Virginia Woolf longed for her room. For men there is the pull of the attic, the back porch. A study if you have money, a park bench if you don't. I remember this passage in a D. H. Lawrence novel in which a little boy watches his coal miner father get ready for work in silence before dawn. The man is doing a breakfast meditation. Watching the coals ignite, watching the kettle, carefully carving his coarse bread. Breathing the coal smoke from the coal he digs all day. The boy watches from the shadows. The boy is alone, watching his father in solitude, enjoying the not-sharing of his space.

The economy of the nuclear family allows for our buried asceticism to express itself. I was always shocked when travelling in India at the utter absence of personal space. Most people are too poor to have personal space. I've made my professional stand on boosting the intersubjective and community-building aspects of yoga culture—as a chosen ideal, not out of economic necessity. But the truth is that I am a solitary person. Sometimes I wonder if I'm a misanthrope who prefers to fantasize about friendship and togetherness than have it. I long for solitude when I don't get enough of it. I can treat my introversion as a spiritual virtue, but it's as much a product of my economic privilege as my temperament.

Then there's the existential angle. When I was seventeen I played Garcin in a scene from *No Exit* by Sartre in theatre class. It was the scene in which he has his revelation: "Hell is other people." I didn't really understand it at the time, but it sure stuck with me. Sartre meant that we cannot escape being constructed by others. Instinctively we know that as our relationships multiply, our capacity to maintain the fiction of our agency and autonomy diminishes. We are trapped in a web of performing what others want us to be, and we love a lover to the extent that we can feel ourselves fulfill their expectations. Ah, the French.

I have clients who have large families in which they can't go for a crap without the approval and meddling of a dozen aunts. Everybody gives know-it-all cooking and child-rearing advice. Everybody polices everybody else's roles—especially gender roles. One Indian guy had to step in and save his younger sister before her wedding when he found her surrounded by forty women tugging at her sari and poking at her hair and jewellry. She was weeping, but they were all laughing at her tears, saying things like, "This is the most beautiful you'll ever be able to be, so you should be grateful for our advice!" And have you ever seen the stack of envelopes stuffed with cash at a big Mediterranean wedding? The extended family supports, for sure, but they are also buying their right to continual intrusion. What a nightmare.

The nuclear family is grossly inefficient. It obstructs group learning and support. But we have to be honest that it also strikes a bargain against the vampiric nature of the tribe, in which older people can keep their sense of relevance or even vitality by retaining possession over younger people's lives. Perhaps the nuclear arrangement is our way of neutralizing generational competition. But it goes too far: people can wind up feeling as though they're not responsible for each other. What are libertarian politics, except the final and bitter triumph of the nuclear family?

When I lived in rural Vermont and Wisconsin there was always the woods, and I could count on seeing no one for hours if I went hiking. Maybe seeing no one allows us to rest the constant demand upon our empathy. Now in this urban centre I need space that I know is mine, available to me whenever I can steal away, laid out with the few things that represent my internal life. The study is my ersatz forest. Nuclear structure and male privilege pays the rent on it. Now our solitude has been invaded by cyberspace. We are alone, but flooded with the alienation of others. We don't really have a nuclear family anymore. We have nuclear-structured homes that house the shadows of all humanity.

Like you, I say to this partner and child, *I love you no matter what*. I shut the shadows out, and say it firmly to our triad, in this private space. It's like an act of faith: something from my religious past. But I know that if we're going to resist capitalism and its alienation we'll have to give up, at some point, the yearning for solitude. Privileged introverts like me will have to learn how to work in shared spaces, shored up, perhaps, by a barter economy.

Christmas is coming. Nativity scenes are sprouting in front of churches. The shepherds and animals gather first. They will surround and support the holy family when it comes. Then the kings, lonely wanderers, always the last to recognize and appreciate the scale of the very small.

love,
Matthew

|||

December 8th

Dear Matthew,

Christmas is coming indeed. About ten blocks north of my house the Portuguese neighbourhood is alight with the most far-out nativity scenes, electric animals glowing on the porches, chimneys wrapped in red Home Depot lights and massive LED candles on every lawn. Mocking the nativity scene should be a Jewish right!

Imagine if we recreated our *own* birth scenes every Christmas. It would be a fucking nightmare. Every house would set their front lawn alight with a theatrical performance: uncles with cigars, screaming nurses, fake blood splattered on the snow, gurneys stored in the basement through the summer brought out for the special occasion and dressed with tinsel. The lighting would be amazing though. We'd borrow those huge overhead operating-room lights, like 50,000 candle power, so bright it would melt the snow, but it would bring to life the massive styrofoam vagina with a head coming through it, and all the neighbours would recognize that head as yours so many years ago. When you'd pull into the driveway, coming home, you'd be greeted by your mother's outstretched legs, and your life coming through the centre of her great garden, your father watching on from a distance, wondering if you really are the saviour, or just another baby like the one next door.

Now, our lawn is nothing but frost with a few holes dug for the spring bulbs we still haven't planted. We've been planting so many other things this week: drawers of baby clothes, homemade salves (the comfrey salve has really helped my joints), maternity bras with strange flaps I can't figure out, new sheets and shelves everywhere.

Your reading at Centre of Gravity last night was straight to the point. Thanks for joining our community and remixing Patanjali. Centre of Gravity started in my garage. I was teaching large classes at the only two popular yoga studios in Toronto at the time. I was also studying Buddhism, practicing on retreat, and I'd just finished my academic studies in psychoanalysis. My son was two and I realized that my interest in possibly becoming a monk wasn't going to happen. I was also going through a falling out phase in the psychology community because they were blind to the social and political fires of the time. I couldn't engage the psychoanalytic community in political action.

I was offered financial backing to start a yoga studio by a couple who own one of the largest clothing retailers in Canada, but it didn't feel like the right model. Still doesn't. On Tuesday nights I started teaching yoga from 5:30 to 7:20 p.m. Then we'd all take a short break and then we'd sit for thirty minutes and

I'd lead the group in Vipassana-style meditation, followed by a lecture. The talks ranged from Freud and Winnicott to the Gita, Buddha or Marx. This all happened in my garage. You had to walk down a dark, unmapped alley to find the blue door. The debate was lively. In the first year there were six of us. Year two, there were ten. Last night we had seventy-five. We are moving in two weeks for the fourth time.

I started getting visits from yoga students who wanted to go deeper in practice through sitting, learning texts and having more intimacy in community. Buddhists who had studied in monastic settings started coming to Centre of Gravity for the feeling of community, less hierarchy and working in a psychological framework they couldn't explore with their teachers. Parents in the neighbourhood came to learn about self-care, and lots of artists, most of whom knew each other, brought their friends.

I tried to create a space where we were a cross between the formality of a temple and the accessibility of a yoga studio. Just the right amount of form keeps things precise and contained. And then we would, and still do, discuss what forms to use and how and who leads. Last night, for example, Rose led the chants for the dead and ill. She gathers a list of names from the community and recites them at the end of class. The list of friends who have died is swelling. Everytime we chant the list I cry. I keep meaning to create a third category. Right now we chant for ill people and those are dead. But I want to start chanting for the 200 species on the extinction list and create rituals for the animals and languages disappearing at increasingly alarming rates.

I'm also talking to one of the students about letting go of our charitable status so we can see if it's possible to try and run a business, with less governmental constraint. Within all the forms I still feel like the community has the energy of an activist group or an artists' collective. People are learning the texts, how to go deep in practice, how to drop into their lives and respond. In other words, we are learning together how to serve. Servants of servants.

It's also a lot of work. This morning I woke up tired. I have one day off (today) and then off to teach a retreat in Wisconsin where I've been working with a group for almost as long as Centre of Gravity here in Toronto. Eight or nine years now. I couldn't imagine doing anything else. I teach in Wisconsin at a Zen centre in a barn. We practice sitting and walking meditation, I'll give a talk everyday, and before lunch I'll teach two hours of asana. Repeat this schedule in silence for four days. December in Wisconsin is the end of hunting season so some evenings while we're sitting we'll hear gunshots in the distance.

It's good writing this down. There is a class war right now between the ultra-rich and the poor. And the losers right now are of course the poor, but also the environment and our collective health. When I started Centre of Gravity I wanted it to be a place of personal awakening. Now I want a space where we can show ways of waking up that include social transformation. Being awake in the middle of family life can be the site of this shift. People say we need to leave a great earth for our kids. We also need to leave awakened kids for this ailing earth. We don't need a revolution. We need embodied rebellion. Revolution replaces one power structure with another. Rebellion would be the moment-to-moment responsiveness of mindfulness, co-operation and creativity, to embody our values and continually model them for our kids and community. Family can also be a space that protects us from the anxiety of being separate atomized selves, or consumers.

When you spoke last night I watched your cheeks. I've seen you with hollow cheeks, stubbly cheeks, worried and tense cheeks. Last night your cheeks were soft, like your wrists and shirt and long hair. Your mind firing on a hundred cylinders. Precise, inventive, confident, wounded, drenched with a thousand pages of a thousand years of philosophy soaking the floor of that big room, seventy-five hearts, and Patanjali's aphorisms crawling through them all, like tiny golden caterpillars.

Last night in my dream Leonard Cohen and I were leaving Centre of Gravity after your talk, and he wanted me to see where he was staying. As we walked to the car we looked over a fence and there was a pool filled with inflatables of every colour. He told me that this is where he wrote his best poems.

"This is how we do rebellion," he said.

Then I could smell yogurt and blueberries and I woke up and Carina was again eating a 3 a.m. snack in bed next to me. When I fell back asleep the dream continued. Leonard Cohen asked me to help him climb the fence. I kept telling him he's almost eighty and he shouldn't climb that high. "Just give me your shoulder to stand on," he said, and he hopped the fence and went to go pick blueberries in his perfect pinstripe suit. The dream ended there. When I woke up I thought about you and how you went to see Leonard Cohen play last week and that I forgot to ask you how it went.

I met him once. I was in Montreal at the Zen Centre which, at the time, was on the main floor of his home. He was putting his suit jacket on and walking down the hall. He bowed to me, and I was surprised how formal he was. I couldn't imagine anyone else bowing outside Japan, and doing so wearing a well-fitted suit. He mentioned that the park across the street looked like it was in a cloud and walked past me to see that park through the open front door. The door was red and his suit was navy. He said he needed a hat and I joked that monks with hair like his don't wear elegant hats with their robes. He laughed and opened his arms as if to demonstrate how fine his suit was. We both laughed and he walked outside.

It's almost 7 a.m. and I'm going to sit now. Some of your lines I'm left with from your reading last night:

" . . . live beneath and beyond the cascade of words."

"The practices of yoga diminish alienation."

"Negative thought patterns can be altered by embodying what balances them."

"Concentration stills alienating thoughts."

"It is Patanjali's close and precise attention that I wish to translate here, while leaving his metaphysics and asceticism behind."

Thank you.

love,
Michael

|||

December 15th

Dear Michael –

Wow, that's funny about the Christmas shit in the front yard.

You were dreaming about Leonard Cohen while I was writing an essay about him. What—are we eavesdropping on each others' unconscious now? What a bromance we've got going here!

Although I hate that term actually. It minimizes something that a century of homophobia has made really difficult—how men express intimacy. It's in that same category of ridicule that makes every domestic man out to be some kind of idiotic bumbler, especially around the house. But I guess that's a little more deserved.

There are these old photographs circulating around Facebook showing how men used to have their tintype portraits taken together. They stand in pairs or triads, hand in hand, arms around each other, this one's hand slipping underneath that one's waistcoat.

One picture was set up by a riverbank. Two friends with matching handlebar mustachios are lying in each other's arms, gazing at the man under the black cape. According to Foucault, "homosexual" didn't even exist as a category of persons to be pathologized until the late 19th century. If that hadn't happened, would these letters between us be a little less rare in the literature of family life? If that hadn't happened, would I have spent less of my forty-two years subtly freezing in the presence of other men—especially men like you, whom I love and admire?

I remember wanting to hug my best friend Jonathan in high school, to hug him and hold onto him. We were so close. He understood me when it felt like nobody else did. The thought of hugging him terrified me. I thought I'd get an erection. I thought getting an erection would destroy who I thought I was. It took me years to learn how to physically embrace friends like you, to make full relaxed bodily contact, to not feel threatened or confused by the love I feel.

Anyway: Uncle Leonard provided the dreamscape for my teenage years, which of course extended long into my first marriage. He offered a perfect balance of explicating, worshiping, and rebelling against all of the old religions of sacrifice. Along with Cormac McCarthy, he's like a chain-smoking bookend upon another age, finding romance in violence and violence in romance, describing the tensions of the heart in such excruciating detail that one has no choice but to seek relief in his images of transcendence: the rose, the window, the lonely wooden tower of Jesus. I loved that a stylish Jew understood Christianity better than Christians. The crucifixion is just another sacrifice of just another son. Every desire has fangs. We are caught in impossible knots of passion. Life abounds in a kind of negative beauty. It's all true. But did this really help me?

My brother hitchhiked in from Montreal last week and took me to see Cohen in concert. At thirty, my brother must have been the youngest guy there. We sat in the arena, high up, looking down onto the little old man in the blue silk suit, prismed and magnified on a thousand LCD screens. I recited the lyrics of every song under my breath, but they felt different to me— someone else's story, someone else's religion. I'd seen him twenty years before and breathed the lyrics then as well, back when they were a revelation to me.

Sitting beside my brother, I had the feeling I get whenever I enter a Catholic Church now. The old piety is replaced by a curiosity in the facades of things. Now, all I see are the chips in the plaster, the cheapness of gold-coloured paint. In Cohen

I can hear the bald mechanics of generating affect that hasn't really changed since Homer. I was glad to hear, two decades ago, that he'd found Buddhism. But then it became clear that he just saw more of the same in it: authority, sacrifice, transcendence. Michael—it seems like you've had an easier time as a BuJew who's able to tell the difference between Buddhism and the Torah.

The thing I said about churches—it's all true, except at Christmas. At Christmas I'm still flooded with rich memory. I can hear the carols in my heart. Especially the medieval ones like "Lo, How a Rose E'er Blooming." Candlelight, poinsettias with their velvety petals, the brightest flutes and reeds from the organ. But it has to stay in my imagination. I can't go in, not even to midnight mass, when the cathedral is darkened. I can't sit shoulder to shoulder with the faithful. I'm swept away by the textures and sounds of this childhood, but I'm queasy around people who are credulous. I can have private epiphanies, but when I'm with a throng of people who all believe or at least pretend to believe the same thing, I feel very suspicious. On the home front, this feeling makes me anxious to raise Jacob free of all that. But of course I'll condition him with other beliefs that I can't even see.

If it stays in the home, the warmth of Christmas is fine for me. For what is *believed* at home, really? What grand story can we assemble from this constant action of cooking and laundry? The family believes in itself, the home feels itself as a home. Maybe routine and normalcy give us an overall sense of *this is the way things are and should be,* and we go to church to have that validated and glorified. Maybe this is why Dylan Thomas nails it for me with *A Child's Christmas in Wales,* which I can't remember having a single church scene, although it's clear that everyone went.

It was coming home from church that I loved most—coming home from the performance of belief. Late at night, with snow, the tree lit up in the bay window, and I was tired enough that the gifts we opened didn't feel exciting as much as austere and sacramental. I remember the quiet ripping of paper from boxes that held a toy car or a book mingled with the quietness of the night.

When I was sixteen, my French Italian girlfriend had me over for her family's Christmas Eve. The night went from dancing to Edith Piaf in the living room, to us sneaking up to her room to come maddeningly close to ACTUALLY HAVING SEX while we were pretending to look at her books, and then being called back downstairs to gorge ourselves on chocolate fondue. Then: french onion soup at dawn, pulling the strings of cheese as far as they could stretch and laughing our asses off. They said we were supposed to keep vigil with the Holy Family. Who can sleep when a baby is to be born? It's like the reverse of a wake. Each second in the world, six women give birth. We stay up all night to balance that labour with whatever feels like abandonment.

I don't know how Alix will rebalance after the pain of her labour with Jacob. She gives a new meaning to my favorite line from Luke, speaking about the mother of God:

Mary kept all these things, and pondered them in her heart.

love,
Matthew

|||

December 20th

Dear Matthew,

Carina came home from the midwife yesterday learning that the baby dropped. It's seven weeks away from the due date so she needs to rest now and, most importantly, she has to stop practicing the affirmations she began last week. She found this app with a quiet British voice repeating slogans like:

> *You have smooth birthing muscles*
> *Double the relaxation of your pelvic floor*
> *Feel your rainbow body*
> *Let your skull get soft,*
> *and so on.*

Carina listened to these affirmations everyday last week, and also before bed—I think she relaxed around her uterus and pelvic floor so much that in the same week the baby dropped, head down, which is great but also a little early. So yesterday I was joking that she needs to stop relaxing and start resting in a more energetic way. Instead of rubbing her belly yesterday I was helping her hold headstands for longer.

Life hurtles forward. A is talking about his coming "little brother." Centre of Gravity is moving this week. Carina's father is having surgery on his hand. One of my teachers, Richard Freeman, has a double-detached retina. My other teacher, Norman Feldman, turned sixty-six and broke his arm this week. Norman's wife Molly, also a Vipassana teacher, called to tell me she is turning seventy and retiring this year. Birth and death, birth and death.

I had a dream that Carina gave birth to small baby with no eyelashes and then when the legs came out they were covered in a soft fur, like a wolf or a husky. The baby slid out between her legs onto a bright white world of ice. We were in the tundra or in Iceland. There was only white and it went on and on, soundless and cold, but Carina's body was warm and pink and gorgeous. It was a pretty sexy dream and when I woke up the sun was bright and our white sheets were warm. Matthew, I feel so lucky Carina and I are together. Do you ever wake up with Alix and feel relief to have found someone you can share this strange life with? I got out of bed with a very naive thought: *I don't want this to change.*

Family wakes us up. Is a new story about spirituality beginning to develop? Is it about the interaction of these old practices that you and I have been trained in and the needs of the modern family? I ask this because the yogic and Buddhist traditions, and the way we create family, both need a new story. It's not only a matter of seeing the troubles with modernity and the nuclear family. We need to be aware of the difficulties facing contemporary parents who are interested in spiritual practice and waking up through family life. Any parent who is paying attention knows that we're living in a time of crisis. All our living systems, ecological and economic, are failing. Matthew: all these themes are interconnected. Economy based on consumerism and never-ending growth is incompatible with the well-being of our biosphere and the health of our family life. Distraction is killing us. What is less obvious is that there are fundamental problems with the stories that underlie these troubles. What I mean by story, which you and I have talked about in almost every email, is our basic understanding of who we are, how we should interact with the world, what family means, and our role in these living systems.

There are stories that haunt me, some that uplift me, and a few that inspire me.

We need a story that is more consistent with evolutionary theory, the insights of modern psychology, the wisdom of sociology, and the tools from our yoga and meditation practices that help us reduce reactivity, transform stress, and transcend transcendence.

One more thing, Matthew, around privilege. We don't live in a land of equal opportunity. Statistically, children of poor parents remain poor and children of upper-class parents end up in those same classes. My grandmother inherited money from her late husband (he died soon after their divorce) and she gifted me some of that money to pay for my university education. Carina has an enormous debt from her education that we're trying to figure out how to pay down. It's been a source of suffering for her and for us. That's just the surface.

You and I are white, hetero, educated and self-employed. That base-line gives us an enormous amount of privilege, and huge blind spots. As our kids grow I wonder how we can explore our blind spots as a family.

When we go to the park nobody assumes we are nannies; when the going gets tough we can find more work; our midwives speak our language; putting our kids in slings doesn't seem exotic; we'll likely find childcare that reflects our cultural background; accessibility won't be an issue for us; Jacob won't be teased for the colour of his skin; we can surf online and find parenting resources in our language; if we decide to have more kids we can find resources to support us; we can get the medical support we need; if we do home-schooling or one of us stays at home for a while we won't be called "lazy"; and when people make assumptions about our sexuality or gender they'll be right, and won't put us in a box that negatively impacts our family.

I think because so many of our friends aren't straight, hetero-normativity is what I'm thinking about most these days. Our family can express affection in public. We can live openly with our partners without explanation. We can talk openly about our family, planning vacations, and troubles at home. We can talk openly about lesbian, gay, bi or trans issues without being told we have a "bias" because of our sexuality. You're planning to be legally married as are we. Our kids won't be teased at school about their parents' sexuality.

Early on, we know our children's race, ability, class and (generally speaking) these things won't change. As parents, we can teach our kids about privilege and provide them with appropriate language and tools to move about the world as socially-responsible and aware beings. We don't necessarily know our child's gender-identity or sexual preference. How we talk about these things could impact how our kids feel about themselves and their possibly divergent-from-the-norm identity or expression.

When I was in grade six my friend Sofia had a lesbian mother though nobody spoke about it. At parent-teacher interviews only one mother came, year after year. Her parents never "came out" and so she couldn't either.

Carina and I think about moving from Toronto, maybe living closer to the ocean, where she grew up, or in Europe, where I'm teaching often. We don't have to think about the status of being together, the legality of our relationship, or having a child taken from us, because of our sexuality. We could live with people who look like us.

I imagine we'll be talking a lot more about sexual fluidity with our kids. At A's alternative school downtown, heterosexual parents raising heterosexual kids *isn't* the norm. And Carina and I are only starting to talk about how these issues can be on the table in our family. Even small things like the assumption that everyone is heterosexual unless proven otherwise, seems an easy one to introduce to kids in a heterosexual household. Or that gender is what you do at certain times, not something you are. This is a Zen way of looking at identity anyways.

love,
Michael

|||

December 29th

Dear Michael –

Yes, I think a new story is emerging. I just wish everyone could participate. You and I are so fortunate to even have this conversation. Imagine two human males in their forties, spending an hour each day writing about their feelings on machines other people get paid a few dollars an hour to make. For us, family can can wake us up in the same way spirituality can—because we have time in excess of our survival needs.

Are we too well-fed to be of real use? Somewhere in the Laws of Manu it says "If anyone suffers injustice, there will be no peace in the land." I want to read letters between two expectant fathers in Syria.

But all this progressive idealism can have its own blind spots to the dark mechanisms of psychic growth. I was reading your thoughts about normativity and nodding and agreeing with everything you say. But then I'm also wondering how our children will need to rebel against our enlightenments. It's so easy for progressive parents to believe that they have achieved a new world, and that of course their children will be the first honoured citizens there. Of course they will accept our ideas! We've done so much work on ourselves on their behalf! Of course they will see all that, and thank us, and have such charmed and grateful lives. All we had to do was to carry them across the finishing line to a new Valhalla and let them be the free indigo beings we know they are. In the end, this might not be so different from the parents of boomers assuming that their children would just take the baton of post-war prosperity and run with it without turning a hard left. Did they really dig their way out of the Depression to watch their children drop acid?

I think of how K told me about spending her early life clawing her way out the country-club Republican culture of her childhood. She became a writer, went to a Quaker Peace College, wore ripped clothes to enrage her mother right to the edge of being cut off entirely, got divorced, found Buddhism, and did a thousand things her hometown wouldn't understand. Through it all, she became her own person, as many do, starting out as a person-against.

But when V was old enough to feel the pull of individuation, what could *she* rebel against? How does a child rebel against the rebel? K and I had both saved ourselves through writing and writing-against, and we shared this dream that V would obviously share our artistic path. Of course she would be progressive in politics! Of course she would be a Buddhist! Who else could she be?

When V was six she started drawing intricate copies of Tibetan Buddhist icons. She enjoyed doing it for sure, but we went fricking bananas over it, rejoicing that we'd influenced this little person along such a virtuous path that confirmed certain values and fantasies. We went so far as to take her to this big Tibetan gathering in Washington D.C. to introduce her to the Dalai Lama's personal painter. We found him on the Washington Mall. He said, "Sure, bring her to India. I will teach her." We were so happy talking to him. V didn't really care. She pulled on our arms, wanting to run away and look for fairies amongst the cherry trees.

Was she doing what came naturally to her as she drew, or was she trying to please artistically-devoted parents? A little bit of both, I'm sure. I wonder whether we gave her enough space. She still makes splendid art, after all that, but it's not the life obsession—like writing is for us—that we fantasized it would be. I think K and I may both have become writers, in part, because as children we hadn't felt like anyone was really listening to us. I think I became a writer so that I could have a perfect kind of internal dialogue, uninterrupted, with someone who accepted me. I'd like to believe that we were better listeners for V. Every generation of parents would like to believe this, I'm sure.

It doesn't matter what the content is: art, progressive politics, environmental activism. It's the form that's at stake: who is telling who to do what. The child becomes an adult, partly, through difference from the parent. For us this might mean learning how to watch our children express their individuation—so strangely!—through a devotion to the dominant paradigm, because they know we hate it, and it would be the most obvious way to say *fuck you* to the people that matter most.

Being able to say *fuck you* is an essential birthright. We always think our job as parents is to instill values, but it's both less and more than that. We have to model the capacity to create values in an ongoing struggle for transparency. When we're talking about the psychic health of our children, we have to understand that the child indoctrinated into leftist artistic values may be no more comfortable in her skin and with her autonomy than the child indoctrinated into the Tea Party Youth. In both cases, the parent has invaded the child. But I do think the leftist invasion is probably more benign, and the potential rupture less severe, because the content nurtures rebellion instead of false piety. It also may nurture empathy and inclusiveness. I know in V's case, she seems to welcome everyone, just as they are, and that makes me happy.

Our children will see right through the self-righteous intelligence of our ideas to feel the anxiety with which we hold them. And *that's* what they'll reject: how we feel pinched and cold about how things should go. They will reject every way in which we close down to change, even we who have changed so much and accumulated such radiant virtue! I think that as progressives we have to be willing to accept that the form of rebellion is as developmentally important as the content. We must hold to new ideas that are just and good, and still be willing targets of all the individuating rage that is to come.

I grew up reading the poet Irving Layton. He wrote this one poem to his son called "For Max Who Showed Me His First Good Poem." In the last stanza he gives a typically grandiose aspiration, some honest fatherly advice, and then acknowledges and invites the inevitable.

> *I fathered you for holier ends*
> *To live with greatness from day to day,*
> *Avoiding the common joyless ruck;*
> *Your emblem the proud scanning eagle*
> *Alone under the pitiless sky.*
> *Be gentle and have a loving heart.*
> *Then kick your dear father in the balls*
> *And go your own way to renown,*
> *Knowing you're one of the lucky ones.*

I think you're up north now, leading the silent retreat for the New Year. Carina is with you: I imagine the bracing cold is good if her cervix is starting to thin early. She should probably kneel in *virasana*—more stable for the pelvis than any wide-angled sitting pose.

Jacob is sleeping now on this Saturday afternoon, as if he has always been here, and yet he is only ten weeks old today. In April your second son will be at the centre of your house, as if it was built around him, begun a century ago, never quite finished, an extension of his body.

Alix and I were looking at pictures of her from the summer before last. She and I had just started exchanging letters. She was off to Europe to backpack for two weeks. She teared up to see them, saying "I look like such a *girl*." Carina, too, will be utterly changed. These women cross a threshold that we can only visualize. We have to cross it slowly somehow. When we do, we find ourselves in middle age.

Alix is newly powerful. She's finding inner resources that I can't quite understand. She's healing herself from the birth with organic rhythms of food and walking, and a profound attention to the textures of sleep. As if sleep was some new territory she can explore in smaller periods of time and in which she's never alone, because Jacob's sleep is always interwoven with it. But not exactly. They cuddle each other to sleep and then wake each other up with rhythmic stirrings that say *I'm still here, baby. I'm still here, mamma.*

She's naturally reaching out to the moms and babies group that our doula organizes. They share their hearts and wonder at their changed lives. They are joined in some great sacrament, stripped of so many prior modes of social performance.

But Alix has also found that there seems to be a natural barrier to how much difficulty can be shared. Perhaps because, after the birth, you can only ever tell your story with the baby present, and it doesn't feel right to burden the child, even if they couldn't possibly understand. She's thinking a lot about what you and I are thinking about: how do we share the hardest things? The difference is that what she needs to share, eventually, is so much more visceral.

Our doula came over for her check-in visit and she and Alix sat at the kitchen table for a long time, holding each other's hands and gazing at each other, while Jacob slept in his bouncy chair. Alix asked for her insight into the labour. It had been so hard and so different from what she had imagined. And she felt shame at the discrepancy between the hoped-for birth and the real one. Our doula sat and gazed at her and shook her head and said very slowly: "Sometimes things happen this way. We don't know why. But you were listening so deeply. You knew something wasn't right, and you knew what you needed. And you knew to ask for what you needed. You did the perfect job. You did what you were able to do."

Then they gazed at Jacob together and were silent.

Most of what Alix does is guided by some silent knowledge she doesn't need to think through, while I recover by writing and thinking optimistic thoughts about making money and giving her things, and setting up a school fund for Jacob. Our sex has become darker, coming in stolen hours, ripe with some maturation I can't understand, as though there's nothing more to hide, ever. Her movements carry the power of the animal she drew in that birth-prep class, an animal that has survived.

I'm researching my book on Ayurveda. I came across this line from Charaka—the compiler of the old Ayurvedic sayings: "The person without a child is like a drawing of a lamp." I'm almost shy to type it. It feels judgmental. There are so many of us now who are choosing not to have children, or who can't, or who want to but haven't found the right partner and aren't comfortable thinking about the in vitro way, or for whom, for one reason or another, it just hasn't been in the cards. Plus there are those committed to conscious childlessness for psychological or environmental reasons. Four years ago, I would have been among them, before I woke up in the middle of the night beside K and realized that I'd just ignored and then deferred the whole question for myself, as though I wasn't really a body of my own, and that I actually did have a burning desire to be a father, and that this wasn't going to just turn off. I see Charaka's line and nod: I was a drawing of a lamp. I'm going to have to really fight not to project this feeling onto the many childless people I know.

It's sad to me, this division that occurs between people with children and people without. I have a good friend who knows he doesn't want children. He drifted away from me as soon as I told him Alix and I were expecting. I even told him I wouldn't become one of those child-obsessed parents who wasn't able to talk about anything else. But I think he looked in my eyes and knew that I was becoming another type of human being. He's right, but I miss him.

It was great to have lunch with you the other day. I understand a little more about the public nature of your fatherhood now, and not just to A and the coming boy. So many people know you, but only in one role. So many people want to know something more about you, and they can't. What a weird and large responsibility you've gotten yourself into. Is it just "right place at the right time?" Who decides who gets to sit at the head of the table in our little burgeoning communities? Over tea I said: "Holy crap: you've become a spiritual teacher." You said "Yeah—who knew?" And we both laughed.

But I was also glad to hear of your positive experiences with your teachers. How Roshi says her practice is "Manhattan," and is bitchy when you flub the koans. How Norman calls you up when he hears complaints about the dharma talks you give. I know that Norman's health hasn't been good. I hope you have many hours left to spend together. I don't really have anybody that stands behind me as a mentor anymore. I've had intense encounters with many charismatic leaders, and they've been both instructive and sour, and they haven't lasted.

Somehow, between Norman and Roshi, you seem to have managed to strike up a good conversation between guidance, support, freedom, critique, and boundary. But the best part about it is that the power structure is tacit and voluntary. I've known you for eight years now, and I had no idea who you answered to. I thought you were like me, having organized life to be responsible to no one—although in the more dangerous and presumptuous position of giving public spiritual advice. But you're not alone, and this is a good thing as you continue to parent your sangha.

Things oscillate so quickly between the public horizon and the private foreground. Then everything shrinks to a very small scale. Two weeks before your son arrives, you'll be flying off to Vancouver and Seattle to talk to hundreds at a time. Your whole center is moving buildings and your books sell thousands of copies. But Carina is breathing beside you, just her, just now. Very soon you'll hold in your arms the focal point of your world, and Roshi and Norman and your uncle and the Centre of Gravity will dissolve into the walls of that stable. You'll be crushed by love for his skin, his fingernails. There is so much work to do in the burning world, and we will do the greatest portion of it in those moments by holding the smallest body of the most familiar stranger. Isn't this where your quiet rebellion will be found? One of the things I love most about Jacob is that he has no plans.

Public and private, vast and tiny, and also, slow and fast. Two days ago, we finally got snow here. It used to be that by New Year's there'd have been a hard snow pack for a whole month. I used to skate in the backyard of my parents' house. The snow came slowly this year, but the climate is changing so quickly.

I went to put on my boots. They were full of wood chips. It took me a minute to figure out where the wood chips had come from. Then I remembered: K had shipped the boots back to me from Cortes this past summer, stuffed into a box of books and work clothes smelling of gas and paint. The last time I'd worn the boots was while logging on the upper hill of what's now her land alone, taking down the dead cedars for firewood and to clear paths. We had both fantasized that one day we would be visited there by V's children, and that we would take them walking through trails that we could take pride in having prepared for them many years before. We shared a long view of a future there. It was an abstraction to me.

Such a horizon can close so very quickly: with two signatures, a notary's seal, and by breaking down the box the boots came in for recycling. It's like a wedding in reverse.

Perhaps this is what Patanjali meant in his chapter on yogic powers in which he says that through meditation the yogi can shrink his flesh down to the size of an atom, or inflate it to the scope of the world. How did we invest everything in something as large as a life together? How does it shrink to nothing so quickly? Expanding out to the whole culture: how did we build this highway system that in fifty years will crumble?

Jacob has started to giggle. He knows me when I visit him and Alix in the morning. He's working so hard at forming this skin, of witnessing and touching the world as a world. He'll fuss and complain to be taken to the window now, or to the next room, to look at new things. His fascination exhausts him, but with help he can find his own sources of soothing. I watch him sleeping now with a thumb in his mouth, and his other hand already beginning to brush at his gossamer hair.

Happy New Year, friend.

Matthew

|||

January 4th

Dearest Matthew,

When you write: *How did we invest everything into something as large as a life together? How does it shrink to nothing so quickly? Expanding out to the whole culture: how did we build this highway system that in fifty years will crumble?*

I've read and re-read these words Matthew. No, they are so much more than words, they are the questions that echo, and will echo for years, through your heart, her heart and through mine too. I don't communicate much with A's mom anymore.

How can we not all feel this way? We love with our every ounce of life, knowing the whole edifice is unreliable. This is the Buddha's first teaching: the task of turning *toward* the pain that comes from unreliability. The Buddha calls this *dukkha*. When the Buddha defines *dukkha* he says: "This is *dukkha*: birth is painful, aging is painful, sickness is painful, death is painful, encountering what is not dear is painful, separation from what is dear is painful, not getting what one wants is painful. This psycho-physical condition is painful."

Being separated from what one loves is painful. Dukkha, for the Buddha, is not just how we feel, it's so much more than that. It's the pain of separation inherent to life. You do not overcome it. You embrace it. This is almost impossible. But you capture it, Matthew, in those questions. *How did we invest everything in something as large as a life together? How does it shrink to nothing so quickly?*

And then there's Jacob interrupting it all with his giggling. When I think of Jacob giggling, I see your face too, laced with a hundred million registers. And I love what you say about falling in love again.

In Zen there's an idea that awakening is when our face falls away. Our social face, our identification with a mask, our clinging to a persona—when this falls away, the moment emerges and we are that moment. Then the whole thing changes. In my work with Roshi, she wants my face to fall away. When mine does, hers does too. My face more easily dropped away when I was one month old or three years old. But I see it happening to my face again as I approach forty. This is what Patanjali calls *purusha*. Of course academics and stiff cardboard meditators reify *purusha* into some kind of pure awareness, when it's really just a reworking of a Sanskrit term that means "a person." When our persona falls away, a person emerges. Maybe the goal of spiritual practice is to become purusha, a person.

The heart of practice is to show your face. It's Jacob giggling and you catching the giggles too.

On retreat last week I gave a talk on Beginner's Mind. I started looking through journals to see where the term Beginner's Mind came from. Turns out the first place that Mahayana Buddhists used that term is when the founder of the Rinzai sect, Linji, used it to describe what happens to your face when you practice: "There is a true person of no rank who is constantly coming and going from the portals of your face. Who is that true person of no status?"

I see the true person of no rank as the one in you who is Jacob and not Jacob. I feel that person in my face when I let everything drop and tell Carina, as I did last night, that I am so proud of how she is carrying this baby, how I see her trust herself in deeper ways, that I'm here for her with my entire being, and that I'm scared and I don't ever want to lose her or say anything to hurt her. And I know I will. This loving is going to hurt. This is *dukkha!* Holy shit.

I have a friend named Koshin who teaches Zen and runs the Zen Centre for Contemplative Care in New York City along with his husband Chodo. They wear robes and shave their heads. They also look like two old babies. They are both taller than me and their cheeks are always well shaved. When Koshin teaches I can see a hundred feelings moving through his face. It's an invisible practice he does, letting go of the ways he presents himself so that when he's in public he allows himself to show a changing weather system as it moves through his face. I admire him for this. More than a year ago he was here in Toronto at Centre of Gravity teaching on death and dying for palliative care providers. He turned to me and said:

"Michael, it's time to shave your face."

"But A loves my beard. I've had it for four years."

"Then *he* should shave it."

That night we went to my student Grant's house and A shaved my head and my beard. We had fun with it, trying on a thousand haircuts from the '80s before my head and face were clean. I had grown my beard after A's mother and I split up. I was ready to show my face again.

The wind has died down outside. I didn't shovel the snow from the back walk yesterday because the white is endless. A fragile paradise.

In your letter you talked about Roshi Enkyo and Norman Feldman. They are certainly mentors to me, much more than parental figures, and I can't imagine doing what I do without them. Sometimes they breathe down my neck and I want to move on from constant monitoring, though actually I've never received feedback from them I haven't needed. The constant feedback has saved me from a lot of trouble.

Carina was my student when we fell in love. We met Carina at a yoga teacher training where I was invited to give a lecture. I was attracted to her but it wasn't until almost three years later that I was overcome. A's mother and I had split up two years prior, and I took A to San Francisco for some one-on-one time. We walked into a store in Mill Valley that sold pottery. We were visiting my father the next day and I wanted to find him a gift. I spotted a lined cashmere scarf and as I felt it with my right hand I knew it was for Carina. The idea shocked me. I took it to the cash and asked them to wrap it as a gift. I didn't tell her. It sat in my cupboard for four months as I debated whether I'd give it to her which was really admitting to myself that I was falling in love. When I told her the story she said it was the same for her. "When I started falling for you," she said, "I thought: *My body was made for Michael.*"

I called Norman to ask him what to do. He said he was so happy. He said this is natural and okay. It was a relief to me. Then he gave us some rules.

1. Tell everyone. Do not keep a secret. Let people know you are dating. Secrets wreck community.

2. Carina has to stop practicing with you for three months. Enjoy the relationship and explore what it's like without the teaching dynamic.

3. Keep me updated.

When I'm with Roshi or Norman my face feels young. A thousand Michaels can move through me. It's exactly what I see in Jacob's face.

love,
Michael

January 3rd

Michael –

Well you've shaved and I've grown a beard. I haven't cut my hair since K and I parted. I don't think of my beard as hiding my face. It feels like feeling my age, growing into a man's body finally, more than a boy's, gaining a little more weight, building muscle with slow reps in the gym, no longer tentative, no longer withdrawing, not needing to clean myself up for anyone. It goes along with not being vegetarian anymore. I was vegetarian for fifteen years, and I think it made me wan, borderline anemic, reticent, halting. I think my spiritual practices have always been partially aimed at taming something, deferring something, withdrawing. Now this beard is growing right out of my face and I cannot pretend to be young or naive anymore. I'm not afraid of meat, and pulling strings of muscle out from between my teeth. I am meat. I am in middle age. I'm middle-aged!

Something happened last night. Alix put Jacob to bed and we pulled each other towards the study to make love. But I felt beside myself, watching, worrying abstractly. Her flesh flattened to my gaze as I watched from miles away. No erection.

I burst into tears as we embraced and Alix asked me what was wrong. The shadows of the previous weeks came into focus: I had dreamt of Jacob dying. My arms were paralyzed. I told her everything.

Alix has been leaving Jacob with me to go to yoga class. She's shaping back up to teach again. I'm divided when she goes between adoration of the baby and visualizing Alix doing vinyasa by candlelight, and worrying obsessively that she will be struck by a car while walking. She hasn't pumped and left a bottle here. What will I feed him if she is even an hour late? I remember reading about a concoction made with goat's milk. In a few moments of internality, my partner has died and my son is starving.

These images have coincided with an avalanche of self-doubt. I'm struggling to reinvent myself professionally, again. I haven't had time to be properly depressed about finishing that last book. I love my research, but can't imagine my own contributions becoming more than a drop in the ocean. Every brilliant book I read weighs me down. It seems impossible to make enough money to pay for everything I want to give.

I think the holidays, along with Jacob's more relaxed schedule, have given me the time to really feel the terror of parenthood, and perhaps existence, for the first time. He has started smiling upon every *Hello*, every time he sees me. He seems happy, calm, adjusted, resilient, and he's even putting himself to sleep sometimes! These early moments of individuation have made me a little less needed, and being a little less needed comes with a quiet flood of powerlessness. He belongs to the world, not me. Alix belongs to the world, not me. The world will take them from me. Of course, day by day, the world and time takes me from myself.

No consolation or fairy tales. The three of us are bound to each other in joy and fear, even though most of our fear is child-like, like you and Carina going on about sharks. The inevitable separations are intolerable before they occur. Then, when they happen, we adjust. No one knows what is coming. I said these things to Alix. After a pause, she said, "I know that feeling."

I sat in meditation before dawn, feeling my breath become even, then thin, then delicate, then almost-gone. A nimbus of warmth encircled me. The cat pawed at the door. He was breathing as well. My attention wandered back and forth between breath and the internal catastrophes of the past few weeks. Breath warmed the catastrophes, and the catastrophes sharpened the breath. Time stopped.

I got up and went to Alix. I looked at her, and a hot erection came instantly, showing the other side.

love,
Matthew

||

January 4th

Matthew,

I'm touched by your letter. The terror of being alone with this living breathing person who can't actually look after himself and also the fright of you dropping away every day you parent. I know the abstract worry really well. And not being able to be hard. You are lucky to be in a relationship where you can lose your erection and use its loss to go deeper with Alix.

I went to see my old therapist Anthony. I hadn't seen him in at least a year. I told him I was feeling defeated by the troubles I was having with A's mother. I thought A and I would have a more independent bond now than we do. It's like he is aligned with her home and losing his connection with ours. I said, "Anthony, I'm losing this struggle to have the role in A's life that I think I deserve."

Anthony said: "Yes, you have been defeated. It's like not being able to be hard. This will make you a better teacher. We need leaders who can feel defeated." I wept.

When you were about to make love to Alix and you starting worrying, abstractly, and your erection was defeated, what was happening in the portals of your skin?

You froze and you caught yourself freezing. Then, you and Alix were able to include what was going on for you. *That* is yoga. *That* is intimacy.

Matthew, when we write to each other for the rest of this time, let's replace the word yoga with intimacy. If I wrote a new version of the Yoga Sutra for family life, the Domestic Sutra, it would go like this:

Healing only happens when we don't freeze.

Healing only occurs through intimacy.

Intimacy occurs when strange parts talk to each other.

Yoga is the intimacy that arises when we don't hold on to rigid views.

Intimacy is beginner's mind, which is the body of compassion.

Oh, and I bought a motorcycle. An old black and yellow BMW 1150GS. Carina is astonished. It looks like a bumble bee on wheels but it's a little louder.

Let me back up.

We have a friend named Adriana Disman who is a performance artist living in Montreal. She wrote to us about her new partner, Danielle, who has a PhD in Tarot and gives readings in Toronto when she visits. Carina went and so did I. She used the office of a psychotherapist nearby and so I walked there alone in the snow listening to my boots on the fresh sidewalk.

She wore black and had shoes with heels and a round face with black-rimmed glasses. We sat face to face and she told me, "Everything you say is confidential. I don't talk about the future. I don't channel."

Then she said, "Keep your feet on the ground when we talk and don't close your eyes."

The next thing she said was that I seemed behind myself and not fully in my body. Over my left shoulder she saw a student of mine who was asking me questions. Then Danielle said, "Over your other shoulder I see a motorcycle. What's with the motorcycle?"

Matthew, I love motorcycles. Since I was in grade one, I've always wanted one. My father looked after an investment property my grandfather owned and the property was a farm where they had a Honda 50cc motorbike. I drove it alone, for a whole afternoon, every time we went. I fell over a couple times but mostly I was so happy riding with my whole body, steering with my pelvis, starting it with the strength of my right leg. It was, I think, my first sexual feeling. It was physical and better than hockey. There was the road, the feeling of the gravel up through the tires and my pelvis, and there was the sky. That's all.

When I'm tired or on a long flight, I'll peruse the magazine stands and look at vintage motorcycles. I never buy the magazines. I've never allowed myself.

"The motorcycle," Danielle said, "is *not* a metaphor. You keep turning it into a metaphor. All your life you make the motorcycle into something else."

Something lifted Matthew. It was so strange. I felt terrified and free simultaneously. There was a candle between us and nothing between us. She was right.

She went on: "You give everything you have to your family and students. You also have this motorcycle on your shoulder. What do you associate with it?"

"Sex. My body. Not thinking."

"I want you to go get yourself something related to the motorcycle," she said. "It's Christmas. Get something towards The Path of The Motorcycle. Get a bike, a helmet, gloves, something."

I came home after the session and Carina just clicked with what I said. "I know, Michael," she said, "I know you have to do this. I hate that you want to do this but I can see you are going to go through with this anyways."

She has alternated between support, fear, anger, and, two nights ago, calling me selfish for thinking about a motorcycle in the last trimester. Then last night she said, "I'm glad I can be angry at you about the motorcycle and also see how it's what you need. But I don't find it sexy!"

"Have you talked to your friends about it?" I asked Carina.
"Yes. I talked to Mielle and Kate and Erin. For a long time.
They all said the same thing: Let Michael get the motorcycle."

love,
Michael

|||

January 17th

Michael –

I imagine it's raining in Portland. You're probably staying in someone's guest room. Maybe a room that belonged to a child who's moved away from home.

After four days of balmy weather in the middle of January, the temperature has dropped again, and ground has hardened. Carina has my number. I hope she's not too shy to call if she needs something.

Jacob is a wonder. He's craning his neck into the world, wobbly. He'll gaze into the middle distance for a half-hour at a time, at trees beyond our apartment window, at the curtain edge before them. His eyes glow: you can see his brain flowering and invaginating behind them. He's vocalizing, and beginning to reach for things. The enormity of learning how to move willfully on the earth is exhausting. Alix is the nap-captain. She intuits his saturation point about ten minutes before it comes, before the neurogenesis has sapped whatever excess protein and glucose he has available and he's ready to crash.

It seems like he doesn't want to nap, until you see that he doesn't really want anything with agency: he's utterly possessed by the growth process, and responding with pleasure or frustration at its bounty. More accurate to say: it doesn't occur to him to nap, until, it seems, he is tricked and soothed into it, by Alix's cuddling, bouncing on the Pilates ball, "99 Bottles of Milk," or bouncing in the bouncy chair, or in the baby wrap against my chest. It's strange and compelling to realize that the drive to be awake is a survival adaptation. Our extended infancies are a liability, and the sooner we awaken to where we are and the faculties we have, the more likely we will survive if our parents are killed. We race against time to learn our interdependence so we can gain a kind of independence.

I think we carry this drive towards wakefulness into spiritual life. But we need to sleep and dream there, too. I liked meditating with your community last month, and how at the end Rose chanted the names of the recently dead, and everyone recited an admonition that went something like *Life is short, do not squander it. Wake up, wake up.* (You'll have to tell me the story behind that text.) I also like your idea about chanting for the endangered animals and diseased earth as part of our family. Someone struck the gong at the end of the mantra, but muted it with his hand, so that the sound was cut short.

It is a wakefulness, I suppose, that eventually allows us to relax. It reminds me that one of the meditative achievements the Tibetans talk about along the bodhisattva's way is called the path of "no more learning." I see Jacob enter that path with every nap. Helped by his mother, with her strange Buddha-like mixture of good humour, irony, and strong earthy arms, along with her own isolation, and the periodic swells of dark memory from the birth. It's hard not to want to be her baby as well, to nudge Jacob aside a bit. But just as often, she needs to be held and cared for. And bounced.

Two nights ago I woke up in the middle of the night shocked at the whirlwind of the past three years. Not so long ago, K and I were wondering where we were headed. An older guy who's been my yoga student for seven years just reminded me yesterday that three years ago he and I stood together on the stairs after class and I told him that I thought that I would never have a baby, that that part of life was passing me by. Eighteen months ago, my marriage began to unravel at breakneck speed, around the same time I met Alix. Weeks piled upon days and nights of sleeplessness as I trembled with the change. Rupture here, braiding there. They overlapped, such that the braid carries the rupture. Have you seen those broken pots that the Japanese repair with cement coloured by gold powder?

I think: *every sorrow and confusion I've ever had, every pain and uncertainty, every year of listless wandering—I would live these all a thousand times over to be where I am now, watching this little boy and his mother sleep.*

The next morning we went for our family walk, which always finishes up at a hipster café where coffee is a total fetish. The twenty-something guys smile at Jacob through their bushy beards and then resume their meditation on cleaning espresso nozzles. The skinny jeans force them into some new kind of slumpy standing meditation posture, lithe and contained. The women who work there have cattails and patchwork skirts and crocheted vests. One made a macrame sling just for her iPhone, although it was for a far more obscure device that I would have ever heard of, probably.

Our tiny family sat in the front window in blazing sun, sweating in our winter clothes. I wriggled Jacob out of his snow-suit and propped him up on the table. It was the brightest sun I think he's ever been in. His eyes adjusted slowly, and he found his thumb to suck. I remembered the first Sanskrit verse I memorized: *sarvatma cha divanatho.* "The sun is the lord of all."

At one point all four milk steamers were going and it sounded like we were at the ocean, and I thought "Cool. Hipsters are like bored pirates."

Then I remembered something so simple and incomprehensible. In the natural order, if things proceed as they should, this baby will survive me, perhaps by forty years. I will die, perhaps in his strong arms. I desperately hope we stay strongly connected. My life has poured out into his, and at a certain point, it will be exhausted. As empty as this coffee cup. Jacob is the lord of all.

I have no idea what world he will inherit. Or how skinny his jeans will be. I suppose there's a limit to how skinny jeans can be. Funny how there's no limit on how baggy jeans can be. I wonder what it all means.

I love to see him in the sun. But I know it is unseasonably warm and wonder if there will be snow for him to take his own child sledding. I wonder whether any coffee, no matter how perfectly prepared or from whatever exotic and drowning location in the world, will console him. I wonder if there will be coffee at all.

Get a good helmet to go with that motorcycle. Maybe you should paint the helmet flesh-coloured so you can look like a big-headed baby-monk tearing down the highway, trailing a flutter of tarot cards in the wind. You could paint serenely closed Asian eyes on the visor in see-through paint. And wear a bunchy black leather robe and diaper!

love,
Matthew

January 21st

Dear Matthew,

My room in Northwest Portland has two windows, one to the north and the other facing west. To the north the fog rolls across the roofs. To the west, five thin birch trees are covered in frost, white on white on white. My eyes are dry but I'm well rested. The people I'm staying with have no children. Their house is well appointed and I'm envious of how clean it is.

For the first five days we study the Heart Sutra, and for the last two days we study chapter two of the Yoga Sutra, particularly the first ten lines.

Yesterday I started the Yoga Sutra talks with my own ever-changing translation, based on my letter to you recently, on The Family Sutra. It goes:

Now is the teaching of intimacy. Intimacy can only be this.

Identification with fixed views is the enemy of intimacy.

Let the imagination elaborate endlessly; and don't hold on.

Then, you are free to be nobody.

The elaborations of your imagination can easily be confused with who you are.

When you are fully in your life, you can't see it.

After class a tall, bearded man with faded denim jeans (there are many who fit that description in Portland) came up to me and said, "I get it. I think I get it. He's basically saying, 'Don't just sit there. Do something!'"

I laughed, and thought to myself, "Exactly." We looked at each other for a couple seconds. His breathing was gentle. Then he told me he came to the workshop because he found out last month his girlfriend was pregnant. He heard I was a father and wanted to hear me talk about parenting. I didn't have anything more to say to him. We just sat there together, in silence, and then he told me that he was really enjoying the retreat and that every night he went home and sat with his girlfriend and told her he was scared. It's terrible but I have to admit that after we spoke I had fantasies that his girlfriend was the one you mentioned, at the coffee shop, who knit a small pouch for her iPhone!

The Yoga Sutra is a text I love because I read it as a map of meditation. It's as dry as reading a map and as insightful. I trust it. The Heart Sutra is a Mahayana text, maybe the most chanted Buddhist text on earth. Some monks try to chant it in Japanese in one exhale. While in Japan, I memorized it in Japanese; with Richard Freeman I memorized it in Sanskrit. I can sort of understand the Tibetan version though I can't make out the middle section. It's such a potent mix of compassion, fear and negation after negation. *Think you love this with all your heart?* It says, *Let go of that too.* The most repeated word is a loud shout: *Mu. Mu* is *No.*

My favourite line is: *without walls of the mind and therefore no fear.*

As the walls of the mind fall away, so does fear. I hear this as, *not adding fear to fear.* And yet after all these years I am an expert at worrying, especially when I wake around 3am to pee and can't fall back asleep again.

Then I worry about my son, I worry about Carina, I worry, in the darkest hours, about becoming irrelevant. I'm not sure what that means exactly. I worry that one day I will lose interest in the city and my friends and I'll want to spend my days walking the shoreline of rivers somewhere far away from cities. I will lose my mind and dementia will set in. I'll be happy, but nothing I think will have any relevance to the culture, the city or my family. It's a strange fog I fall into when I don't sleep, which is rare, and mostly happens when I don't eat well. I see myself with a large parka and a lumberjack shirt, counting birds on the horizon, talking out loud to myself, and running out of money in a catastrophic way. Someone will have to come find me because I'll set out for a morning walk and get lost. I'll stop writing and reading. My grown kids will understand but nobody else will. I worry about how attractive this is and how strange. Sometimes I worry about how my parents worry about me. Sometimes I worry about making a living at this strange occupation I've chosen. I love worrying. At 3a.m. I can worry about anything.

Twenty-five hundred years ago the Buddha listed five fears:

1. fear of death,

2. fear of illness,

3. fear of losing your mind,

4. fear of loss of livelihood, and

5. fear of public speaking.

I would add the fear of your child dying before you. I think of a Japanese proverb that says: *Fear is only as deep as the mind allows.* Even knowing all this I wake up at night and worry a lot. I worry about people. There are so many people I love to worry about.

Carina called me in the middle of the night. She said she could feel her pubic bones coming apart and they were burning, and the burning was spreading like a ring around her pelvis. She was scared so Kate came over and slept in A's bed downstairs. Today they are making soups to freeze.

She called again this morning and the pain had passed.

I told her to focus on Wednesday (I get home Tuesday) and we will have the baby Wednesday. That seemed to be the most helpful thing I could say: visualize Wednesday. I guess it's hard to visualize a day, I thought to myself after, but it seemed to work. Maybe I should have said: *visualize a cork plug, don't let yourself relax, keep that baby close to your ribs, imagine stuffing something like wine bottles or cabbage rolls or wrapping presents that aren't going to be opened EVER. Imagine you have a big bowel movement coming but you have no privacy.*

We are pretty sure that the boy's middle name will be Winter. I saw an email came from Carina at 3 a.m. with the week's forecast. Wednesday it's supposed to snow in Toronto. I imagine Carina giving birth in the snow, in our backyard, in one of the beds of frozen kale. Wolves gather round instead of midwives and we roll the baby in the snow to clean away the excess blood and then he crawls up onto Carina's breast and starts suckling. She's lying on animal fur, maybe from a bear, and the trees are swaying in the wind but we aren't cold. The neighbours are sleeping. The cars are frozen in their parking spots. We are the only humans in the city who are outside, breathing crisp air, and Carina howls and so do I. The baby cries and then stares into Carina's stunning eyes. Have you ever seen Carina's eyes? They start out brown and then there are these psychedelic yellow lines, like the kind you see in butterfly wings, moving out from the dark centre. I think her eyelashes came from a deer. This vision I have of an outdoor winter birth is far better than those Russian water birth videos from the seventies with that shitty maroon upholstery and those ridiculous fur hats and the glass birthing tub that made the couple in the video look like two mammals captured for Soviet study.

I get home Monday night and teach at Centre of Gravity on Tuesday. Then I have to go give a talk to medical students at the University of Toronto, a radio interview on CBC, the first day of the online meditation course is Thursday, a board meeting Friday, and then meeting with my editor sometime on the weekend. Somewhere in there I want to walk in High Park with Carina everyday, make love, and sit in the garage with my new motorcycle. The gas tank is empty. I just want to clean it or start it. I've started reading blogs about vintage BMW motorcycles and how to care for them. I've stopped making yeast infection recipes. The yeast is gone! The recipe was a success. Matthew, we should market this recipe for women with yeast infections. We could bottle it and have a logo similar to the logo for Wonder Bread, but with a line crossed through it. Can't you see the advert with you and me on the back of the *Yoga Journal* cover holding up the bottle of yeast killer we invented?

Last week I ordered new robes for Zen practice and a pair of denim jeans reinforced with Kevlar for motorcycle safety. Hilarious combination. I didn't tell Carina. She seems happy not hearing about the motorcycle even though she sees the new helmet in a box beside the laundry sink.

Here in Portland, I've been waking up early to do a quiet yoga practice. Thirty minutes of standing postures and then an hour of supine postures. The main practice I learned from Richard Freeman is mapping pranayama patterns during asana. So in every posture I'm working on following the inhale up through the soft palate where it feels like the ethmoid bone floats. The exhale drops down into the center of the pelvic floor and after the pause at the end of the exhale, the inhale draws the center of the pelvic floor, energetically, up behind the navel. I'm working on finding these patterns in supine postures because next month I'm having knee surgery for my torn meniscus.

I have to pack my things for teaching now. The classes are held in a new centre—a renovated funeral home. It's perfect.

Love,
Michael

|||

January 24th

Dear Michael –

Okay, that baby needs to come right away. You're getting a little slaphappy. It sounds like you're not sleeping enough. But who am I to talk?

There are bulbs in the frozen earth that will come up. Memories and fears in the garden of the body: they will become visible as well. Everything hidden is revealed, and when it is, it shows that more is hidden. Your baby is so close to arriving! Everything trembles! Carina, your house crinkling and popping in this arctic front, A in his restless sleep, and you on your wobbly knee.

The week before Jacob was born I joined Alix in her trance as much as I could. We had such quiet between us as the hours passed. For long stretches we would just look at each other. The gaze was similar to gazing at the baby now, and it felt like it was doing the same thing: imprinting. I made all of the herbs for her that warm and mobilize the womb: strong teas of pennyroyal, cinnamon, and saffron. I fed her bowls full of okra, sautéed in ghee. I added garlic to cut the ghee taste. Maybe she knew instinctively how big Jacob was: he didn't need any more ghee. But I thought it would be good at the end, for lubrication.

They say in Vedic astrology the knee lives in the tenth house of career and public presence. It's said to correlate to forward movement in personal dharma, because it's the first part of the body to break the forward plane of movement when we walk. I was taught to ask clients with knee injuries if they were reconfiguring their working lives. Or maybe knees just commonly blow out as we enter middle age, which is also when we're all considering changes in direction, if we're lucky enough. Either way, it sounds like you're going through something like that.

Thanks for reminding me of the ethmoid bone you referred to when you were talking about yoga. I had an Iyengar teacher who used to speak about it. For a long time, I've just felt it as the "cave of the eye socket" deepening as the soft palate relaxes upwards, so that the eyeball isn't reaching out across the forward plane, like the knee. Sometimes it feels as though my eyes could open in reverse, pointing back into my skull. I imagine seeing a mountain lake, at night. Yes, I have seen Carina's eyes.

Your first letters to me talked about how this time around you would cultivate your own support. Maybe you've done it. You've prepared a home that feels like it's yours. You have the freedom to retranslate old yoga books more adventurously than I do. You have an injury to take care of. Good teachers keeping an eye on you. A board of directors to relieve you of decisions. And a bumblebee BMW, bought at the best time. Baby Winter will be four months before the roads dry up enough to ride it. You'll be able to get away for a few hours a week, into history and wilderness. You probably won't even think about it until the hour before you kick the crank.

Because maybe the baby will support you as well. I think you wrote about how the smell of A's head comforted you in a way you couldn't explain. I don't mean like that. I don't think you need comfort in the same way you once did.

love,
Matthew

January 27th

Dear Matthew,

Dōgen quotes an old koan that I just remembered this afternoon:

> "One time, the old Zen master Huineng asked a monk,
> 'Do you depend upon practice *and* realization?'
> The monk replied, 'It's not that there is no practice and
> no enlightenment. It's just that it's not possible to
> divide them.'
> 'This being so, know that the undividedness of practice and
> enlightenment is itself the Buddha Ancestors.'"

The unbroken lineage of realization, according to this monk,
is practice. Practice and enlightenment are not two things. You
don't sit still or do good ethics so that you can get enlightened.
It's the other way around. Our actions are expressions of our
awakening. When I say family wakes us up it's another way of
describing the inseparability of practice and awakening. We
practice family because we are awake. We are awake because
family demands it.

My backyard is white. It's minus ten degrees Celcius and I
haven't been out in a few days. I must have caught a cold on the
plane when I returned from Portland on Monday night. Tuesday
morning I woke up, practiced, wrote a lecture, and bought insur-
ance for my motorcycle. Run down and happy, I spent the afternoon going over the bike, checking tire pressure (low), opening
the gas cap to check the gas (lines frozen), and double-checking
the electrolyte levels in the battery (dead). Impatience got the
better of me and I broke the plastic clip on the fuse box under
the seat. There's work to do before I get it running.

As I washed the grease from my hands in the basement sink,
I felt as if I was fifteen again, working on cars (my summer job),
and I imagined that I'd build a little workshop out in the garage
with my old tools, and start working on the bike myself. In one of

the black German cases that comes with the bike there are special BMW tools, a manual, and some stray bolts. I've arranged them on a plywood plank like an altar. A desirable displacement of identity.

So I have engines, tires and an old wooden garage built in 1918, with barely a foundation, a leaking roof—all in all, a perfect little temple. You know, my father loves motorcycles—he has two—and when I was young we worked together on cars and bikes and anything we could find. I'm back with the ancestors. Do we all grow into our parents as we age? I took to stillness and my father took to riding and business. I understand more now what he must have felt taking two hours away from the family and being alone with a machine, the wind, the garage. Anything to reconfigure our thinking is worthwhile, I think.

Now, five days have passed and I'm in bed. Carina and I both have colds and we spent the last twenty-four hours in bed together, lying around in different rooms in the house, being quiet. We downloaded a David Darling record and Van Morrison's *Astral Weeks* and watched the light move across the hallway and into the bathroom. Maybe I needed to get sick to stop everything and just be home, here with Carina and the baby. Van Morrison doesn't sound as good now as he did when I was stoned, at seventeen, driving in the car in the middle of the night, with Sam, my tomboy girlfriend. Or maybe Van Morrison never really sounded that good, except at exactly the right moment, in Hollywood films, when the only way to make a scene work was to play "Brown Eyed Girl."

As we went to bed the other night, Carina asked me to guide her through the hypnobirthing meditation, but I told her that I was too tired and my throat too sore. She told me she was upset that I wasn't as connected to her body as she imagined I'd be. She's wanted more massage. I told her how hard I've been working, that I needed rest. She said she was disappointed that I haven't been able to connect more with the baby. At first I was really upset, but I realized she just needed me to stop explaining myself and hold her, in the moment, massage her feet, rub the new homemade oil she made into her belly. She wasn't asking for a lot. For three days she's been making salves and various other concoctions and then, once they were finished, setting them in small glass bottles. She leaves them around the house, mostly in places where I'd find them, like my dresser. I didn't pick up on the cues. She was saying: *I've made these salves, rub them into me, I need your hands.*

Carina has been working as a chiropractor. She set her office up in our living room. Now that she's down with this cold, she's realizing that it's time to stop working and focus on the baby. But her enormous student debt is such a weight that it's hard for her to stop working, and just as she begins to entertain the thought, she hears her father's Finnish voice warning her to work, work, work. I have that voice in me too. As Buddhist as I might be, I'm a very productive Jew. I feel lucky that when Carina wants to stop working we'll be fine. It's the first time in my teaching career that I can work intensely for a week and then have the same amount of time off—to rest, or get the house ready, or, maybe the greatest privilege, to be able to take five days off with this nasty flu.

Carina and I are having conversations now about her staying home with the baby and what it's going to be like with me travelling and teaching. She thinks a dog would be the solution. She gets worried that being alone at night, with the baby and strange urban noises in the alleyway outside, will keep her from sleeping. My body recoils when she says the word "dog." I see her in her slippers, walking the naked baby in the snow, to the dog park, with baby shivering at her breast, and then, she drops the leash in the shit, and the baby is crying, and it's midnight, and the snow is coming down harder and faster, and I'm in another country. Or, it's 4 a.m. and I'm woken up by the dog, even though I need to sleep and the baby has been up all night. No dog, no dog! I'd have to start teaching twice as much just to afford all the dog food and the vet bills, and the baby will be ill all the time because he has to go out with the dog and he won't be dressed well because we spent the clothing money on dog treats or raw vegan dog food from that natural juice company in Santa Monica.

When I'm teaching, I try to hold nothing back. Sometimes when I get home, I have a lot less energy than I had when I left. I'm finding myself more exhausted these days. We've found making love in the morning is much better than the evening for this reason. But Carina is showing me my shadow. I have an easy time explaining my lack of intimate physical energy, but actually, I just need to find it. I need to find it for her. I bought the motorcycle, after all. I somehow manage to practice every day. I have an assistant doing bookkeeping and emails and someone helping me edit a new book. There's no reason I can't look more closely at how I'm using my energy. So, since that conversation about the more intimate touch she desires, and since we've been sick in bed, I've been massaging her feet, giving her prenatal perineal massage, and talking to the baby through her swollen skin. It's showing me I need to slow down. It's so funny how I think of myself as a calm and focused person and then sometimes I catch myself in a momentum of speed and distraction where my hands can't get slow enough to touch her, her tissues, softly, listening, intuiting what she needs.

This must be what Dōgen is referring to in quoting the koan about everyday practice not being separate from formal practice. He says something else too that's worth mentioning: "When practice does not fill your whole body and mind, you think it is already sufficient. When your practice fills your body and mind, you understand that something is missing."

Something always remains, something gets left out. No matter how much we think this pregnancy is in our hands, we know it's not. I always have this feeling around animals: no matter how much I think I know them or their habits, there's always this other part that is vast and mysterious and can't be known. These days I feel this way about everything. No matter how much I know how Carina thinks or how she walks and sleeps I actually have no idea who she is. When I'm truly present with the process of this pregnancy, I realize that I don't really understand it at all.

Now the tea is on, the low winter light is fading behind the garage, and Carina is carrying wet clay to the kitchen table. She's been working clay to make bowls and plates. The bowls are oblong, like her belly. We haven't been this quiet together, in our own place, since we met. I want to spend the next week like this. I have so many deadlines. And, we have to continue the conversation about money and what will happen with her work as a chiropractor when the baby comes.

Carina turns to me holding the wet clay pot:

"How many centimeters is this?"

"You mean, how dilated is it?"

"Yes."

"Four centimeters," I say.

We laugh and stare at each other. The furnace turns on. I get up to make more tea.

love,
Michael

|||

January 28th

Dear Michael,

As I write I'm calling and clucking at the cat. When I'm up early, Krishna is torn between snuggling beside me and wanting to curl up with Alix and Jacob. Either place would be warm and loving, but he doesn't understand why there are two. So he sits in the kitchen between our two rooms and cries. Still, cats are way easier than dogs. Dogs smell bad. Full disclosure here: there are few things I dislike more than a happy, stupid, smelly dog. Sure, they're cute and lovable but I get conflicted around them. I've had so many friends who love their dogs and love having their dogs lick their faces with the same tongue they use to lick their balls and asses. Yuck. Don't get a dog, or I won't come over: you're too good of a friend for me to pretend to like your smelly dog.

More snow is coming down now, before dawn, and I imagine it's covering the bike tracks to your shed.

How many places can we be in at once? You're fifteen, the shed dates to the Great War, and maybe you dream of a student having an anxiety attack in Vancouver, where you're off to next like some kind of Buddhist paramedic, hoping Winter holds off for another week.

Maybe this is a different type of being-present: to be aware of so many things, over the broadest sweep. Carina's attention can't help but be the inverse. Winter's head is pressing on her cervix after all. There's nowhere for her to go within herself but to her slow dilation. The world is shrinking for her, I think. I remember when Alix's first practice-contractions began, she disappeared from the surface. When they accelerated with active labour, looking into her eyes was like looking into a dark underwater cave. This is where her sound emerged. She only came to the surface when she had to ask for help, when she knew she couldn't do it alone.

Holding her, wrestling with her through that night, I stood guard at the edge of something. I was aware of the time down to the minute: whether the broth was boiling on the stove, where my car keys were, whether the doula was hungry, the weather outside, where Alix's shoes were, how young the backup midwife was. When Alix reached for towel bars and furniture to pull on to disperse the overwhelming power of the contractions I guided her hands so that she wouldn't rip the tiles out of the wall.

Indians speak of Shiva inhaling and exhaling the universe into and out of existence. I think it's also a description of the attention that expands and contracts. Isn't it amazing that Carina is beginning to contract muscularly as her attention contracts to the diameter of a few centimetres. She follows the exhale down to a single vanishing point. You're not there, but still inhaling the world, as you need to, to watch over. And to manage the details of the house, as she winds her chiropractic practice down, and worries about her student debt. That debt belongs to both of you now. We take on each other's pasts. Too bad Shiva can't exhale student debt out of existence.

I know why you got upset when Carina confronted you about wanting to be touched more often. I think many of us have been there as partners: to feel accused of being absent or of not connecting when we are connecting in a different way. It's felt to me for a while that this basic contrast in the structure of emotional contact gets caricatured as "He can't settle down," or "He can't focus on what's important," as if there were a single way to be intimate. I think it's very hard not to reduce the scope of the intimate down to a single point when the center of the perineum is the center of the world. When baby is born, another sheaf of single, crucial points arises. His cry, his mouth, the nipple. It's the crucial scale of the very small. When Alix is able to go down the street to a yoga class these days, she feels like she's travelling to Europe.

There isn't a single scope for intimacy. For years before my first marriage dissolved I had a similar issue to what you describe with Carina. I would sit with clients all day and then teach my heart out late into the evening. I was close to people all day long. I would come down to the apartment from the studio and my partner would look for a connection. I would focus on the tea kettle. I was spent. I had given too much away. Not to harp on it, but I really don't think that being vegetarian served me there. I notice that almost every long-term vegetarian client I have struggles with vitality and libido. I look at them and think to myself: *you need blood.*

She would say: "You have time and energy to love all of these people." It's important to note that 'all of these people' were for the most part women. She would ask: "Don't you want to come home to me? Am I not the heart of your life?"

I was baffled and irritated. I told myself I was absolutely supporting the heart of my life. Through work. I thought constantly of how more income would mean more time off, more time together. (And on and on, like you said.) All the money went into the house and into the busy dream that someday, somehow, a perfect time would magically emerge.

Over time I realized that my capacity for closeness declined because I was finding my creative life elsewhere. Our interests were diverging, and while it had been clear that we weren't going to have a child, this suddenly meant something quite different to me. As K withdrew from the business we had built together, we shared even less. She took the lead in going to the lawyer to dissolve our LLC status and giving up her director's role. I have come to feel that some kind of material responsibility is important to psychic growth in a relationship. This is perhaps a hidden form of fertility.

I still wanted sex, but not closeness. I experimented with porn, which made me feel like an empty shell. She found out about it and was so hurt. It was easier to indulge my guilt and apologize profusely than to actually talk about what was happening to me.

I felt like we were treading water. V had left home, and K and I virtual-parented her by phone and email. Our writing interests grew apart. I tried, like in the old days, to help her with editing her novel, but my heart wasn't in it. I was as professional with my feedback as I could be, but what she really needed from me was basic emotional support, which I was less and less able to give. What we shared began to dwindle, and I think fantasizing an idyllic retreat to Cortes was a way of trying to paper over the hole. I wasn't even forty years old.

I still think of that shed out there on that island. Your shed reminds me of it. But yours is different. You'll use it to fix your bike, and to teach A and Winter how to fix bikes. Like your father did. What was I going to do all the way out there, on that rainy island? Who was I going to serve or teach with the old tools I collected? I remember sharpening my axes and spades every day on the stone grinder. I had to be my own little boy out there, marvelling at the spray of sparks.

Here's an old Tantric recipe that might jack up the night for you, if you take it over a few weeks. At 5 p.m., blend three raw eggs with a heaping tablespoon of raw honey, and a half-ounce of brandy. It's like candy. Also good right before bed. Before meditation, it drops the mind into your heels.

Your chemistry together might change entirely when Winter comes, and aphrodisiac therapy might not be at the top of the list. But in a way, it can serve any task: that she sees you not only standing and watching at the threshold of her circle, but knows that you are alert.

love,
Matthew

|||

January 28th

Dearest Matthew,

The due date is still more than a week away.

Your last letter really touched me. I'm thinking about the little, yellow, wooden home you and K shared on Cortes Island. I was there the summer you split up. I was teaching at Hollyhock Retreat Centre and my old friend Everest took me on a windy drive to go visit the writer Ruth Ozeki in her writing cabin not far from where you and K had a house. Ruth pointed out the house you guys owned. Then we went to see the incredible modern post-and-beam house that Everest designed for the American artist Alexander Calder. His family was out and since Everest designed the house, she took me there for a tour. The woodwork was seamless, the windswept trees and the topsy-turvy elevation of the property wanted you to stay, to rest, to make home. The house had long straight lines but it felt pulled out of the ground somehow, earthy, spacious, right. I could live there easily. It also made me think about Carina's debt and how I'd never be able to afford an island gem like this, or the lifestyle that comes with it. I went down to the docks and ate an oyster off the beach and watched float planes come and go. I've always loved the old Beaver floatplanes from the 1940s. There are a dozen of them on Cortes Island. They deliver the mail to all the adjacent logging towns and the hundreds of outposts east of Cortes in Desolation Sound.

The next day K and I had a beer at a restaurant on the bay, near the Klahoose First Nations reserve. The restaurant reminded me of so many rural Canadian bars: run down, bustling in the summer, struggling all winter. The exterior wood needed white paint a decade ago and the rest of the building was covered in one kind of siding or another. We faced the bay. K's hair was red. She talked about writing and I talked about taking a break from writing. I wondered where you were. The water had such deep blue undertones and the sky was whipping so far overhead, the clouds looked like quick kid's sketches. There was something we weren't talking about. How could I have known you two were coming apart?

When A's mom was pregnant we rented a modest cabin north of Toronto on the Magnetawan River. The river runs from Algonquin Park, four hours north of Toronto, due west, and empties out into Georgian Bay. Everyday we swam and I loved being in the water with her. She sat one afternoon between two sets of rapids and she looked young—younger than I ever remember her. I was twenty-seven and she was thirty-seven. After a few days we went driving in our old Volvo wagon. I'd picked up a map of forgotten pioneer roads and we followed the map until we came to an old gravel road that crossed some bridges, through a three-way intersection, and passed by old farms and a church. The church was white and abandoned. I stopped the car and got out. The ground pulled me in, as if I were being told to stop everything and lie down. I did. I lay on my back next to the church and studied it from below. A hundred years old. Nobody around. The forests behind my head were thick and silent. Past the gate a line of twenty or thirty aspens trembled. It was July and hot and the wind was just right.

I wanted to live there.

We walked to the farm across the road and an old woman answered without opening the door fully.

"Am I supposed to know you?" she said.

"No. I am interested in the church."

"Nobody goes there."

"Does someone own that place?" we both asked at the same time.

"Yes, a family. They had parents with farms here once. Now they have an antique store in Toronto."

She told me their last name. A few days later I called the family in Toronto and told them A's mom and I were pregnant and maybe we could rent or buy the church since nobody seemed to go there anymore. I named a price: $20,000 for the church, the acre of land around it, and all the contents.

One month later, on the due date, they called. *Yes.* We called the doula, asked if we could leave town, researched the nearest hospital, and drove four hours north. When we got to the church, the first thing I noticed was that there was bear shit by the front door. I knew it was a sign. We bought the place. I put it on my credit card.

I loved being up there, finding swimming holes, making espresso on the woodfire stove, pumping water from the well nearby, chopping wood, watching horses in the fields. A's mother was so happy there. After three summers, I started feeling like I still wanted to be up there, but not for the whole summer. And I wanted friends to visit. And email. It was something I kept struggling with. I loved the stars and crisp wind and being far from the city. But in the third summer I started longing for the company of others. I was feeling more and more isolated. I missed my friends and wanted A to have his friends up there too. And I have ambition. I love teaching and writing and being with friends who are making things in their lives.

So when you talk about Cortes Island, the place of your lost summer home, I understand. It's not exactly feeling like you've retired too early, or that you can't play the game of the isolated writer (we've both done that!). It's about some kind of aloneness that emerges at a time when the creative juices are getting fired up. *Practice needs to be shared*, I wanted to yell. There was a poverty there that wasn't at all related to my own love of being alone. It had to do with the fantasy of getting away, the isolation of a nuclear family, a partner who was struggling to find her niche, and a strange sense that if I were to truly follow what I held deep in my heart, our time in the woods would look nothing like it did. We'd have big parties followed by weeks alone. A small canoe for adventures. A motorcycle. I'd write and we'd have time together and time apart. Friends would visit with their kids and I wouldn't cook every meal.

Eventually, as you might know, the separation was so acrimonious that I gave her the church, hoping it would resolve things. It didn't work. Hopefully one day it will be A's. And hopefully A will do something with it that meets his needs, even if it means turning it into a social space. Or he might need to sell it because the church is my story.

After I gave the church to A's mother, I took a last visit there. I invited everyone I knew who had kids. We played a wild game of archery in the graveyard across the road, we drank wine through the night, and at one point there were a dozen kids climbing trees. I was single and I kissed my friend G, which created all kinds of trouble but knocked me out of the depression that had dogged me since the split. The next day we swam and cooked and did it all over again. It was joyous. I attached a string of paper lanterns to a boat battery that I had hooked up to a solar panel and the whole place glowed like never before. I saw how the church could be used and then I said goodbye.

After A's mother and I split my heart was broken. A piece of me will always be broken after that. The split also saved my life. So the abandoned church stands for all of that: joy, suffering, being torn apart from everything you work so hard at. The church now stands for unresolved conflict. I'll always feel that the relationship ended more painfully because we couldn't resolve our troubles. She kissed someone else. Three days later, I was in pieces at a friend's house and she called me and told me it was over.

The jagged question of my separation from A's mother will probably hang around a good long while. Chinese Master Hsuyun said, "A thousand thoughts give us the opportunity to come back to the question a thousand times." Our separation is still my koan.

Tonight Carina and I are cooking and we rented a Wes Anderson film. The early contractions have stopped for now. A is at his mom's. The furnace is running and Carina is working on her clay bowls though one is turning into the shape of a bird. Outside the yard is still white and the snow on the tree makes me think there's something like a snow language that shrubs understand. They read the patterns on each other, like the way one-year old kids communicate with words. Maybe our sons will hang out with each other. I miss A when he's with his mother but it's nice to have a quiet house. It won't be this way much longer.

love,
Michael

P.S. As for the bourbon and raw egg yolks: Richard Freeman showed me a pranayama practice where you rest at the end of the exhale and then when the mind is really stable you swallow your saliva and visualize/feel the saliva dropping down the central axis, like nectar, and dripping onto the pelvic floor. It works for the same purpose.

|||

January 31st

Dear Michael,

I was awakened at four this morning by a howling wind whipping the trees and clattering siding. I felt an immediate terror for my professional life. What if my books are riddled with errors and faulty assumptions I'm unaware of? The wind called out the fraudulence of my trying to be someone. It has also come with an eerie weather change. It was fourteen degress celsius at the end of January: a record high for Toronto, and then a record temperature plunge as the wind began, bringing another wave of cold and wet snow. I feel disorder—personal, social, environmental—breaking over me in waves.

But then I heard Alix's naked feet on the tile—running. She came into the study beaming: Jacob had slept through the night! I hugged her elated naked body close. She went to pee and then skipped back to bed. I sat down to meditate, and it didn't take long for the breath to show me the texture of my fantasy against the texture of the now. At the end of the exhale I felt your silence—there were two business emails yesterday that you didn't answer, uncharacteristically—and I wondered if you were in labour together, and I felt Carina's downward and outpouring pulse riding the violent wind. This humid wind is good for birth, I thought.

Your son is crowning, maybe, and my son now owns the night. Or we'll see. He's eating enough at one time and his digestion is slowing enough that he is sustained through the dark hours. His stool is coming less frequently, and is thicker and darker than the mustard that filled those newborn diapers.

I saw that it seems to be in the nature of things that I should give my sleep, perhaps for the rest of my life, to my children.

I know of that old yoga teaching that Richard describes, and I've practiced it as well. *A-mrt*: the undying. I think the *rt* at the end is cognate with *rta*, the word for "season"—an unfolding of something. I think it comes down into English as "ritual." In Ayurveda it is used to describe any rhythmic thing like menstruation. But the fact that *rta* connects bodily and environmental rhythms is exactly what some old yogis were rebelling against. They didn't want to see themselves as changing and corruptible. A lot of them conceived of the body as a sealed machine for generating immortality, beyond the seasons. The saliva, consecrated by the breath, becomes an elixir that will build other tissue: semen especially, which of course they couldn't "spill." The lore is filled with heroes who evolve shining bodies of light while fasting and ingesting nothing but saliva—which is nothing but themselves, as it were. They report incredible bliss, as they wither away.

But the eggs-and-brandy come from the interdependence paradigm, which says that virility and libido and energy come through relationship. My friend Miles in Vermont had about a dozen hens, and they hid their eggs all over the acreage. You had to go out and find them. Steal them, really—the hens would defend them with squawking and scratching. I hunted the eggs thinking about the protein they carried that I needed, thinking that perhaps my sexual dysfunction was simply a nutritional issue. I ate a massive amount of raw eggs, and things didn't improve. I ate so many raw eggs I gave myself hemorrhoids. They create downward heat. Of course writing so much doesn't help the old anal veins either.

I think meditation is in part a hyper-refined digestive process. The parasympathetic takes over. You can feel pulses and secretions. If the breath isn't wet and smooth, the spine gets stiff. Belly-breathing massages the vibrantly-coloured organs of digestion. The neuroscientists in Wisconsin have studied brain waves in meditation, but I bet that hormone levels are probably radically changing, redirecting the attention of the tissues towards love, tissue repair, resilience, plumpness. I think the MBSR people have measured cortisol reductions in meditators, but I'll bet that's just the tip of the iceberg. I'll bet ten minutes of that mental stillness and alertness that makes the mouth water and the hands glow is flooding the flesh with all kinds of creative juice. I used to work hard to get that feeling. Now it just washes over me when I watch Jacob wriggle around.

We're always digesting *something*. Saliva is made from rain, salt, banana, mango, grain, broth, bone marrow, egg yolks. Thoughts are made from breath, neurology, social mirroring, the virus of language, trauma, memory and pleasure. The

Ayurvedic books are big on the balance of *ahara*—input—and *vihara*—output. The world transits through us and we transit through the world. There is no world outside of a series of inter-penetrations.

It makes me think of your church, and how it sounds like you were starving there. *So small amongst the stars,* as Leonard sings. Did you really need to get so small? It sounds like you were hungry for friends, work, email and eggs. Maybe a family being alone in the natural world is not enough. It's a fantasy. Where does it come from? Swiss Family Robinson? *See the plucky triad bivouacking through the forests, befriending bears, staying safely within the childhood of history.* Maybe you spent so much time alone sitting on your meditation cushion that once you had a family, you needed something else. Amazing that you, so attuned through study and training to the ways the mind works, had such a hard time communicating your deepest needs to your partner. Maybe the masks we put on for our lovers are even harder to crack than those we wear for our families.

I remember on Cortes that I couldn't receive email except on my phone on the very tip of the island, so I would leave my writing or the garden to go for a run twice a day on the muddy shoulder with the phone slapping against my thigh, heading for the ferry dock a mile away. I'd turn on the phone and watch the reception bars light up, and I felt I like I was eating. There were notes from students and clients, employers and respondents to my writing.

I can't believe you owned a busted-up church with A's mother! Part of me wants to make a cash offer to buy it anonymously through an agent. If I had the money. And then you could go there with A and Carina and Winter, and we could come too, and everybody could share the wood stove to boil our soup. It just seems too sad to lose. But I'm sure it's not a good allocation of funds to buy into our history again.

We took Jacob to Doctor Donna for a check-in. He's watching everything now. He is wide open, drinking the world in like milk. Donna palpates his soft white belly and his scrotum and bicycles his legs to see that his hips are good. She has known Alix since Alix was a teenager. Donna used to palpate Alix's belly with her strong farmer's daughter's fingers, fifteen years ago.

I'll bet Donna's old enough to have heard of the raw egg thing. I'll bet that some of the Orientalism that you and I harbour is just displaced nostalgia for the earthy and more cohesive knowledge our wandering families have lost over the past century.

love,

Matthew

||||

February 5th

Dear Matthew,

Yesterday I came home and the hot water was running in the kitchen. I called out a few times and Carina didn't answer. Concerned, I went upstairs and Carina was falling asleep. She forgot about the dishes she'd started. Then a few hours later I walked outside and saw glass under the car. In the strong wind last night a large piece of glass that was leaning against the old garage shattered. Carina drove the car right over the shards of glass without noticing. I can see she's turning inward now.

7:12 a.m. The windows here at the Vancouver airport are dark. The view is split into tinted quadratic fields and I feel far away from Toronto. It makes me think of my father, and how he flew here after my parents split up—how this was the first thing he inhaled, the deep blue mountains of dawn, the grey skies, the smell of saline air. Even from inside the sealed airport, you can feel the heavy rains of the west coast, towering coastal mountains, storms, old trees. Four days away from Carina, one week from the due date, I'm so ready to take a break from teaching and just be home.

When my parents ended their relationship they took my

brother and me for dinner and afterwards we went to my father's architecture office in an old brick building on Richmond Street, in the heart of downtown. We walked quietly up the six flights of stairs. My parents weren't speaking. My father turned the overhead office lights on. I knew why we were there because I knew of the affairs. My father had told me everything. My brother must have felt something was off because he kept looking at me and holding my gaze. We learned how to talk without talking. We still do.

My father showed us some of the buildings he was designing, airbrushed on large sheets of translucent paper, and there were foam models everywhere with small plastic trees glued to them, like the ones glued to my old trainset at home. The white models were littered with small plastic figurines, hundreds of them, glued to the foam models of buildings that hadn't been built yet. Everywhere there were miniatures, little scenes a small-scale couple standing beside a red sedan, reduced men in suits standing at the exits of buildings, a petit dog and fake grass.

In my father's office that night, I didn't know I was angry. I wondered why my mother wasn't wearing makeup as usual. My mother had no idea how much I knew.

"Your father and I are going to separate," my mother said.

"Aren't we telling Sunny?" I asked, wondering why my sister wasn't there.

"She's only seven. Your father doesn't want her to know yet."

My brother didn't say anything. He just kept looking at me. I wondered if I was supposed to feel a certain way, or maybe he didn't know what to feel so he looked at me for as though I were a gauge he could trust. Maybe he wondered why I wasn't surprised. The whole family was numb, until we walked back down the office stairwell, the wooden stairs groaning under our feet, and my mother, walking behind us, started to cry. I didn't turn around.

Two years later, my parents had split, and after selling the house my father came to visit me on the west coast. I was at the University of British Columbia, studying philosophy and experimenting with psychedelic mushrooms. My father and I drove out to Tofino and camped in the rainforest. But it was hard to connect.

Matthew, I started walking away. It felt like the whole project of trying to speak to my father, to be with him, was going to be impossible. On that trip I would often leave my father and walk alone, studying the ocean, feeling the beads of water accumulate on my face and hands, one with the ocean, the furthest point of the continent, the birds on the coast unhinged from everything.

That's when this thought struck me, a thought that I first had on a canoe trip at summer camp when I was ten. The natural world is wild, it doesn't care about humans, and it's also home. Also this: we are so close to some people. We share the same body, and yet sometimes we can't rest with each other.

Around that time, a lifetime ago now, I stopped taking drugs and discovered yoga practice and began psychotherapy.

Twenty years later I think often about my father. He's one of the most important people in my life. His red hair has turned grey. I call him every week. I understand him more than anyone else I know and for that complexity I'm grateful. He rarely visits. Mostly we get together one-on-one and when we hug I grip him so tightly.

love,
Michael

|||

February 10th

Dear Michael –

A few weeks ago you asked, "Do we all grow into our parents as we age?" I think we have our answers: yes and no. You are the resourceful son of an architect. You've made a career for yourself out of thin air. Who could license you for what you do? You're self-reliant. But you're self-deconstructing, not self-destructive. You're self-aware to a fault. And you've struggled long enough with the avoidant patterns you inherited to turn them into something else—a kind of political resistance. You long for an intimacy that used to be scarce.

It's actually amazing how deeply you and I can bond over family life, when our fathers seem such different men. I have my share of missed connections and temporary estrangements with my father, but not to the depth you describe. My dad is likely more progressive than yours in politics, but far more conservative in personal risk. Having affairs would have been absurd for him. Not to mention exposing his child to them—he would have died of shame. He can get angry and wear his disappointments on his sleeve, but I've never seen him act out.

Maybe in part this means that if I'd had your father, I don't think my relationship to K would have lasted seventeen years. I think my dad's manners wired me for forbearance and a loyalty that often doesn't know when to let go and give myself and others space. You have struggled to do what your father couldn't do in relationship, while I've struggled to do less of what my dad does. Bonds and expectations can be too loose or too tight. How rare it is for us to hit the sweet spot.

I feel like I'm just discovering my father again. My formative memories come from when I was about four until I was about eight. He was orderly in all things. Everything had a routine, which comforted me early on, but then chafed me so hard when I was a teen, it was one of the reasons I left home so early. He was very particular about bathing—I remember him scrubbing me between each toe when I was really little. Then drying between each toe with great attention. He told me later that he'd learned this in basic training for Vietnam. The drill sergeant showed them horrible pictures of athlete's foot and said that if any of them contacted this while in training after his fair warning, their tour would be extended.

I remember my dad teasing me—he'd been the youngest of ten children and I think he was teased constantly as a child. He coached me in baseball, which meant we were glued to each other's sides through the long summers. There was always somewhere to go, a practice to become better at something. He had keys to the batting cage at the field, and would take me there in the evening and feed ball after ball into the pitching machine. The constant repetitions are inside me, and have played out in so many ways. I've felt it in how I've written and rewritten, compulsively. In how I've chanted the rosary through certain low times in my life, or practiced asanas to wake me up when I've been numb. It's here even now, in how many of these very sentences I've reworked to describe him. But I've learned how to surrender to the fact that I won't get it right. Enjoy my failures, even. I don't know if he's learned to do this, or if he would ever want to.

He is slight of frame, which meant that he towered over me, until one day he suddenly didn't. I've been physically bigger than him since sixteen. It's hard to understand being larger than one's father. One has to imagine taking up space in the world beyond him. When you are a boy, what is beyond him? I'm glad you had your uncle.

I remember my father working in the study on his Ph.D. thesis in Russian history. It was all about state-caused starvation during the Russian Civil War of 1918-1921. Unknown numbers of peasants died. They were eating unspeakable things in the end. I had no idea of the topic at the time. I was just enthralled by the very notion of Russia—so far away. It felt like my father was from there, and that he was going the old country every afternoon in the curtained room. He used to tell me about how the peasants used to hold sugar cubes in their teeth and suck hot black tea through them, even in the hottest weather on the steppes. He told me: *When it's hot, drink hot—it will cool you down.* I sat quietly beside him as he poured over yellowed books, mouthing the Russian as he read, compiling notes on thousands of index cards. Some cards were light blue and I wondered how the notes on them would mix with the notes on the ivory-coloured cards. I scratched my finger along the leg of his desk, and furniture wax came off under my nail. I liked sharpening his Number Two pencils, and watching the shavings curl into my hand and stain my palm with lead.

I remember idyllic hours, but he was studying a massacre, knowing as all historians do that it was one of countless massacres. He was researching freight train manifests—the nuts and bolts of how grain was exported from a famine-stricken land or hoarded by landowners. He was researching treachery and propaganda. Perhaps his orderliness is a response to the chaos of history. I'm sure it also carries the echo of a mother who, in taking care of her tenth child whom she birthed at the age of forty-seven, had enough energy to pay attention to the broad strokes of his character development, but little left over for anything but the pragmatic routines that had proven useful through the years.

There were piles of black xeroxes, smelling of ink and alcohol, printed out from the microfilm machines at the library downtown. He had a small microfilm reader on his desk, projecting sixty-year-old Soviet newspapers onto an eerie grey-blue screen. When he left the study I would gaze at the backlit Cyrillic characters, mystified that they could form a language. I'd smell everything: the books, the index cards, the electrical air coming from the fan of his microfilm reader. He taught me one Russian phrase. До свида'ния. *Do svidanya.* "Until we meet again."

He abandoned the thesis when it was clear the field was in recession, and that he could earn a reliable income as a high school teacher. Before long, he was appointed as the librarian of a Catholic girls school. When my school had a teachers' conference day, I would go to work with him and sit amongst the books for hours, and watch him field dozens of questions from the kilted girls working on their essays. This was pre-internet, or course, when things actually had to be searched for by hand, and when you just assumed that you needed a guide. My father loved guiding. He typed the thousands of index cards that mapped his realm. The radio in his office was always tuned to classical music.

I absorbed something in those hours that I'm still learning: data comes in various forms of unequal value. It takes a long time to collect it and assess it. There's so much sifting. So many points of view to reconcile as the picture comes together. So many agendas confounding our clarity. A single aspect of a single story can take a lifetime to describe honourably, and it's so hard to do that they'll call you Doctor once you've done it. As if you could now heal that part of reality.

All of these repetitions, within these limited ranges of motion, showed me how nothing is ever finished. With patience and meticulous attention to detail, we may slowly come to a fuller view of what has happened, of what has happened to us. The very effort of caretaking alone may someday bend the world towards justice. Cultivating memory is an implicit act of faith that says *We can do better*. In every page of microfilm, there is always a sentence or two of reason and hope, too hard for the naked eye to read. You make your father sound like he had many things he needed to forget, and not enough patience to really discern what was worth hanging onto.

Since Jacob was born, my father has become more real to me, as I have become more real to myself. I think I'm closer to imagining what he must have felt and still feels about his two sons: a wordless blend of shock, recognition, confusion, devotion. And then—something that will come later for me—a sense of withdrawal from a future that belongs to Jacob. More and more I will recede into memory and familiarity, and Jacob will have to bear his own newness in the world, as I once did. *Until we meet again.*

love,
Matthew

February 13th

Matthew,

10:08 a.m. Cooked a kale and feta frittata, took lots of time sau-
teeing the leeks. The snow is still here. So, nearly, is the baby.
Contractions started yesterday at dinner, got stronger through
the night. At midnight we walked through the icy park and then
I convinced Carina to go back to sleep at 2am. We woke up at
7 a.m. and the contractions have almost subsided. I'm tired but
I want to clean. I am so excited. I want every corner of the house
to be clean and organized. I want to fold shirts, organize the
cutlery, and I just found myself using a rag to clean the top of
the washing machine. Carina likes a very soft touch on her back
during contractions, figure eights around her sacrum, my fingers tracing her skin. She's wearing yellow long underwear that I
found years ago at Salvation Army, a black bra, and she is beautiful. So beautiful.

Last night at Centre of Gravity I thanked everyone for their
support. I said *This baby is all of ours.* I said, *Some of you can't
have kids and some of you won't have more kids and some are
not intending to have children and yet this baby, our baby, is for
all of us.*

If I'd been just a little more manic I could have gone farther.
What I really wanted to stand up and say was, *Listen everyone,
this baby is going to save the world!* I cried a little.

This baby is for the snow and time and winter. This baby is
winter.

Will update soon. Now I need to go get bagels for the midwives in case they get hungry. And we have no olive oil.

love,
Michael

February 13th

Dear Matthew,

9:23 p.m. Feb. 13th. Hours away from Valentine's Day. The moon is an orange waxing crescent and Carina is glued to it. Her contractions have been quiet all day. A came home from school and then the contractions got stronger, we ate dinner, then A and I cleaned. And cleaned some more. When A first started flossing before bed I had him lie down, then I took over—making sure his teeth were sparkling, as if this were the last opportunity to get his teeth cleaned, maybe for years, and I was playing dentist. He seemed so small. Carina dimmed the lights in his room. He said he's not as excited as us. I said of course not. "How could you be," I said, "you've never had a brother. You'll see, it's going to be beautiful and strange and you'll feel so many things." He asked if he could have the licorice stick Carina bought him. He's been chewing on it all night like a younger teething version of himself. We've all been in bed. The duvet smells like detergent. I cleaned it today. Did I tell you A and I washed all the duvets?

love,
Michael

|||

February 14th

Dear Michael –

I've had a cold and now a mild fever since Tuesday night. I cancelled my clients today. This is the first hour I've been able to rise above the ache in my joints and mental fog to write. I've been grateful for the pause, extra time in bed with Alix and the chubber, Jacob. He has a red-and-white pinstriped sleeper that makes him look like a porky peppermint candy. I call him peppermint piggy and tickle him and he laughs and finds his thumb. Things are freezing back up outside. The sky is slated and snow is splattering by at a sharp angle. I think of every faucet in your house, running. Hot water to bathe her. Cold for her forehead and mouth. One tap just running for the sound of it.

So many men are out snatching up last-minute bouquets from the florists today. Carina is opening like a rose.

I tell Jacob he has a friend coming. He makes blubbing sounds and pounds his toy piano. I want to communicate so much to him, and I am anxious around this. But my real job is to resist smothering him with my forty years of emotion. That will be your job too. The stuff about your father is a lot to process. I hate that word: processing. Have we only started using it since computers? As if memory is a problem to be solved, and not some chaotic weight that immobilizes you in one moment and then vanishes with the simplest shift of weather or perspective.

You'll be surrounded by the birthing women soon, if they haven't all piled in already. If I'm recovered, I'll come whenever you want if you need someone else to stand with, someone else who knows both your love and your distance. Part of me wishes I could be there as the one person who witnesses you. I imagine your face breaking open as Winter emerges. The women in the room will understand and feel Carina. But who will witness you? There's a hundred films of you online, and people have your books by their beds. But who will see your face then, and see the sweat soaking through your birthing shirt?

I'm halfway across town and I want you to know that I can see you.

love,
Matthew

February 14th

Matthew—

2:59 p.m. Laboured until 2 a.m. last night. Kate was here in the bedroom with us. Andréa brought her camera and filmed. Waited as long as we could to call the midwives. Spent almost two hours in the old iron tub, pressing Carina's hips inwards during every contraction and kissing. In the last twenty-four hours we've kissed for longer and in more ways than we've kissed in our almost three years together. She had an orgasm on a few contractions. I got in the tub with her for a while because I didn't want her having orgasms without me! We called them contractogasms.

After the midwives came the contractions slowed and I guess one needs more privacy for contractogasms because the midwives are all business! I went to bed downstairs. Kate slept next to Carina. Andréa slept on four zabutons in my office. She used the small pillow from our Japanese meditation bell as a cushion for her head and a towel as a blanket.

Today the contractions are intense though spaced far apart. Carina was given Gravol to rest this afternoon. It's a marathon first phase. A chewed on licorice, set his walkie talkie up in our bedroom, and slept through the night with the static hissing in his ear. In the morning he cleaned his lunch bag, I made him lunch and my good friend Steve came to pick him up and take him to school. When Steve came in the door I cried. When Kate brought me her beet soup I cried. When I saw Andréa sleeping I had the urge to kiss her forehead and tell her how much I loved her. I did it from the doorway instead. I have a lot of energy, I feel strong, and anything anyone says seems like the sweetest thing in the world.

I haven't left Carina's side all day. A hot water bottle between us. Now she is listening to those birthing affirmations she had to stop listening to when I was away. Mostly I'm guiding her through breathing. I had rehearsed a guided relaxation script she liked but now I'm just making it up. Sometimes I'm not sure if she knows it's me next to her. *Exhale, release your buttocks, release your jaw, keep your voice low, double your relaxation. Soft hamstrings. You're like a marionette with strings released. Go deeper still. Then slow down the inhale and let it spread between shoulder blades. Keep limbs loose. Release your legs through feet. Snow melts on the earth. Snow melts Carina, snow melts. Think of the colour orange and take another breath.*

It just started snowing. 3:10 p.m. Carina lit some sage. It's winter.

love,
Michael

February 14th

Dear Michael –

Our letters just crossed. You have such good help, and are giving such good help. You're giving her all the non-reactivity and softness that you've ever learned. How amazing what you have learned to give. Everyone's breathing along with you both. It is snowing, but I can also hear runoff trickling in the gutters. Eat as much of Kate's soup as you can! It's okay to cry in front of all of those women. I think there's something different about crying in front of Steve. I'm not sure what it is.

love,
Matthew

February 15th

Olin Winter Stone
7 lb, 5 oz
12:08 p.m.
St. Joseph's Hospital
Toronto

|||

February 15th

Wow. Long life, Olin Winter Stone, and family! I don't know what else to say.

love,
Matthew

|||

February 18th

Dear Matthew —

Olin Winter Stone is three or four days old—I can't keep track now. We moved into the yellow room with bay windows so that Carina doesn't have to go up and down the stairs. My training is paying off: cooking, cleaning, laundering everything in view. I chant to Olin when he cries. I'm sleeping in my office under the off-kilter Buddha. Carina needs a lot of reassurance that going to the hospital at the last minute was the right thing to do. She really wanted the baby at home, in our bed.

Olin's face changes by the hour and his suckling is pulling the plates of his head together. His white wrinkled hands are now the colour of the rest of his body. His head smelled like hospital lube for the first two days and now the baby smell is coming in and I can't stop nuzzling my nose into his neck folds. You know the smell I'm talking about?

It's too early to write about the birth. Maybe you and I never will, though for different reasons. Our birth certainly wasn't traumatic but it's still not ready for words.

I found a record by a piano player named Nils Frahm. It's called *Screws*. We have it on all day and night. It sounds like Eric Satie in even slower motion, played in the rain, or solo piano being played in the hull of an old boat. Carina wakes me once in the night either to get her goat yogurt or help change the diaper. If I sleep at night I am fine to serve in the day, or at least my moods are stable and I can focus. She is too sore to massage. The menstrual pads you made for Alix that you passed on to Carina are doing wonders healing her perineum. We are settling into a routine and even from within it I find myself envying the menstrual cycle of women, the pruning and planting rhythms of gardeners, the habits of bears, these mysterious trends that connect us to the great cycles of nature.

There are hard berries on the pine tree.

When I wake in the night it's in the grip of some strange terror. It lasts a couple of minutes—it's this feeling as if there is danger and everything is wrong. It's deep in the psyche, far below time and thought. Then I hear the piano in the other room and I'm soothed. Something terrible is behind my dreams and it's not near consciousness in the day. It only appears as I'm waking. A kind of terror. This happened when A was born too. I recall it from childhood also. I wake up like I'm a scared kid. It doesn't show up in the morning, only in the middle of the night.

I feel raw at night. In the daylight I feel calm. I love Carina and Olin and the snowy park out the window. At night my mind goes pawing into time and grabs darkness by its jagged edges. Why such rough messages in the night?

Who am I? My name is Michael Stone. I have two sons. I've fallen in love with a beautiful woman, more stunning than the first girl I ever loved, the one with red hair who lived at the top of the red brick hill up the street from my house in 1983. My initials remain the same, the scar on my left knee is getting fainter by the week, my fantasies have changed, and I'm not anxious like I was when I was younger. My friends without kids say things like, "Maybe after the baby you and Carina will start going out again" or, "When will she go back to work?" But we can't go back. None of us can. When you recover from being ill you think, *Now I'm going to go back to how I was before.* When we get ill we try to heal ourselves so we can get back to how we were before we were sick. But the time of the broken leg or the fever is completely that time when we were in it. Having a baby is the same. This time is fully this time. We don't go forward into another time. I woke up suddenly aware that there isn't anything that isn't this moment. Just this moment, we have nothing else. It's true and it scares me.

Carina is reading Mary Oliver poems to Olin right now. The snow turns to rain. The wind is quick and from the west. These are good hours. This is a long season. I don't like the night.

love,
Michael

|||

February 20th

Dear Michael –

I know the smell. Jacob was born by caesarean and the hospital smelled of detergents and sanitizers and plastics, but I could smell him from the beginning, or I felt I could. In his neck folds, and his fontanelle. I think it's the smell of life itself, before the skin thickens to hold it in. The skin thickens by keratinizing—by dying. How strange is that.

I was so happy I could drop by the day after Olin was born. It was like the house had given birth—everything wide open and flush and damp and messy. A let me in. I said to him *Congratu-*

lations big brother. He looked down at his Lego helicopter and grinned and shrugged. I imagine he feels so much he can't allow himself to show yet.

I stood at the kitchen door watching you stir perineal tea in a big mason jar, not noticing me. I remember that careful, absorbed, wide-eyed attention. I could see you as a child, maybe seven, earnestly doing something for your mother. I bet you felt you had to compensate for your dad even then. Then you saw me and I showed you the bagels and gluten-free banana bread and chai and date pickle I brought and you said I should go upstairs to the yellow room.

The day-old mother is the strangest combination of full and empty, whole and broken. Carina was radiant in the sunlight. Her voice was deeper. I could hear a rasp from the loud sounding echoing from the labour. I could see she was in pain with every movement as she sat up, but so full of things that the pain was peripheral. Like she almost didn't have room for pain. She tucked Olin close, rooting in his sleep, ruddy and peeling. I know he was born vaginally, because he's all squishy. So fragile. Can you believe we survive any of this? I hugged her tight. I had planned to sing *Happy birthday Momma* in her ear but I couldn't say anything because my throat caught. I speak to thousands of people per year in lectures and then my voice is just gone when there's something to say.

Alix and the bubster were waiting in the car outside so I had to dash. I stopped A in the hallway and said *So what do you think buddy?* He shrugged shyly. I said his name, slowly. *You have a brother, little man.* He shrugged again. I don't know why I was leaning on him, calling him out. He didn't seem to mind. I think I wanted to say hello to my own ten-year-old self. I was remembering when my brother was born. It was impossible to understand. My brother was so precious. My mother had complications in the hospital and I was really worried about her.

I had night terrors as well for the first few weeks. I was deeply shaken by Jacob's birth. I couldn't believe they'd gotten through it. Part of me had had to prepare for them to die in a very explicit way. As in: *In a few hours this woman might be dead in front of me. What will I need to do first?* My brain fixated on her Moleskine notebooks.There must be twenty of them in a cardboard box, filled with writing from over the past decade. I thought of dealing with her clothes and underwear. When we first met, she was wearing a long green dress.

I wonder if this dredging of fear happens quicker for new fathers than for mothers. The mind is open and clear with simple service, and I think everything can flood back. We watched her give birth, and we're standing there at the sidelines, and something is happening to our bodies as well, but it's hard to say what, and because it's so much more psychic we have space to recollect terrors that the mother can't yet afford to recall. We get to go to the sink and wash dishes, and have our own separate thoughts. It can happen really quickly. Sometimes just unlocking my bike to ride to work gives me a whole country's worth of space that Alix never gets.

I actually have written about Jacob's birth. I started writing early on the morning that Olin was born. I hadn't heard from you and I knew he was coming, and I was worried for you, and my own memory started flooding back. So I have it sitting here, an unsent letter, and I won't send it until it feels right. Maybe never. Maybe like me, it will take you four months to be able to write about active labour, Carina, Olin's head emerging. Maybe we can exchange those stories on the same day.

But for now, everything is new, and you have endless days of simple work before you.

love,
Matthew

March 1st

Dear Michael –

Olin is two weeks old. I can feel your house stitching itself back together. You're getting ready to go back to Vancouver to teach, and I imagine you're making provisions for Carina to have help. When anything big like this normalizes, I'm always amazed at this firming-up, a kind of hardening. The birth is like weeping, and it goes on and on until it's done, and then there's a shuddering sigh, and the brain feels suddenly clear, and you can wash your face and get back to chopping vegetables.

Births and deaths smash the repressions of the everyday. They are the raw material that slowly dry into knowledge, but a knowledge that cannot fully prepare you for the wetness of the next experience. After you and I went to see the psychoanalyst Adam Phillips speak last week I've been reading the book of his you lent me. I think you lent it to me for this passage: "Knowledge does not answer questions. Questions answer questions."

I doubt I'll ever carry on in the same way. I wonder about my own capacity to harden. I'm sitting in a drab hotel room in Houston now, about to present on yoga and social activism at a conference with lots of smiling people selling yoga products. I'm starting to travel for work almost as much as you are now. I think I understand your early years with A a little better. My hotel room overlooks a highway. There's an endless stream of pickups and SUVs.

I had to leave Alix and the baby yesterday, and it really hit me. I was melancholic on all three airplanes. Somehow, packing my bag felt less like collecting together the things I needed and more like raiding the apartment, stealing things from this woman and child. I think there's surface-guilt about leaving her with a baby who devours time and attention. I really hope she doesn't get exhausted. She's running a marathon. There might be a deeper guilt in me that the freedom and anonymity of travelling will be a pleasurable contrast to the intimacy of the babypad. But I don't think this is it. Really, I just miss them, as though I've been the child in the home, and I'm not sure how to consider myself apart from them.

I don't think you have quite the same feelings here. You told me the other night on the phone that you took the motorcycle out for a spin. I think part of you is already nomading again. The first picture you posted on Facebook of Olin after the birth was of him swaddled in a receiving blanket, asleep on a meditation cushion, and your caption read: "Here's where you tuck your kid during meditation practice." I realized: *Olin's already portable*, and he won't have to struggle against being the vanishing-point centre of family life. Of course you're doting on him and will forever, but he is a second child after all, entering into a stream that's already flowing.

I lie awake thinking: *How can I give Jacob exactly what he needs? How shall I show the world to him? How can I nurture all of his strengths?* Like some sort of panicked creator-god, imagining that I'm responsible for everything (how grandiose) or that my effort to show him the world is not the actual world that he will first see: a father's effort can be a kind of anxiety. Adam Phillips asks: *What is the drive towards knowledge a drive for? What does knowledge cure?* I can already feel that I want my son to know my knowledge, to be the center of my hopes, the inheritor of all my recipes and cures, and that this may terrorize his questions. I want to really be awake, and not do this.

Sitting beside you, listening to Phillips speak last week, I was struck by so many things, but perhaps most of all by him quoting the psychoanalyst Harold Searles: "The child suffers from not being able to cure the parents." I would like to give Jacob less to cure in me. This means way less doctoring on my part. And becoming more curious about what my fear is than in my skill at getting over it.

love,
Matthew

March 3rd

Dear Matthew —

There are these pinnacle moments of total simplicity where I'm humming a melody and running my fingernail along Olin's purple foot and then an hour later I'm finally getting out of bed with him to put more soup on. We are protected in slow time.

A few days later it's the same. And then we make our first steps outdoors to walk the icy park and the following day I'm showing him off at the coffee shop. Little by little the miracle is normalized and in less than a week, when Olin is three weeks old, I will indeed be on an airplane to Vancouver to teach, staying in a hotel room on Granville Island, watching Olin for three days on Skype. I want to be a man in a film getting on my wild horse, to cross the desert in search of sparse food for the family, or go hunting for furs to keep them warm in the blistering winter. But in the end I'm looking at their photos on my iPhone, sending home money via e-transfer and talking to them daily on Skype. And the worst hardship I'll face in my journey is what size espresso to get at Starbucks so I don't get constipated on the airplane.

I have a clear memory of standing at the Vancouver airport exactly eight years ago, talking on a payphone with A's mother. She was down and exhausted. She had little if any support. I was teaching on the west coast for a few days and I felt dreadful being away. But while we were talking on a payphone, a floatplane took off not far from the airport terminal. The sky was crystal clear and the saline air was perfect. I was happy to be away and I was upset. I couldn't figure out why I was oscillating.

A few things were happening. First, she was becoming resentful that her own music career had all but ended as I was suddenly being invited to travel and teach. I was frustrated that she couldn't look after the baby without me, even for just a weekend, and also that we had no support as a young family. In retrospect I see that we were living a model of family that was isolated and without a social network. Looking after a tiny baby alone was exhausting. So many people need to do it this way. At the time I was upset with her though I think now it was an impossible situation. My suggestions that we ask for help fell flat. Meanwhile, I was happy to be off teaching and making enough money to cover the costs of our simple lives. I was dangling at the end of a payphone trying to dial us back in. She resented my work and I, her dependence.

There is no doubt it's harder for the person who stays home. When you come home from Texas, Matthew, you'll have met so many new people, some of your talks will have reached people deeply (and you'll be moved by it) and sometimes your teachings will be clumsy (and you'll need to digest that, too). Alix will have been home with the baby, trying to keep a routine, while you've been navigating connections, hotels, awful food and delays. If you're like me, though, something in you feeds on that liminal space: stolen hours at 30,000 feet to be alone and think and prepare. I wrote my second book on airplanes. After A was born I wrote a book a year for four years.

A's mother's resentment was not just about my travel. It had to do with so many things that I still can't grasp. So I have radar that's up all the time now, being careful that Carina has support, that we are both in touch with what we need. Carina and I talk about this all the time. I think the stay-at-home mother scenario hurts both people in the end if there's no support for the mother to step away and do other things.

Last night Carina was up a lot with the baby. Her parents are visiting from B.C. Her mother rocked Olin from 3 a.m. to 4 a.m. and her dad took over at 6 a.m. At 7 a.m. I woke to A crawling into bed with me, asking if he could sneak into Carina's room to get the iPad so he could play video games for a while. I said if he crawled in without making a sound, and if he could do it without waking anyone, he could play video games for an hour. For fun, we both got on our hands and knees, stealthily crawled into the room, got the iPad from the cabinet and just as we made it out the door, Carina and Olin heard us and woke up.

The house is full to bursting. The support is coming from every direction: Carina's mother, Marlene, has the kitchen totally organized, Carina is finally bathing, I'm cooking in a clean kitchen, and the midwives call to talk with Carina. Carina's imagining becoming a midwife. Because of her chiropractic studies, she could likely do an accelerated program. She's been talking about it every day since the birth. I can see it. It's such an obvious fit. We keep looking at programs online and tuition costs.

When I went for coffee a few days ago, I bumped into our midwife and I told her about Carina's fantasy of being a midwife. She said, "I'll meet with Carina and talk her out of it! Most of the women I work with want to be midwives right after they give birth!"

I asked why she'd talk Carina out of it and she said being a midwife is tricky with a young family. Especially if one person has to travel for work. The lack of sleep is impossible sometimes, she said. Since our midwife is a single mother of two kids, one thirteen and the other a few years younger, she had to get someone to come live with them. The way I understood the arrangement is that this woman she met lives with the family and is available before 9 a.m. and after 3:30 p.m. in exchange for food and accommodation. She said if Carina were a midwife you'd need someone to live with you and help out in some kind of arrangement like that, just like her parents are helping us now.

So now Carina is imagining this midwifery role and I am all caught up in this idea of having someone live with us. I love it. I am enjoying having Carina's parents stay with us. Anyways, what started as a conversation about Carina's midwifery fantasy has now turned into a really great conversation about expanding how we think about our family, and trying to find a way to have someone come live with us. Our generation doesn't do this much. I feel in a tangle. On the one hand having enough space in our home to invite someone like an au pair to live with us is such a position of privilege; we are closer to the 1% than we like to believe. On the other hand the idea of the cereal box nuclear family, with dad dressed to go to work and mom helping the kids get ready for school is impossible for everyone. If family is a social creation for raising kids, there are certainly a thousand ways to do it. When social forms fail to fit people's needs they break-down and reform to meet the needs of the people. But with family, it's working backwards: We're stressing ourselves out living up to a form of family that's not possible anymore.

In our current economic model employers pay a wage but bear no responsibility for the social costs of this generation of workers. Then, within the family dynamic women primarily perform the unpaid and often invisible work of raising kids, cooking, and health care. Parents together then have to make the difficult decision as to where to leave their kids when they are at work because the shrinking social net means grandparents and extended family aren't nearby to help. Capitalism's need for the private, self-sufficient nuclear family creates oppression on all fronts.

Carina is up. I hear her moving under the covers. I'd better go check in on her and Olin. He's gained over a pound this week. Oh, by the way, so many people are asking me, "What do you do with an infant if you want to meditate everyday?" So, I am documenting all the possible places where one could tuck a sleeping infant during meditation practice. So far the back of the meditation cushion is best, but also between my legs, under my desk, and in a sling.

love,
Michael

|||

March 4th

Dear Matthew —

I have a few minutes alone and don't know what to do with myself! Carina's parents have everything under control and Olin is asleep. You're likely on your way home from Texas now. I used to take the red-eye flight home when I was in the far west teaching weekend workshops and retreats, but now I wait until Monday. The red-eye fried me. But again, as we were talking about, I carried this guilt for being away and felt I had to come straight home and get to work as a dad.

I was irritable all day today. I watched it coming to a head with small quips and rising impatience, until I realized I haven't done any physical activity in a week. I lay down to rest and remembered walking by a place on Ossington called Academy of Lions, a crossfit training studio. I had no idea what that was so I called them and they said there was class in an hour—a free introduction, in fact. A packed his binoculars, a helicopter magazine and a new novel by Meg Tilly. Carina's parents made lunch for her. I wore my old running shoes and arrived to find everyone decked-out in full workout gear.

A started reading and then checked in on me while I tried skipping rope. It was horribly embarrassing—I couldn't get two skips at a time. Two people were coaching me from either side and I was jumping and hopping and trying to use my arms. *Stop using your arms*, they yelled. *Just your wrists! Jump higher!*

Meanwhile A, out in the café, was shaking his head, laughing while watching me with his binoculars. Ten minutes of skipping and I thought I was going to throw up. I was hallucinating images of Buddhas drinking espresso and throwing up. Then we threw medicine balls up a wall for ten minutes, followed by jumping onto a three-foot-tall box, over and over again, up and off, backwards and forwards, landing with knees turned out. I had a headache and my eyes pounded. After that we did some strange version of push-ups called burpees and the small, strong teacher came over and told me I had good yoga moves but that they wouldn't get me anywhere in crossfit and I had to get more focused, stay tough, and jump higher when I clapped my hands. "Don't clap your hands like a yoga guy!" he yelled over the music. A was still shaking his head at me from the lobby.

We finished the class with kettlebells. They told the guys to get the heavy blue kettlebells and the girls to get pink ones for an exercise called "clean and jerk." All the exercises were named after sexual maneuvers. I picked up a pink one. I won't even tell you how long I lasted except it was shorter than this sentence. It was the hardest physical activity I've done in a decade. And also, the squats and swings with kettlebells were fabulous for my injured knee. I hated it and I think I'll go back.

I came home starving and A was laughing and he told Carina and her parents all about what he saw, the way the instructor yelled at me, and how I chose the pink kettlebell rather than the blue. We were on the floor laughing. Carina's father told me fishing stories. A asked if a friend could sleep over. I put Olin on my chest and we slept for an hour while A played more video games on the iPad in his room. When I woke, the snow was falling in slow motion and Carina's parents were teaching A Swedish.

Recharged. Sleep and laughter are good medicine, especially with a few kettlebells.

love,
Michael

|||

March 5th

Dear Matthew —

I'm on the ninth floor of Robarts Library preparing for tonight's lecture. It's the eighth week of talks on Shantideva's eighth-century text, *A Guide to the Bodhisattva's Way of Life*. I'm in front of a pile of dictionaries and commentaries. When I woke early this morning, I went online to see how much kettlebells cost.

Last night before bed, Carina said she thought I wasn't relating to her parents or A. "You're bouncing off people." I inhaled and there was the knot—the one I tried to find working out on Sunday—and it rose up into my throat before the tears came. "What's wrong, love?" she asked and ran her hand through my hair. Olin was between us, feeding.

We lay on the bed.

"It's too embarrassing to say."

"Say it. You've had it with you for days."

I cried.

"Tell me, Michael."

"I'm scared I'm going to give everything I have to this. Every ounce. And then it's going to end. You are going to walk away."

I cried and she held me. Olin came off the breast and fell asleep.

"Now with Olin I realize how present I was with A and then I start thinking about how badly it all ended with A's mom."

"This is different now. You are ten years older and I'm not her," Carina said, with Olin snoring against her chest.

I just lay there crying, Matthew. I couldn't stop. It felt so good to cry. I felt like I was being indulgent too.

"I can't cry longer."

"Yes, you can. Michael, you are superman. You can do anything. I can't believe it sometimes. But I love this. I love you when I see this part too. I love you."

I kept crying.

Waking up this morning I felt cleaned out. I drove Carina's father to the airport, went to Mysore class to practice, and now I'm at the library. In an hour I plan to pick up flowers and go home and spend the afternoon with Carina and Olin. Work is about to pick up so these feel like my last spacious days. There are tears in the background all the time. I hadn't realized that behind the joy of this birth, I was carrying around a lot of old images from A's birth. Images of A's mother saying it's over. I have to hold those images really close, but not too close. It seems the kettlebells are pulling old memories into the light.

I dreamt last night A and I were riding motorcycles down a thin trail across a field at dusk. They were small 50cc bikes like the one I had when I was a kid. Olin and A were behind me, Olin on the back of A's bike. The sky was wide. There was a stream nearby and Carina was at the farmhouse. It was like a farmhouse I visited once in grade one. I was proud of A's riding. We were all going home—the boys—to see Carina. As I was riding towards the barn I closed my eyes and saw stars. It was like the sky was inside me. I said to myself: *It was there the whole time.* I repeated it a few times and woke up: *It was there the whole time.*

Love,
Michael

|||

March 6th

Dear Michael –

Days are short as far as getting clear goes! I think the time lag speaks to some alienation from the body. We know long before we know. The ice starts melting a long ways away first: high ice covering the mountain stream, exposed to the sun. It was there the whole time!

It took me five years of shutting down in relationship to really understand what shutting down was and meant, and what someone can do to pretend it's not happening. A whole host of intimacy survival skills—forced and flawed—can pour into a widening gap. I do think, like you're suggesting, that we spend the long days or years of our confusion doing metaphysics, exercising our brains everywhere except in honesty.

Poor old body—so ignored, so overwritten, so perpetually honest and supportive. What a wonder that we can dissociate so deeply, and it keeps breathing for us, or for whoever we're pretending to be. It must love us. I guess when they ask us to watch the breath they're saying, *See how you're here and loved, even when you feel exiled and rejected.*

Had you felt you were bouncing off Olin as well? Is he a danger to commit to? How does his birth change your relationships? I think of how A's gestation and birth not only exposed the rifts between you and A's mother, but how as you look at him now you must see the wall that exists between you.

How strange that A looks so much like his mother. Identical, really. And that you cannot talk with him about her. I'm starting to see what a deep groove this is. He is the breathing proof of both the love and the catastrophe of that relationship. But what a terrible thing to say. Of course he's so much more than that. He's a boy with elaborate Lego, precocious language, repressed anger, a delicate frame, and his own irreducible mysteries. Olin and A: they're part of your story, and they are also unknown.

When I go to kiss or fondle Alix now, Jacob gazes at me with the largest eyes. If I touch Alix's breast, his eyes widen even further. It feels like he is watching how I approach and commit. He learns attention, dependence, distraction. His gaze is so open and penetrating at the same time. In moments I want to turn away. He has come between Alix and me as well, changing us both, inheriting our world as it changes. At his birth so many things died, not only the many old parts of me I've described, but an aspect of the relationship between Alix and myself also died. We can no longer be completely open possibilities to each other, if we ever were.

The full meaning of the fact that Alix and I knew each other for only four months before we became pregnant is starting to dawn on both of us. If there's an answer as far as we can know it now, it comes as we watch Jacob play or sleep and smile silently at the astonishing changes, and commit to the enjoyment of changing. In September, Alix will be starting school to become a psychotherapist.

Recently we've both had dreams of being cast in plays, not learning our lines, not going to rehearsal, and showing up on opening night, empty and humiliated. She was cast as Juliet, and tried to fool everyone with lines from *A Midsummer Night's Dream*. I was cast as Ulysses and given a white robe, and I wasn't even clear on the story. I tried to cover up by convincing myself that all I had to do was to sail the boat and watch the horizon. It didn't work.

What is the root we share that gives Alix and me a sense of longevity? What is this connection we feel, so old, but so eccentric, as our story? When I met Alix I felt all of my repressions begin to quiver. I didn't sleep for weeks. She appeared to me in half-dreams. I couldn't see all of her, but I tried to, so she fragmented but also surrounded me like a cubist figure. When I could finally form thoughts about her they said, *I think I know this person. I know her people. We love the same books. She is so rich with life, and pleasure, and she's impious, and curvy, and she's been waiting for something. But she is also unknown to me.* I was parched before I touched her. Part of this story has now become a human being. The word made flesh, as they used to say. And then comes all of the work, the plain work, the boring work that binds us closer, as a soup will thicken with cooking.

I laughed hard at your crossfit saga. Just goes to show: there's a lot yoga can't get to. We should go together some time. Or maybe to that crusty old boxing gym on Dundas West. It's open twenty-four hours. I wonder who boxes at 3 a.m. I went there with my friend Stuart once, and could hardly walk for a week afterwards, or lift my arms. I loved it. Especially punching. I hadn't punched anyone hard since I was fifteen. The guy deserved it.

love,
Matthew

||

March 16th

Dear Matthew,

Thanks for picking me up at the hospital yesterday. I've been avoiding this simple knee surgery for three years, hoping it would heal through massage and some yoga practices, but I think taking A snowboarding upset the joint in an unrecoverable way. A simple meniscus tear. I was only afraid of the general anaesthetic, not the surgery. Anyway, I'm resting now, the swelling isn't too bad, and I'm not in any pain. I can't walk so I'm reading and returning emails.

Carina had to get A from March Break camp because A's friend's cat died and so her parents couldn't get him. I found myself going to the hospital alone by taxi. I didn't think anything of it until I almost cried when I saw your car pull up. I was watching the circular salted driveway from the second floor hospital window.

Last night after you dropped me off, A and I had a talk. He's been unhappy about the plan of flying on his own to meet me this summer in British Columbia for a two-week vacation. That was the tip of the iceberg. It turns out he doesn't want to be away from his mother. This story is endless.

"I can't be away from mama."

"Maybe we should just go away for a week. But remember, last year we were away for three weeks."

"It was terrible, I missed her and the trip was terrible."

"If you didn't miss your mother when you were away that would be strange. It's *important* you miss her."

"You don't understand, I love her more than you. I don't want to hurt you, it's just that . . . "

"It hurts. It hurts me," I said.

"I don't want to hurt you."

"I want you to really think about this."

"I have. I don't want to be away from mama."

"You're almost ten."

"You just don't understand."

Another transitional night in our home, Matthew. But this time I kept thinking: *No, Michael, something has to change.*

This morning A came into my bed. His skin was warm.

"A, I can't do this anymore."

"What?"

"All this negotiating about time and where you live and us taking trips."

"I just love being close to mama. It's different." He sat on the side of the bed.

Matthew, finally, like a wave cresting, it came out of me:

"A. How about we take a year off from anything new. You have two parents. We both love you. But you know what, it's too stressful for me and you and everyone. I am not going to take you on trips. For at least a year. This summer you don't have to come on vacation with Carina and Olin and I. You can have all that time with your mom."

"Yes. That's what I want. That would be great." He starts stroking my hair. "I don't want you to feel bad." He cries.

"I love you. I'm sorry this is all so confusing. But now you're ten. And now you need to make your own decisions. I've been trying for five years to have equal time with you and I won't anymore. If you say you want more time with your mom let's try it."

"I'm sorry."

"A, you don't need to make me feel better. It's not your job. I feel upset. You feel upset. It's okay. This is intense. This is big. But this summer let's try something new. It's so much all this planning and going back and forth every week."

"Yes. That's what I want."

"To me," I say, "it's painful. The idea of not being with you all the time. But I think I would be easier, no?"

"It's what I want. I want to live with mama."

love,
Michael

|||

March 18th

Dear Matthew,

I'm still waking in the night with worry. How did A's mother and I go from loving each other to despising one another? All week A and I have been talking about travelling together and his resistance. He has internalized his mother's stories and now he filters our arguments through them. It's like his cognitive brain has been taken over by his mother's voice, but there are all these moments when his hand reaches for mine, or he crawls into bed with me, and his body is saying: *I love you, I need you.* When I pick him up or drop him off at his mother's house he never kisses or hugs me. He wanted to go see the film *Formula 1* about Nikki Lauda and James Hunt. In the dark, cold rep cinema, he held my hand the entire time.

There are a lot of people in and out of our house these days. Others have commented on the way A can be so negative about our house and so affectionate at the same time. Their eyes corroborate what I'm seeing and feeling and it really helps me stay sane.

I've been aware of the psychoanalytic notion that a child has to fight and try to kill one parent, but without that parent dying. That's been my view on it all along. If A can feel me fighting for him, that part of him, however unconscious, will stay strong, even if it's not allowed to speak. The part of him that loves me and has to hide it can still feel me supporting him. But now he is turning ten. I can't protect him as much. So now I've started to talk to him more about this gap between what he tells people about our relationship and my experience of us. I'm also trying to open up the conversation about how enmeshed he is with his mother but it's impossible. It stresses him out. It's keeping me up, too. I feel like he's a knot in a rope that his mother and I are pulling and after five years or more it's time for me to stop pulling my end. The knot is getting too tight.

Carina and are fantasizing about leaving Toronto if A doesn't live with us.

love,
Michael

March 19th

Dear Michael –

It was so good to visit you and Carina on Sunday afternoon, to hold Olin, to watch Alix hold Olin and remember that Jacob was so much smaller such a short time ago, to see Jacob reach out and try to hug Olin on the blanket where we laid them both, to see Alix's fairness in the wash of sun. Your table is blessed by that late-winter sun through the floor-to-ceiling windows. The sun kisses every disorder, from your bandaged knee to the rumpled kitchen. Leonard Cohen is always talking about dancing on a broken knee. I think it's in a poem, a novel, and a song. The sun fell right on you as you filled in the details of your challenging time with A.

Is A too young to know his own voice yet? Do we even get to have our own voices? Is every voice fashioned through mimicry? How are children made to twist and dance to the distorted music of our resentments and needs? Loving you has become taboo for A. He's conflicted in loving you, but he does.

I hope that someday I have some kind of unthreatening role to play in his life. I fantasize us sitting in a rowboat together, fishing. I'll say, "I want to tell you what I know about your father . . . " I imagine him tall and willowy and listening quietly, and that some of this stress and sorrow will lift.

I have some different news. I noticed palpitations in my heart on Thursday afternoon. It was an hour before I was to give a presentation. It raced and thumped arhythmically, loud in my ears. A disjointed swirl of wind in my upper left chest. Perhaps I imagined the faintest tingling in my left hand. I lifted my left arm—was it numb? Was it heavy? I couldn't tell. My tumbling pulse sped up, slowed, sped up.

I went for a walk and some deep breathing, and my pulse calmed down, and then I gave a talk to a room full of women on using Ayurveda to prepare for birth. I came home and Alix was asleep. I ate something and went to bed in the study with the orange alleyway streetlight beaming in through the window. The palpitations woke me up at 3:30. I sat up in meditation posture and breathed deeply and watched my breath come and go and lengthen and soften and asked my heart: *What are you holding, what are you hiding?*

I thought of Alix and Jacob and how I mustn't die, but of course I could easily die. Jacob knows me now, and I could die.

My mother's father died after *six* heart attacks that started in his forties. I thought about how I don't have his profile. I stopped smoking at twenty-six, after five years. I was vegetarian for fifteen. I don't eat fried foods. And on and on, bargaining with myself, tallying my health virtues, taking inventory or how much chai I'd had over the past week, listening to my pulse, consoling myself, preparing: for what? The streetlight poured in its orange witness.

I didn't want to wake Alix—we're both sleep-deprived—but I had to. I found my clothes in the dark and sat at the edge of the bed. She bolted upright and asked me what was happening. I told her I didn't feel right in my heart and she started to cry. I kissed her and slipped out into the dark morning to find a cab. I took a book with me. I smiled to myself. *If I'm having a heart attack, I'll need to have a book with me. At least I'll learn something. I bet the waiting room has a comfy chair in a corner by a window. I bet there are not too many people there this early in the morning. If the TV is blaring I'll ask the nurse to turn it off so I can concentrate on my heart attack and my book. I'll need a pencil too, to make notes in the margins. And a snack. I wonder what Ayurvedic foods are good for heart attacks?* Holy cow—nothing like a little chest pain to show you how neurotic and self-protective you can be.

By the time I saw the triage nurse I was feeling better. The palpitations had softened and spread out through my chest like a warm pulsing wet spot, and I answered *no* to most of her questions as she took my blood pressure and pulse and sucked on her double-double coffee and tried not to roll her eyes. I said things like: *I wouldn't call it chest pain—it's just a very odd, disorganized feeling.* She looked at me blankly. I could tell she didn't want to admit me, but policy forced her to. I declined and walked out into the gathering dawn. The arrhythmias shuddered to a stop over the next several hours, but picked up again at 8 a.m. I decided to go to the walk-in clinic. I felt more relaxed about it. They gave me an ECG. The four lines looked smooth and regular on the pink graphed paper. The baby-faced doctor looked at me, looked at the printout, put the printout in the recycling bin, and said, *Have you been under stress?*

Of course there's stress. Not hearing from V now for almost nine months, and not knowing who I am to her now. I'm giving up my office space because the rent is exorbitant and I'm not sure where I'll see clients. I don't know if I can get a mortgage. What will Jacob need? Every time I straddle my bike I think of my friend Jenna, who was killed as she rode her bike two years ago. She was five months pregnant.

I don't know if something began to crumble in my chest on Thursday. I generally believe that I'm stable and resilient, that I can breathe through anything. But the unconscious is ironic: whatever beliefs I have about my strength conceal the iceberg of what I don't know. You can't breathe away the future. You can't breathe through death.

The more I watch—myself, Alix, my clients, my breath, you, you with A, Jacob, Jacob with Alix, Jacob burying his face into her neck now, the news, Alix alone in the afternoon light—the less eternal I feel. I am touched by everything. And used, and worn away. Witnessing erodes me, like bones bleaching in the sun.

love,
Matthew

|||

March 31st

Matthew,

Home from Montreal, my knee is healing well, and after an exhausted day yesterday, I am feeling good. Four days in Montreal left me tired, mostly because I didn't have much time alone. My knee has disrupted my morning practice routine.

Olin was fussy last night and Carina wanted to wake me up but she didn't. She knew I was really tired and not sleeping well generally. Then this morning after I took A to school, Carina was coming down to the kitchen and told me she wanted to wake me up, and should have, but didn't know if it was okay. "When I'm not working a full day, it's fine to wake me," I told her, "just try and let me sleep if I have a really full day the next day." I made her breakfast, finished the laundry, saw one student, got on my bike and now I am here at the library.

Also, I feel guilty being out of the house in a world of adults, riding here on my own and getting rest. It reminds me of you in Texas. We need to step away to support our families so this guilt of being out of the house is unresolvable. Carina looked fried. I have fantasies of coming home with a magnificent supper and flower arrangement. I could walk in the door after being away for most of the day, having finished all my writing and emails, maybe even completing a new book, and in my bags are a hundred pounds of groceries, Carina's favorite ice cream, and fresh laundry. It's so easy to overcompensate.

I woke to the sound of Olin crying, A running himself a bath, a squirrel scraping the pear tree—the whole house rumbling. There was beef broth on the stove, a bottle of lemon water next to my pillow, and just as I was noticing all these details, A came in and told me to get up and make him some food. "Please," I said, " just say please."

We are under the very last days of snow.

Brick house. Softer ground.

Carina has things to say at the end of her eyes.

Last night I left grapefruits on the counter so we could make juice.

The library is very close to home.

Like you, I've had strong sensations through my heart. Twice, both in the middle of long teaching intensives. They occurred the year when Carina and I started dating. As I was inhaling, I'd feel stress in my heart, right inside the left cavity, the same strain I felt during descent once in an airplane. It first felt like a muscle being stretched and my instinct was to inhale and go with the length of the sensation. Then the sensation turned more electric and inhaling and exhaling didn't help. The wires felt tangled up. I pictured my heart, and muscles a few layers deep, beneath the pectoralis, around the pericardium, and there was stress developing around my heart, and so I shortened my breathing, thinking the shallowness of the breath would alleviate the building stress, and there was urgency, and I told myself, *your left hand isn't going numb, your balance is fine, it's not spreading*, but even though I was doing every breathing technique I knew, the cramping didn't stop.

Then, all of a sudden, the strain ended. I inhaled and exhaled deeply and it was gone. Worried, I continued teaching and later told Carina. After both instances we went to the hospital. When you complain of a stitch in your heart, they're quick to rush you into a small room with an EEG machine and hook you up. "The spasm has vanished," I told them, though they quickly taped electrodes to me. Carina and A sat next to me more worried than I.

There was nothing wrong that they could see. "Must be stress. Must be panic." They had a few other ideas, mostly around stress and panic, and after the second round I went for a physical and walked for a while on a treadmill while an elderly doctor monitored the computer. It was in the old brick hospital Carina visited a year later, when she was pregnant and discovered a bladder infection. It's the same place where the Doctor announced to A that Carina was pregnant.

Life throws these unexpected curveballs through the body, and no matter how much we sit still, practice breathing, take care of ourselves and our diet, still the body has its own logic, and it's the site of the unpredictable. Like the time I grew a round golf ball on the back of my head. Benign and strange. The doctor booked me for surgery and I recall listening to the sound of the scalpel cutting a thin line in my scalp, and removing the round white invader. I asked the surgeon to see it and it was exactly as she described, a round moon that had taken residence in the thin layer that surrounds my skull.

Or what about the time when I was in seventh grade and I invited Sarah to lie with me in the third floor bedroom on Elderwood, the house where I grew up. I thought I wanted to have sex with her. We kissed and she took her shirt off, then mine, and she began undoing my belt and just as we were about to go further, I could hear the sounds of my brother downstairs playing with his friends. They were running from the front door into the backyard, around the driveway, and back through the front door. I could see their shoes tracking globs of mud through the house. And then I couldn't get focused again on the task, on kissing her gorgeous arms and navel. And that was it. The feeling was gone. My body was in two places at the same time. She had a beer in her bag, it was warm, and we drank it. Then we walked to her house in the dark, smoking cigarettes, and it occurred to me that she wasn't the one for me, wasn't the person I wanted to date, regularly or forever. We kissed goodnight and I walked down Vesta Drive, back to my house, and thought about the way I didn't want to go forward with her, even though I hadn't yet had intercourse, and though my imagination wanted to, she wasn't the one, and my body was saying so. The distraction of my brother running through the house allowed the distraction of my body to show itself. Maybe these messages come from the heart or the stomach, but not the brain, I thought, the brain was too high up for this kind of knowledge.

When I look at my hands typing these words I'm surprised that these are the same hands that felt Sarah's breasts, the same ones that chopped wood on a canoe trip that summer in 1986 and sliced the right thumb—a scar that's almost disappeared—the same hands that learned how to drive a car, how to bow in temples in Japan, and the same ten fingers that held A's small body when he was born.

This must be the same heart, too, that was crushed when Neri didn't want to go on a date with me in seventh grade, when my uncle Ian died and I was the only one to speak about him at the funeral, when A's mother met another man, and yes, the same heart that very slowly, with great fear, started opening to the possible return of love. There is no duplicate heart. This is the heart that knew, when Carina and I met, that love was visiting my life again, when I was scared that this bruised organ with its perfect language was telling me something I didn't want to hear—that love is possible even when things are broken, right in the centre of a wound, and that my job was to simply show up. When we spoke of moving in together, the forces in my heart started wrenching away the old bits, the ones that were injured, not just from the separation three years earlier, but from the whole line of separations and wounds that were layered in some corner of my chest. A chest with a number of locks. A living reliquary of bruises, lacerations, joys and fears. It was this heart that was hooked up to an ECG machine that, like the ECG machine you encountered, could not possibly read this kind of stress.

love,
Michael

|||

March 31st

Dear Michael –

I'm glad you wrote today. It's forced me to find time alone and breathe a little deeper. So many thoughts have piled up to share with you: the meaning of Easter to me now, how my relationship to my father is changing, memories of grandfathers. How unknowable Alix has become to me, how strong. But we had to take Jacob to the clinic early this morning because he has the beginnings of an ear infection that won't allow him to sleep more than a half-hour at a time, and that makes everything else fade away.

We have to move, because now there's no place for me to work, or to sleep soundly. Up until last week I was sleeping in the study and Alix was either in the bedroom with Jacob or on the couch outside the bedroom. She was up twice per night and I was able to sleep for maybe four hours at a stretch, but more importantly I could wake up at 5 a.m. as I always have, cuddle them a bit, do a diaper change if needed, and then get to work in the study that no one else needed.

'I'he study gets the sunrise and the bedroom gets the sunset. As the days grew longer, putting Jacob to sleep at 7 p.m. meant getting black-out drapes for the west-facing bedroom. We realized that our whole first summer with him would consist of sitting in a dark apartment in the evenings, with no access to our western balcony. We knew we had to move him to the study. He adjusted fine, though he continues to breastfeed a few times throughout the night. At Jacob's first waking, Alix moves from our bedroom to the study to sleep with him. But now I don't have a home space in which to visit clients and I also gave notice on my office space this week: I can't afford the rent and lack of flexibility. I could make do with the bedroom, I suppose, but it's not good to meet with clients in the room where you sleep and have sex. I'll have to start working at the library as well. I'm barely keeping up with my course and lecture preparation.

Alix pinches my arm and says I've had the most productive five months of work I could expect for having a newborn, and I know she's right. I wonder whether her explosion in workload has somehow added to my anxiety about my relevancy. What she's doing seems so much clearer. Why can't someone pay her a living wage for this incredible skill? Why does making money for me feel like making stuff up and hanging on by my nails? I can't get Adam Phillips out of my head: I am terrified, and I think expertise is my solution. But I could also use a study, and a return to more structured hours. And somebody to help with cooking.

We put in an offer on a house three days ago. It had the space we needed, but we weren't completely sold on it or the neighborhood. The bidding process took all day. I had to cancel clients and we had to drive Jacob around for hours. We were outbid. Jacob's naps were scrambled. Perhaps this is how the virus slipped in. The emergency room doctor confirmed that fluid is swelling behind the tympanic membrane of his left ear. No bacterial infection yet. He isn't running a fever, even though he feels hot to the touch. I'll give him some warm garlic and mullein oil drops. I hope it helps.

I have an appointment with the cardiologist tomorrow. Like your guy, he's ancient. But I have to cancel it—it looks like we'll be bidding on another house. I think I'll be okay for another few weeks before hearing what this old specialist of the heart has to tell me.

Love,
Matthew

|||

April 1st

Dear Matthew,

Your family is tuned in. I think when kids grow up they understand the world in the way they experienced their parents understanding them. And more than that: for us it's a practice to tune into the needs of our lover, our kids, ourselves—and the ratio is never right. I know you're always thinking about this as a father and as a partner.

While walking with Olin today I thought about dying and birds and hills. We were at Forks of the Credit, a winding path along a frozen river just outside the city. This morning Carina said she had to get out of the city, had to see nature. She is exhausted. In the car she cried and could barely form sentences. She doesn't feel like herself. The weather was miserable.

We walked along the frozen river with Olin but I was totally distracted. I was imagining Olin after my death. Then I thought about loving him and what that means. I started saying to myself: *You are your love. And that love is mixed up and filled with trouble and joy. The way you've loved and the way you've fallen apart, and the way you've loved again and again is actually the very path of love.* My relationship with A is strained beyond both of our means to heal right now. Maybe I'm distracted and talking to myself in this way because I need to soothe this rift I'm feeling with A. How can I spend these full days with Olin without thinking about how close A and I were in those early days? I wish A could see how I am with Olin, like the way I was with *him* at this age, but I have the sense he isn't able to see this. But is that true? Can he really not notice the gap between the things he says about not wanting to live with me and the affection of our home? Or is A at a developmental stage where he just can't see that?

I love watching Olin's body, the way he turns his head to initiate a rollover, leans onto one elbow as he picks up the other, his collar bones turning like slow motion propellers, eyes looking up at the pattern of our dappled kitchen light spread across the ceiling, repeating patterns down the wall. He begins turning over, from the eyes through the pelvic floor and then suddenly, he's made it, into another world, an entirely new perspective, almost a new life. Even in a mirror none of us can see the way we move, the way the hamstrings contract when we walk or how far the chin moves forward as we step off a sidewalk or put on a knapsack. I told you about Sam, whom I lay with, in the dark, when we were teenagers. One time when I undid the buttons on her shirt, from bottom to top, the curtains opened and her breasts were there, in the faint light of the basement. We were turning fifteen. Neil Young was playing on the stereo next to her upright piano. I reached my right hand toward her breast and she interlaced her left fingers into my hand, stopping my movement. I looked her in the eyes. She said, "Just look. Look at my body. I can't see it the way you can."

I never forgot those words and they became a koan for me. I wondered if she meant she couldn't see what I saw, or she wanted to know what a boy thought, or she wanted to see me wanting her, or perhaps she wasn't sure if her breasts, those newly forming parts of her increasingly swollen body, were beautiful. How could she know? How can any of us know? When someone takes your photo, or you look at the thumbnail of your face on Facebook, you can't see most of what animates your image, the gestures of hands and the firing of those little muscles along the scalenes when you inhale fully, the way one hip shifts to the side as you take a step forward, how some people lead walking with the knee, others with the hip. These details are the details of movement and life, of a unique personality, appearing right now in Olin's movement—onto his belly, again onto his back, like rolling sideways down a hill, in the snow, for the first time: the ceiling, the floor, the wall, the shadow, the ceiling. He giggles. Genetics may move him forward, but he's inventing this movement in his own way, like the way he crawls, without putting his knees on the floor, like a bear, like downward facing dog in motion. Now he studies the shadows on the ceiling. Then he farts. No, it's not a fart. I have to change his diaper.

I hope the visit with the heart doctor goes well. And that you all sleep well tonight. Tomorrow we meet in the afternoon and I'll give you a big hug.

love,
Michael

|||

April 8th

Dear Michael –

We bought a house! 266 Scarborough Road. 1920s, well-preserved, with a backyard, a five-minute walk to Alix's parents' house—so helpful!—and a ten-minute walk to the beach. I'm excited to move. I hope it's the last time for a good long while. But that's not what's on my mind this morning, so early.

I was talking to Alix about noticing how A always calls you Michael instead of Dad. Something about it was sticking in me, and I asked her what she thought. She said that not calling you Dad or father erodes the generational rings. I asked her what she meant. She said that when she was a child she had the very clear impression that she was at the center of multiple rings.

Her parents formed the most immediate ring around her. Beyond that was the ring of her grandparents. Beyond that—a dim sense of the people beyond and before her.

When she was three, she and her family went to visit her mother's parents in West Virginia. She remembers the entire trip in crystalline detail. She says it was in her grandparent's house that she realized that that outer circle was weakening and dying. The sprawling ranch bungalow was built as recently as the fifties, but it seemed older and dark, filled with antiques, humming with her grandfather's war trauma. The room she stayed in had this horrible seventies wood panelling with huge varnished knots in it that looked like eyes. The staring walls and the shadowy corridors conjoined self-awareness with death-awareness. Her new aloneness coalesced one morning in the bathroom, sitting on the toilet. She realized quite suddenly that her parents would someday die. She finished her poop and emerged into a new stage of life.

I imagine seven of us—you and I and Alix and Carina, A's mom, K, and K's first husband—standing in a circle around V and A and Jacob and Olin, hands joined. The circle has strong and weak links, flowing with love and anger and joy and trouble. As the children grow we have to give them room. We'll have to loosen the grasp. When they have their own children, and place them at the center, our ring will be further thinned. e'll have to let go entirely. The ring will fray first at its weakest bonds. As we die, more alone and internalized day by day, we will transform into photographs to haunt those at the center of the circle. The most riveting pictures for them will be the portraits. The solitude of the portrait carries the knowledge of the broken ring.

It's five in the morning, and the robins are singing. Our sleep has been really broken. Jacob's ear cleared up on its own, but then Alix got a flu and couldn't keep any food down. But last night we slept well, and the robins are singing.

When my sleep is allowed to deepen after a stressful period, I usually dream vividly. Last night I had two dreams about K. In the first, I had to phone her about a tax issue. A man picked up the landline. He had a broad and pleasant voice, and said that he was happy to finally make my acquaintance. Suddenly we weren't on the phone at all, but I was standing in the kitchen in the house on Cortes Island, and this tall and handsome fellow, my age, was shaking my hand vigorously. K came slowly around the corner, smiling, a little shy. The man was saying " . . . and we have great news to share with you." I looked at K and she nodded and said, "We're expecting a baby." I was so happy for her, and rushed to embrace her.

Then the dream jumps and I'm walking down Queen Street in the Beaches and I see K. She pauses and stiffens, uncertain as to whether she'll speak to me. I try to be warm and inviting, and I ask her if she wants to meet Jacob. "It will be sweet," I say. "He's a beautiful boy." She seems to soften. We arrive at the driveway of our home. Alix and Jacob are inside, and I invite K to enter, but I stay on the porch for some reason.

As soon as she enters I feel a deep sense of foreboding. I wait, feeling helpless. It's taking too long. I have a feeling of menace. Why am I staying outside? What terrible thing is she telling Alix about me? Is it true?

Then the door opens and Alix is holding Jacob and ushering K out. Alix's lips are pursed and she's flushed and sweating. Jacob is wide-eyed. K is wearing a strange smile, and I fear that she's been cruel in some way. I asked Alix, "What happened?" Alix shook her head and continued to usher K out the door. I turned directly to K and asked, my voice rising, "What happened?" Enraged, I seized her by the shoulders. Her body was light and yielding. I picked her up, and realized she was made of straw. The dream person, accusing me and threatening me, is mostly myself.

Alix has started writing again. About mothering, and her new life. Jacob sleeps for an hour in his bouncy chair, and her fingers fly across the keys. Her eyes burn.

We're going to own a home together. I wonder what we'll become. I hold her strong earthy hand tightly in this ring. There are no pictures on the walls yet.

love,
Matthew

|||

April 24th

Dear Michael –

Very busy with home-buying stuff. Paperwork, taxes, the lawyer. I'm selling off my books and supplies because I won't keep my store anymore. I have to buy a better bike for the commute from the Beaches. But I wanted to tell you about yesterday evening, because everything stopped for a moment.

Jacob and I walked Alix to the studio to teach and then walked home in the blaze of the late April day. He sits up straight in his stroller now, pointing the way. He looks like he's driving. He takes everyone and everything in. He has a knit cap with dangles on it. Two older Italian gangster-type guys pointed at him and said, "Hey-o! It's the king!"

We arrived home and I brought him up to the apartment. The sun was streaming in through the front bedroom window. I sat him up in the middle of the bed, on the white duvet, and took his sweaters and socks off. Krishna jumped up and flopped down at his naked chubby feet. Jacob greets the cat now with a cackling laugh and then reaches out to grab fistfuls of hair. The cat loves it, loves his little brother. But yesterday, Jacob cooed and kept an open hand while he stroked Krishna's tail. He fell into a kind of reverie. His eyes were on the sky and the sun, he hummed a little, made soft hissing sounds, felt the sun on his face. I was there, but distant to him. The cat rolled over, and Jacob gave his own purr.

I wanted to hold him there forever. I will have to hold him lightly. He is prior to the mind. He is prior to problems, the negotiation of relationship. He is at once completely dependent and radiantly alone. Of course I'm projecting something. His eyes are curious, but he doesn't need to learn anything instrumental. He pats his hand on his thigh. He stares at the fading sun and mouths new sounds. *Wa wa wa. Ta. Da. Da da. Ma.* The spell lasted for an hour, until the sun dried up. And then he came back to the immediate, focused on me, fussed, seemed to ask me where mummy was.

At the end of *Sheltering Sky*, Paul Bowles asks: "How many more sunsets have we yet to see? Maybe a dozen?"

love,
Matthew

The Following Spring

February 8th

Dear Matthew —

It's been nine months since we last exchanged letters. It's February and I'm on a delayed plane heading to Portland via Chicago. I teach for four days and then fly to London, England. Carina is visiting her family in British Columbia. The snow is blowing sideways across the runway and there are machines everywhere: snow-blowers, de-icing robots, the tug that pushes the plane backwards towards the runway and re-fueling trucks. Out beyond the oval windows it's like a miniature Lego world in a wild white storm.

Olin is obsessed with spoons. He always has one in hand as he crawls upstairs, nurses, eats or opens cupboard doors. I take it away when he bangs on the glass door facing the backyard. For his one year birthday Carina decorated his orange carrot cake with four large spoons in the shape of a W, for Winter, his middle name and his native season. This morning when I went to kiss him in bed (he was sleeping in), he was clutching a spoon in his left hand. I find spoons behind the toilet, in the heating ducts and in the wash. A found one in his schoolbag.

In the morning Olin wakes quickly, sits up with his spoon, and Carina unpeels his velcro diapers to give him air time. As soon as his diaper is off he takes downward facing dog and looks up backwards at his penis, maybe checking to see it's still there. Then he turns around, slides off the bed on his belly, lands on his bum, and then takes off, crawling to the bathroom to either unroll the toilet paper or look down the iron heating vent. Whenever he finds something small, he carries it to the bathroom and drops it down the vent.

Carina and I stayed up late last night because I'm off to teach for three weeks in Portland, London and Gottenborg while she goes west to be with her family. Our pillow talk was imagining a new way of dealing with birthday gifts after Olin received some great knitted sweaters and socks from friends, but a ton of plastic toys from family. We started drafting a letter to family members explaining why we don't want any more plastic, with photos of a beach we went to with A in Mexico that was littered with coloured plastic bits—toothbrushes, tampon parts, bottle caps and miscellaneous electronic parts. The letter ends with ideas about the things we'd love to receive—namely, money for Olin's education and wooden toys. It led to a story I read in a short little philosophy book posed as a self-help manual cleverly entitled, "How to Worry Less About Money." It's talks about the Jennings family who decided to give up Christmas and birthdays and, instead, saved their money to go on interesting holidays. They gave up gifts like high-status objects in favour of an education on the road. Carina and I imagined not getting each other gifts we had to purchase, and the same for Olin and A. Instead we'd save the money, put it into a travel account and dream of simple vacations we could take to strange and wonderful places. Number one on the list was renting a tiny cabin in Joshua Tree National Park and wandering around in the desert carrying Olin in a knapsack, and sleeping in heavy wool blankets under a thick blanket of stars.

Carina and I are away from our home because we're having the walls plastered. The crew is also sanding the old wooden stairs and prepping for putting the house on the market in March.

Last summer I was feeling burnt out with light sleep, too many hours in a tube hurtling through the sky and organizing community in Toronto. I was worried about A all the time. Then I realized that if A was going to live with his mother full-time, maybe I didn't need to be in Toronto, this city where I've spent thirty-nine years. It was a thought I'd never allowed myself to have. Would leaving Toronto feel to A like an abandonment? At the very point at which A is telling me he doesn't want to spend time with me is it fair to make it that much harder for us to see each other? Or will he actually thrive on the space between us? Is this the space he's been asking for, because we've been tightening that knot? He seems to be less stressed now that he's seeing less of Carina, Olin and me. Maybe A's mother will say to him that if I was really interested in being with him I'd never leave to be closer to Carina's side of the family. Is there a point at which I have to stop guessing and just look at what I need to thrive, literally, me, as a human being? I was lying on my back under a blueberry bush in Carina's parents' backyard in British Columbia, exhausted and sad. She lay down next to me and said: "Do you want to move here? Answer quick: *yes* or *no*?"

I sat up, she sat up, I looked at her and said, "Yes."

The decision was made. We are moving to the west coast, the place where Carina grew up.

When Olin was born, I felt a new wave of urgency about the world he's growing into and the one I'm leaving for him. Every living system is in decline. Climate change is real. On the grass in Carina's parents backyard the whole thing came together: I work in cities, I need to triple my efforts into translating these Asian practices I've studied into forms that will offer radical values and practices to an ailing world, and I need to live rurally. Trees, water, imagination, family. I know the buzz of street life intimately. The alleys I know are veins in my body.

The biggest concern with moving out west is how it will impact my relationship with A.

Months ago, I went to see the best child psychologist I'd heard of, and after three sessions of explaining all the dynamics and how much I was missing A, she said: "In these situations, as much as you think you need to fight for A, by age ten he should be individuated enough to want to spend time with you." She went on to say that as hard as it will be for me to hear this, I should "step back and give him a chance to make his own decision."

I thought she was crazy. I left her office and dialed Carina and said that I was through with the appointments. But now, a few months later, I realize the psychologist was saying something impossible for me to hear at the time. The child needs to be able to move between the two parents' homes without guilt. This means no dirty looks, no grilling them after a visit, and no idealizations of one home over another. The question is how much stress A feels in moving between our two homes. Does his cortisol actually rise when he crosses my threshold, despite all of my care and concern? When he is with his mother, is the stress of my enmity with her a distant problem for him that does not invade their bubble? Ironically, because she has managed to create the simplest family narrative for him, regardless of how accurate it is, does her home give A less stress? If he is able to rest there, will he eventually feel strong enough to make his own choices? Will my leaving give him breathing room? Perhaps there isn't anything left for me to do but let him know constantly that I love him and that my door is open.

Carina's older sister is pregnant with her third child and her younger sister is going to come stay with us when we move and help out with Olin.

We move in July.

yours,
Michael

|||

February 14th

Dear Michael,

I can't believe you're moving. And to an island, as far west as you can get! You're going for different reasons than I did years ago. I'll miss you so much. We've written all of these letters, but I think we'll always feel as though we haven't spent enough time together.

Alix and I are watching Jacob grow a sense of being an "I" before our very eyes. Six weeks ago he had the words *da-da*, *na-na*, *pa-pa*, *moon*, *dog-dog*, *monkey*. He says *dog-dog* in a growling bark. He very slowly came to *mama*. We can see how Alix is still the larger part of his own body and self. Naming her means separating her off.

At the play center a month ago he became fascinated with a baby doll and carried it around tucked close to him for an hour. So we bought him a doll for home, and my parents donated a toy stroller my niece used to use. The stroller is bright pink and covered with Disney princesses. Jacob pushes the baby doll around in it and babbles and sings. He bumps into furniture and the doll goes careening on the floor, plastic head first, and Jacob says *uh-oh!* and then picks the doll up, brushes it off and plunks it down in the seat, and starts all over again. In the evening while Alix is putting Jacob to bed, I'll sit on the couch with the doll beside me, both of our faces lit up by this glowing screen. The baby doll stares, unimpressed by these letters. It's a little creepy.

We were reading about the stage they're speculating on in which a boy mimics the mother's actions as the first part of being able to step away from her. He was able to call the doll "baby" pretty quickly. But when we showed him a picture of himself, he would say *mama*! Then he slowly transferred the word *baby* to the photos.

Some days it sounds like he's on the verge of full-on sentences. Whenever they start pouring out, the subject-verb-object construction will deepen its groove, and the world will come into focus for him as the workable but also painful conversation of self and other. Alix and I can feel ourselves inoculating his brain with the self-concept whenever he points us out as *dada* and *mama*, and then we ask him, "Who's the baby? Where's Jacob?" Sometimes we point at his little chest, and I imagine he is slowly feeling a subtle knot develop in there somewhere. The knot that says *this is me*. A knot that can get painful in the throat, or maybe later it's at the root of that stress in the heart we've both felt on our either sides of being forty. I'm haunted by your description of A as a knot that you and his mother have been pulling the ends of. We can make each other so tight. *Jacob, I promise to try to not make you tight.*

When we say, "Where's Jacob?" he covers his eyes with his hands, as if by not seeing us, he becomes invisible. Then he throws his arms wide open with a laugh and we say "There he is!" when what's really happened is that he's able to see *us* again. We, who contain the more clearly-defined, tightly-bound selves that he is learning to mirror.

It's been the longest winter ever, with three ice storms that knocked out our power. One lasted for several days when the temperatures were minus twenty and below. Our old house needs a massive insulation overhaul and I'm going to see if I can scrape together the money to buy a wood stove for the next power outage. I think they will be more frequent. They say the Gulf Stream is collapsing.

My mother had her hip replaced, then her knee. Recovery has been painful. Her appetite has shrunk. But every time we go to see her with Jacob she lights up and I can see the woman I have my first memories of. Tall and blonde, bright smile. She's become even more vociferous in the pursuit of excellent objects for Jacob. Especially doll's houses furnishings. She buys hand-made rocking chairs and tea services so tiny he can't play with them yet for fear of swallowing. She wants to give him the textures of a bygone world: tiny little hay bales made from real hay, a Model T with a steel body, baby's breath flowers dried to look like bouquets of white roses in a wee living room more splendid than she ever saw as a child. She wants Jacob's brain and heart to be absorbed in detail and fine quality. She was a schoolteacher, and watched generations of children grow up in an increasingly digitized and plastic world. She is a protector of the real.

My dad looks like he's about six years old whenever he sees Jacob. They ape each other and giggle and cackle. It's weird to see that the arthritis in his hands means that he has to hook his wrists under Jacob's armpits to pick him up and cuddle. The body and the heart can live in different eras.

Both of my parents are sharp as tacks. Writing letters to editors and city councillors, keeping their meticulous inventory of the civic machine and continuing their dogged 20th century liberal contribution to a world that has moved far beyond their well-reasoned outrage. Jacob will learn more about them in time. When we drive home from their house in the twilight, he gets sleepy and murmurs his names for them— Gammie and Gobbie—over and over again. *gammiegobbiegammiegobbie*. And then their names plus his favourite toy at their house—a little Vespa scaled to the doll's house. *Gammiegobbiegammiegobbiemotocycle*. Then he's out like a light.

It would be hard to overstate how helpful Alix's parents have been. They live really close, and have made themselves available for taking care of Jacob whenever I'm away for work and Alix needs a few hours for herself—now increasingly for the papers she's writing for her psychotherapy program—or when we want to sneak away for a date. We feel shy on dates.

Jacob adores John and Cathleen. Jacob insists that John carry him everywhere. Cathleen gets down on the floor with him and teaches him to roar. They pretend they're lions eating antelope brains. At home Jacob will Jacob will periodically yell *Na-na!* and drop to his belly and start lapping at the floor, eating those brains.

After one of the ice storms, they were bringing him home but the wheels of the stroller froze, so John picked him up and carried him. He chose his path as carefully as he could, but turning a corner his feet swept right out under him in a full pratfall, landing on his back. He managed to keep Jacob held in front. Cathleen was following close behind, and when she reached to help them, she slid over into the pile. Jacob started bawling.

They got up and brushed themselves off. John held him close as he sniffled. There was a full moon. Cathleen pointed at it and called out, "Jacob, look! The moon!" Jacob gazed up from Papa's arms, and was comforted.

It's almost a month later now and every once in a while Jacob will look up from the book he's flipping through and yell "Pa-pa! Uh-oh!" and then make a crashing sound. And then: "Na-na! Uh-oh!" and another crash. And then he'll get quiet and point to the sky and say "moooon." Jacob is telling stories about his life and his people. He's building myths.

Today is Valentine's Day, and the old flower shop at our corner is festooned with red roses. Chintzy red foil hearts are taped to the windows of the cafe and bookstore. So it feels right to tell you now about a different kind of red.

I'll start right at the end of Alix's ten hours of crushing obstructed back labour and the escalating fear and holding each other all night and wrestling through her excruciating contractions that came one minute apart for the last eight hours of it, without any dilation at all. She finally got the epidural and was able to stop crying out, and they began to roll her away for surgery, soaked in sweat. Our doula said to me, *You should go to the bathroom before you go into the operating room. You have some time.*

I said, *I also have to phone Alix's parents. She can't go into surgery without them knowing.* We didn't draw this part in birth prep class.

I stood in my soaking shirt in the cold stairwell and got John on the phone and I almost froze. I wanted to weep on the phone, to reach out to just one other man and say: *It's so bad, John, it's worse than anything I've known, I'm so frightened and she's in such pain and danger.* But I kept it together, because I didn't want him to suffer, even though he'd probably have a clearer grasp on the statistics of labour mortality and more capacity to calm himself than I. It occurred to me that I should phone you but I knew I didn't have time and now I think not being able to show myself to anyone in those hours wound up that spring of tension in my heart that sprung last year around this time.

But I did have one man to share it with. As I walked out the stairwell and turned the corner towards the surgery I heard someone shouting: *Where's the father? Where's the father?* I think I sped up even though it didn't quite register that they were talking about me and that I was becoming a father in that moment. I could see the bright light pouring out of the open surgery door on the left side of the hallway, and to the right side stood a short stocky Filipino man, grinning broadly, holding a scrub gown open for me like a tailor holding a suit jacket. As I got closer I realized he was saying through his beaming smile, *Are you ready? Are you ready to meet your baby?* And I looked him in the eyes and froze for a moment and then said, *Yes.* He slipped the scrubs sleeves on me and turned me around to tie the tabs and I wanted to turn to face him again and ask him if he was a father and how his children were, and did he have to leave them in the Phillipines when he came here, but he was pushing me to the hand scrub station beside the door.

After I dried my hands I looked up through the door and saw the most brilliant red colour I'd ever seen in my life. I didn't know what it was at first. I heard someone say, *Is that the father? Get him in here.* And I took three steps into the room and realized that I was staring into the flesh and blood of my lover. Thin sheets of skin were stretched up and back and tented open by gleaming retractors, and gloved hands smeared in the brightest blood in the world worked in a flurry around the opening.

In psychology and yoga and meditation we speak of "openings" and here was the material fact of opening. When you love a person you try to get deeper inside them to see what they are about and then if this happens you're suddenly gazing into this tangle of movement and I can't tell you how bright that colour is.

Doesn't this capture everything we've been sharing? We're always looking into the scarlet abyss of our lives, trying to see what's there, who's there, who's emerging. How one person comes out of another, witnessed and helped and even saved by so many. I was gazing into this body I love more than my own, opened up so that I can see purple organs, a sheen of fat, the pulsing arteries of whatever it is that motivates her voice and the movements of her gorgeous eyes.

I was staring, and then I heard Alix's voice say, *Matthew, are you there?* I couldn't understand where the voice was coming from, because the open wound didn't seem to be forming words. And then I realized that the speaking-and-head-part of Alix was on the other side of a drape and I was supposed to walk around and I would see her there, and I tore my eyes away from her open belly as they were starting to cut open her womb. She was there with a plastic cap on, flushed, beautiful and sweating still, her arms pinned down in cruciform, now trembling with the medication pouring through her. Something in me mirrored the Filipino orderly outside the room as I switched roles instantly from terrified pilgrim to confident caregiver and felt this smile pour out of me and I said, *You're doing so wonderfully, I'm so proud of you, you are such an incredibly good mother and our baby loves you so much.* And I hugged her awkwardly however I could grab onto her as she was strapped down to the table and covered her with kisses, and she kept saying over and over again: *How is baby? I want to see baby.*

And who are these people in white, up to their elbows in blood, prepared by generations of doctors? Who is this anesthetist standing at my shoulder, calmly looking at his dials and digits on just another Saturday morning for him? There must have been twenty doctors and nurses in the room. Probably three centuries of experience among them all. Where did they come from? What happened at their own births? Are they finding their own lives in this moment, in this red, under these lights, as I am? Did we consent to this opening? To Alix being rocked back and forth as they pull baby firmly out of the small incision? Is this compulsory trust—when there is nothing to do but trust—what religions mean by grace? And suddenly there was the kind and stern nurse, all business, plopping this incredibly fat baby into my hands, and saying in chorus with the whole team commenting giddily about his size and weight: *Well, he wasn't going to come out any other way!* He was so heavy.

I had one moment to show him—a him—to Alix before someone took me by the shoulder and pointed me out the door to the recovery room, carrying him. I told her, *We'll wait for you,* and she said, *Okay, I'll be there soon. Take care of baby.*

I paused to watch the bloody hands deep inside her, sewing up the dark redness I will never forget and will love her for. Baby wriggled in my arms and I turned to leave because I had this sense that he wanted to be away from the light and noise. *I registered his first need.* But then I looked back and saw in Alix's eyes that she was confused. Every impulse she had to reach out for this baby that had just been taken from her body was thwarted. She struggled under the straps. The separation was too quick and too soon.

A month ago we saw photographs of a caesarean birth in Australia in which the team had figured out how to support the birthing woman so that she could draw the baby out of her own womb and hold it to her breast while they stitched her up. This is a better way for sure. Other folks have figured out that baby's bacterial flora benefits massively if you immediately swab their skin with gauze that has been innoculated in the mother's vagina.

My heart has felt okay since last spring, but it's taken a full eighteen months to really take stock of how deeply wounded Alix was by that night. She's an incredibly strong human being, but no one recovers from a night like that quickly. And in a way, the stronger a person is, the more resilient they project themselves to be, the longer it may take for them to realize just how much they are hurting, and how much they need help. It wasn't clear to Alix until just this month how much she'd still been buzzing with a hypervigilance that was sleep-depriving her and not allowing her to dream. She's had to do a lot of things to help settle her ringing nerves, especially at night, but the thing that has helped most has been to slowly take account of and begin to verbalize just how difficult it was. Every few days we have small conversations about it while Jacob sleeps. We're writing the story together, a little at a time.

The real mystery is in how that day will live on in Jacob's body, his cells. Alix and I can talk about it with each other, but what will he feel, beneath what he can say?

The cognitive self wants to soothe with logic and statistics and diversion, but the flesh will keep us awake until we remember, and meet that memory with some kind of renewed dignity. The strangest part is that these two layers can't heal at the same time. Alix says that no matter how much fear she felt in the moment, she never totally lost awareness of the fact that she was in a modern hospital, and that this was the best place to be. Of course that awareness was broken by the pulses of back-labour contraction, when there can't be any thought at all. At the height of her pain her voice shook the hospital. *My spine is breaking.*

But she says that somewhere the thread was intact: she knew she wasn't likely to die. I never lost sight of this either. But we couldn't feel it. The primal self can't understand the safety of hospitals. It is not evolved to understand things. It feels death immanently, and does everything it can to protect and avoid, from violent resistance to going numb.

The hospitalized birth-trauma that can split us is a microcosm for every other way in which the cognitive self negotiates with its existential condition, I think. The rationalisms of economy cover over the frantic need for food. Diplomacy covers for perpetual war. Trade agreements normalize outright theft. Maybe one of the things that you and I are doing, Michael, is figuring out how the visceral truths of yoga and Buddhism— that death is always near, that relationship is the only activity of meaning in human life, that we have no choice but to seize the moment without any assurance of what the outcome will be, that we are animals, clawing at each other to survive, and that this is the strange root of love—can somehow dialogue with this flattened affect of modernity, in which we have trained ourselves to think and perform as if everything is okay. This performance has a cost. We miss each other personally, and we cover our ears against the desperate cries of the oceans and forests. Old St. Paul was delusional in too many ways to count, but he wrote a beautiful thing to the Romans: "For we know that the whole creation has been groaning together in the pains of childbirth, until now." We don't want to hear the groans, or remember them. We think if we hear, we will lose heart. But I heard Alix and I listen to her now, and I have a new sense of courage.

Alix is very pointed these days about her reasons for being in school for psychotherapy. She wants to be part of a conversation of greater transparency around birthing, because the way our culture talks about birth widens this split between the primal self that feels the crisis of the moment, and the cognitive self that does whatever it can to repress and reassure with its default stories. It limits the broader conversation—either birth was a wonderful underwater dream with Russian fur hats, or we don't really want to talk about it. Well-meaning people say to Alix, *So tell me all about your wonderful birth story!* Alix would pause and say, *Well, it was intense.* So then the person would change the subject, or say, *Well—you've got a healthy baby and that's all that matters.* That's the cognitive social brain trying to do damage control for the primal self. It doesn't work. It's a way in which we unwittingly close down to the experiences of others. We all need more support than that.

These days, this story of difficulty feels so remote, because all I can see is how perfectly tight and unique the bond between Alix and Jacob is. They wrap around each other. They are in constant dialogue. His language blossoms to mirror hers. She has these broad facial expressions of surprise and delight that he's learned to mimic flawlessly. Every time he transitions from one activity to another, or from Nana and Papa's house to our house he reaches for her and intones with great dignity and insistence, "momo", which means he wants to nurse. Alix's body is his home and touchstone. When he calls out in the night all for her, she hardly wakes up to drift to his room and into his bed. Sometimes I peek in before dawn and see Jacob actually spooning her, although he's only really big enough to curl around her bum. In the morning, they separate again, each day more softly than on that first day of his life. Each day is a gentler birth.

Every morning now my writing is interrupted in the best way. I wish it would last forever. I hear Jacob waking up, chattering with momma, and then padding down the hall, yelling *dada, dada*. I pull him up into the bed and we tickle while Alix pees. Then she runs down the hallway in the nude and jumps in with us. When we've had enough tickling and cuddling, Jacob sits up and mimes out some story from the past week, like how we went to Riverdale farm and a sheep scared him with a loud bleat, but he hung onto mumma and then me and it was all better, because then we saw the chickens sleeping. Then he points to my bum and laughs, saying *bumbum*, and then points to momma's bum, and then his own. We count bums, and belly buttons, and when the light hits Alix in a certain way I can see the faint scar on her lower belly.

This summer we're getting married in our backyard. You and Carina and Olin will be there, two weeks before you move out west. Last night Alix had an anxious dream about the wedding. It was the big day and she hadn't decided on what she wanted to say for vows. She woke up and told me the dream and I held her and she said, *Maybe we should make the main part of the vows a period of silence. Most of what we feel we can never say. So maybe we should ask people to feel that with us a little.*

So we wanted to ask you, Michael: would you guide the group in five minutes of silence? Not as a teacher, but as a friend. You lead meditation retreats all over the world, but this is just in our backyard, a few minutes of being quiet together, letting people feel whatever they feel about love, family, time, time passing, how much we depend on each other, how alone we can feel in these mysteries, but how we can share that aloneness, how everything is woven together.

We'll be in nice suits. Carina will bounce Olin, who makes really, really loud squeaking sounds when he's excited. Jacob will be in one of the grandparents' arms, pointing at flowers and balloons and trying to direct traffic. Maybe Alix will be holding red roses at her belly.

love,
Matthew

February 15th

Dear Matthew,

Today is Olin's one year birthday. I'm in London where it's windy and everything is grey. I'm thinking a lot about starting over, birth and death, the way Valentine's day and birthdays appear and vanish, adding up to something impossible to pin down and deep enough to make me miss home. Before I left I was sleeping in my office and I think when I come home I'd like to try sleeping in a shared bed again, with Olin between us kicking me through the night. Olin's mostly nursing but he loves picking various things off our plates at mealtime: mostly squash and chicken. When we visited Carina's parents out west I fed him blueberries from the yard, which he loved, and then blackberries too, but the seeds in blackberries upset him. His first foods were leaves and grass and sand in the neighbourhood sandbox. We fed him a little egg yolk once which he loved. Since babies are often low in iron we made him liver thinking it would be the perfect food and Olin responded with a record-setting projectile vomit.

I'm staying in a third floor walk-up in Primrose Hill, in the northwest of London. The sun comes in through the tall windows for thirty minute periods and the rest of the day is a moody grey. The birch tree outside looks cold. Across the way is Chalcot Square, a small park for kids, lined with an iron fence, and kitty-corner to this house, across the park, is a tall purple house that belonged to Sylvia Plath. She lived there after she met Ted Hughes, gave birth to her children in that home, and died one block from here. Her suicide was tragic, but when I walk by her home, with large windows facing east, I imagine a home that one lives in for a long time, and a park the kids get to know, like the ravines I trampled in down the road from my childhood home, the one where all my memories are placed, where my parents moved to begin a life, and where my parents' marriage unraveled. 14 Elderwood Drive. We had leaded windows and over the doorway, etched in stone, were two wings, like those of Batman. Just above them, on the second floor, was a small leaded window with a curve on the top, where I first remember watching people—other families, the bus, the world beyond our home.

Maybe because we're moving, I'm making these little mental films of our family living in new scenarios. Walking around this neighborhood in London, with houses well beyond my own economic means, I picture Carina and Olin at home as if we lived here. He's playing on his own with wooden blocks, Carina is working on her writing, and A, possibly at university, is coming soon for dinner. I'm cooking. Our station wagon is parked on an angle, like the others, our upright bicycles are locked to the fence, and on the roof, a vegetable garden, some old chairs, and an umbrella under which Carina and I sit and read when the kids have gone to sleep. We have four or six kids. Sometimes we all sleep on the roof, under the moon.

Today I walked from the top of Primrose Hill, where you can easily make out the trains in Camden, the density of buildings along the Thames, and a hundred churches and cathedrals, with their tall spires, poking what was once the realm of God. Now the higher realm of the sky is the home of the Shard, the Shangri-La Hotel and the banking industry. These are the new gods.

I walked through Regent's Park and followed an elderly couple walking a black dog over a bridge. They were wearing matching green rain boots with black pants and they each had identical scarves, in different shades of red. He had a thick grey beard and she wore lipstick. They looked at each other as they walked and talked, engaged, peaceful, thoughtful, taking care with one another. He listened, she spoke. She listened, he spoke. He looked at her, she held his hand. They turned around to check on the dog. His right sleeve was worn, his jacket possibly fit him a decade ago, now he's shrinking away from its form, his body moving into that phase where ambition has dissolved and the muscles soften around the bones.

I followed them, as I said, for a while, trying to commit details about them to memory so I could tell Carina: *This is us, this is who we are going to grow into.* I have no desire for a home in Primrose Hill, for the car parked at a perfect angle, for one home that I live and get old in—I know these things change.

But the walk, with Carina, and the two of us interested in what each other is interested in, maybe visiting London, but it could be anywhere—I see it, like one of the visions that I have every so often, together, older, still working on love.

Now the clouds are exactly the colour of an oyster, and I'm checking to see if it's time to Skype Carina again. She is in British Columbia visiting her family and checking out the area we plan to move to. She's unsure about when or how she'll start working again. She's been wondering about studying osteopathy. Right now it's possible for her to stay home and that feels like the right thing for our family. When I'm away from home it's obviously much more work for Carina. Carina being home also makes it possible for me to work, travel, and write, and it's giving Olin a stable base. Being with her family is one kind of support and it's good for Olin but it doesn't always make it easier for Carina, mostly because how she parents and how her parents support her aren't always in alignment. Yesterday they said, "Don't you think you're carrying him too much?" or "Shouldn't you just let him fuss about something for longer?" It makes Carina feel defensive but stronger about her parenting values.

Carina both loves and feels conflicted about not working and being at home. Deep down there's a fracture, as she describes it, and she thinks it's cultural. She feels with me earning the money she has less decision power. If she wants to buy herself something she feels guilty about it. Spending money is complicated without earning the money herself. It's something we're starting to talk about, but communicating hasn't been so great lately. I've been getting impatient a lot, interrupting her half-way through sentences, and cutting her off. It's hard for me to talk about money also, but more than that I've been moody and not listening very well.

On Skype, I watched as Carina's mother slid a soapy bucket across her kitchen floor, Olin crawling after it, and then, from a squat, he stood up and took his first steps. Olin walking, Carina clapping, me hollering on the webcam. A long distance celebration. I can't focus as well on Skype as I could when I held the heavy black handset of the old rotary dial phone with my eyes closed, listening to every nuanced word of the person with whom I was speaking, because long distance made things fragile and precious. Skype makes the visual more vivid but makes me feel much further away.

I have so many dreams of how I should be, what I can give them, how it should all go, and where we'll all end up. I feel presence and absence, attachment and distance, and like I'm always trying to show as much love as I feel, even though old habits, anxiety, and technology get in the way. Through it all I've come to see how the tensions in my home have always mirrored the tensions in myself. And that I depend on how they've always made me grow. This is how I continue, day by day, with something that feels like faith.

There is nothing special about family, my family, your family. We are in line with every human being that's ever lived. The particular family in whose web I was born was formed by the lives of the families into which my parents were born. There is birth, death, joy, craving and love. Carina and Olin, and A and A's mother, have opened me up to a belonging I couldn't have discovered any other way. No matter how much we disagree today, I loved A's mother enough to make life with her.

Once when I was ten I was standing in line for a ferry to take our family to the island in the Toronto harbor where my mother's father kept a boat. My mother was pregnant with my sister and my young brother Jayme was behind me trying to fish a packet of gum from my back pocket. My father bought our ferry tickets and as we waited in the cool morning air I saw others in line. It felt as if, for the first time, I was seeing other human beings, members of other families. Their faces, their different body types—some with thin legs and others with blonde or grey hair—two young girls who must have been twins, both wearing the same red tights; everyone with packed lunches and hats of different shapes, freckles, goose bumps, fair skin, dark skin, a woman with a cane, the sun overhead, and none of us seemed special.

My family blended in with this long line of humans waiting for a ferry—all of us having been born and all eventually going to the same place, a place none of us can know—the horns from the boat filled the air and a small Cessna was landing at the harbour runway. Everything was in its right place and everything was heading in the same direction. In my body I felt something new about life: not my own life, but about the whole parade of humans moving through the world, of which my family was only one small part, but the largest part of the world I could ever know.

Love,
Michael

Matthew Remski teaches yoga philosophy, restorative yoga, ayurveda, and is always writing. He's a stepfather of 17 years, and a new father with his partner Alix Bemrose. He lives in Toronto. www.matthewremski.com.

ALSO AVAILABLE BY MATTHEW REMSKI:

POETRY
Organon Vocis Organalis (1994)
Syrinx and Systole (2010)
Rosary: or les Fleurs du Mālā (2014)

FICTION
Dying for Veronica: A Sub-Catholic Dream with Mind-Music (1997)
Silver (1998)

NON-FICTION
(with Scott Petrie) *Yoga 2.0: Shamanic Echoes* (2010)
*21st Century Yoga: Culture, Politics, and Practice: A critical
    Examination of Yoga in North America* (contributor, 2012)
*Threads of Yoga: A Remix of Patanjali's Sutras with Commentary
    and Reverie* (2012)
Studying Ayurveda: A Manual in Progress (2014)
*What Are We Actually Doing in Asana? Reports and Meditations on
    Desire, Pain, Injury, and Healing in Yoga* (forthcoming in 2016)

Photo © Eugénie Frerichs

Michael Stone is a renowned yoga and buddhist teacher. He is the author of numerous books on yoga, meditation and ethics. He teaches internationally and lives with his family on Canada's west coast. www.michaelstoneteaching.com.

ALSO AVAILABLE BY MICHAEL STONE:

Awake in the World: Teachings from Yoga and Buddhism for Living an Engaged Life

Freeing the Body, Freeing the Mind: Writings on the Connections Between Yoga & Buddhism

Yoga for a World Out of Balance: Teachings on Ethics and Social Action

The Inner Tradition of Yoga: A Guide to Yoga Philosophy for the Contemporary Practitioner